I0868138

Osaka Modern

HARVARD EAST ASIAN MONOGRAPHS 403

Osaka Modern

The City in the Japanese Imaginary

Michael P. Cronin

Published by the Harvard University Asia Center
Distributed by Harvard University Press
Cambridge (Massachusetts) and London 2017

© 2017 by The President and Fellows of Harvard College

Printed in the United States of America

The Harvard University Asia Center publishes a monograph series and, in coordination with the Fairbank Center for Chinese Studies, the Korea Institute, the Reischauer Institute of Japanese Studies, and other facilities and institutes, administers research projects designed to further scholarly understanding of China, Japan, Vietnam, Korea, and other Asian countries. The Center also sponsors projects addressing multidisciplinary and regional issues in Asia.

Library of Congress Cataloging-in-Publication Data

Names: Cronin, Michael P., author.
Title: Osaka modern : the city in the Japanese imaginary / Michael P. Cronin.
Other titles: Harvard East Asian monographs ; 403.
Description: Cambridge, Massachusetts : Published by the Harvard University Asia Center, 2017. | Series: Harvard East Asian monographs ; 403 | Includes bibliographical references and index.
Identifiers: LCCN 2016028796 | ISBN 9780674975187 (hardcover : alk. paper)
Subjects: LCSH: Popular culture—Japan—Osaka—History—20th century. | Public opinion—Japan—Osaka—History—20th century. | Osaka (Japan)—Civilization—20th century.
Classification: LCC DS897.O815 C76 2017 | DDC 952/.1834033—dc23 LC record available at https://lccn.loc.gov/2016028796

Index by the author

♾ Printed on acid-free paper

Last figure below indicates year of this printing

26 25 24 23 22 21 20 19 18 17

For my parents, Cornelius and Rita Cronin,
and in memory of my sister Mary and brother Neil

Contents

Contents

Acknowledgments

I would first like to thank Jack Halberstam, who was teaching at the University of California, San Diego, when I moved to that city after eight years in Japan, wondering what to do next and curious about academia. I would not have begun the work that led to this book without Jack's encouragement.

At the University of California, Irvine, I had the good fortune to study under Jim Fujii, who always seemed to know when to offer guidance and when to let me wander. I am forever grateful for his confidence in me. My research on Osaka originated in a paper written for a graduate seminar on the city in literature co-taught by Jim and Ted Fowler. I thank them both for inspiring and guiding this research. I am also indebted to the other generous scholars I studied with at UCI, including Jonathan Hall, Susan Klein, R. Radhakrishnan, Serk-bae Suh, Duncan Williams, and Bert Winther-Tamaki. I benefited greatly from a dissertation writing workshop sponsored by the Social Science Research Council, and I thank the organizers, the other participants, and especially the faculty advisors, Takashi Fujitani, David Leheny, Susan Napier, and Corky White.

At the College of William and Mary, I found a collegial department and an ideal senior colleague, Rachel DiNitto, who read my work, encouraged me to teach my research, and protected my time so that I could finish this book. I am grateful for her support and friendship, and for the model of her professionalism. It is serendipitous that my other two colleagues in the Japanese Studies section at William and Mary—senior language instructors Tomoko Kato and Aiko Kitamura—are Osaka natives.

They have answered countless questions, and I thank them for their help and patience. Thanks also to my other colleagues in the Modern Languages and Literatures department, especially Rob Leventhal, Jorge Terukina, and Calvin Hui, and to my colleagues in the Asian and Middle Eastern Studies program, especially Eric Han, Hiroshi Kitamura, and Sibel Zandi-Sayek.

Several friends and colleagues have read drafts and offered advice as I wrote and revised this manuscript. I am deeply grateful to Mimi Long, Keith Vincent, Tomiko Yoda, Ken Yoshida, and an anonymous reviewer for their detailed comments. I would also like to thank Micah Auerback, Roy Chan, Steve Chung, Itoh Hiroshi, Ji Hee Jung, Su Yun Kim, Mary Knighton, Diane Wei Lewis, Michele Mason, Masuda Chikako, Sasagawa Keiko, C. J. Suzuki, and Leslie Winston. I have benefited enormously from their friendship and support.

I am grateful for the generous financial assistance I have received from the Office of the Provost, the Office of the Dean, and the Reves Center at the College of William and Mary, and from the Japan Society for the Promotion of Science (Nihon Gakujutsu Shin Kōkai), the Northeast Asian Council of the Association for Asian Studies, and Kansai University's "Naniwa" Research Group. I am also indebted to the Reischauer Institute at Harvard University and the Center for Japanese Studies at the University of Michigan for granting me access to the libraries at those institutions, which has been critical to the completion of this work.

I thank Kawamura Minato, of Hōsei University in Tokyo, and Nakagawa Shigemi, of Ritsumeikan University in Kyoto, who kindly sponsored me during research fellowships in Japan. Special thanks to Hashizume Setsuya, of Osaka University, for his generosity and, in particular, for providing the cover image for this book from his remarkable collection of art and ephemera.

I am grateful to Bob Graham and Deborah Del Gais at the Harvard University Asia Center for all their assistance in the latter stages of this project. An earlier version of chapter 3 appeared in *Japan Forum*, volume 25, number 1 (2013). Other material from this book appeared in the *Proceedings of the Association of Japanese Literary Studies*, volumes 10 and 11.

I would also like to thank my parents, brothers, and sisters for their patience over all these years of research and writing, including long stretches far away from them. Special thanks to my sister Kathe for reading chapters and offering helpful suggestions.

Finally, I thank my partner, Tomoyuki Sasaki. I would not have begun, and could not have completed, this project without him. I am more grateful than I can say for his advice on every aspect of my research, at every stage, and for his constant support. In the Osaka of my own imagination, he is always by my side.

Note to the Reader

The following terms come up frequently in discussions of Osaka, and a basic understanding of them at the outset will be useful:

The word "Hanshin" refers to the Osaka-Kobe metroplex. It is a portmanteau word combining alternative readings of the second character in "Ō-saka" (or "*han*") and the first character in "Kō-be" (or "*shin*"). Sometimes "*Kei*," an alternative reading of the first character in "Kyō-to," is added at the front to include that city ("Keihanshin"). The suffix "*-kan*" means "between," and "Hanshin-kan" refers to the area between Osaka and Kobe, specifically the suburban neighborhoods that were developed there beginning just after the turn of the century. The cosmopolitan bourgeois culture that flourished there at that time, and that provides the backdrop for Tanizaki's *Sasameyuki*, is called "*Hanshin-kan modanizumu*" (modernism).

"Kamigata" refers especially to the premodern and early modern high culture of the Kyoto-Osaka region.

"Kansai" and "Kinki" are two terms for the broader region within which Osaka is located, comprising the prefectures of Nara, Wakayama, Kyoto, Osaka, Hyōgo, and Shiga. Kinki also includes Mie Prefecture, which some do not include in Kansai. Kansai (literally "west of the barrier") carries a more cultural connotation, while Kinki has a geographical connotation, referring to the area near Kinai—that is, the five historical provinces around the ancient capitals of Nara and Kyoto. Kansai is the more common term in everyday use, and it is the one I will use throughout this study.

* * *

The use of "m" for syllabic "n" before labial consonants (as in the place names "Namba," "Semba," and "Hommachi") is prescribed by the traditional Hepburn system of romanization and is widespread in Osaka—for example, throughout the subway system. It also more accurately indicates the usual pronunciation. However, in keeping with current standard scholarly practice, I use the modified Hepburn system, which prescribes "n," throughout this book; thus, "Nanba," "Senba," and "Honmachi." Where the person or institution being named has indicated another romanization, I respect that preference (e.g., the *Asahi Shimbun*). The names of major cities generally familiar to readers in English appear without macrons in English-language text (so, "Osaka," not "Ōsaka"; "Kyoto," not "Kyōto"; and "Kobe," not "Kōbe"). Macrons are used where appropriate in less familiar place names (e.g., "Hyōgo" and "Tennōji"), in Japanese text, and in all personal names.

Introduction

Osaka as an Idea

Any city comprises manifold cities. Social class, race and ethnicity, age, gender, personal history, and other considerations help determine the city that we come to know. And we know a city in manifold ways. We inhabit it as a collection of spaces: streets and alleys, waterfronts and canals, neighborhoods and squares. We traverse it as a set of itineraries: commutes, after-dinner strolls, convenience-store runs, and subway rides. We experience it, too, as a sensorium of voices and noises, tastes, smells, sights, and touches. We encounter it as a series of individuals who belong to populations and types characteristic of cities or of that particular city. Above all, we know a city as a set of practices that subsume these other knowledges as we catch a taxi or jaywalk or carry a police whistle or join a festival crowd. Time multiplies these knowledges. The city changes constantly, and memories of the city last week or last year lend depth to our fresh impressions as we judge this city, today, against those earlier cities of memory.

In addition to such immediate knowledge, we also come to know cities through the mediation of cultural production. Novels, films, television programs, and songs either set in a city or about someone who has come from a city or longs to get to a city help shape our knowledge of that place, whether we live there or have never even visited. Sporting events, news stories, advertisements, and more ephemeral media also contribute to this knowledge. The same considerations that shape our knowledge of the physical city also delimit this imagined city. Whether we recognize a city described in a novel or a film—that is, whether we find it authentic—depends on how we have come to know it. Like the physical city, the imagined city is subject to constant change. New ideas come to dominate while others recede, reflecting changes in the physical city as well as the waxing or waning influence of various social groups.

In the process, certain ideas condense and gain sway within social imaginaries, including both national and local urban imaginaries. That is, these ideas of the city contribute to "the way people imagine their social existence, how they fit together with others, how things go on between them and their fellows, the expectations that are normally met, and the deeper normative notions and images that underlie these expectations," in Charles Taylor's words. These communal ideas, which are "both factual and normative" and neither exclusively materialist nor idealist but "both at once," help shape "a common understanding that makes possible common practices and a widely shared sense of legitimacy" at both the local and national level.[1] In this way, they "solicit recognition of membership in a collectivity," as Chris Berry has argued.[2] And these ideas of the city can be deployed to serve various ends and interests, including both national and local interests. They can also function, in Arjun Appadurai's words, as "a form of negotiation between sites of agency (individuals) and globally defined fields of possibility."[3]

The idea of Osaka that arises from the present study will depend in part on how we approach that city. We might start out from the old capital of Kyoto to the east and travel in the genteel comfort of the Keihan Railway, with its well-upholstered seats, pleated curtains, and a pretty framed print at the front of each car. We could switch to a local train and get off at Nakanoshima, come up to street level, and find ourselves by the river. The light off the water, its smell, and the sound of a passing *bateau-mouche* all remind us that this was once, and in certain spots remains, the *mizu no miyako*, or "capital on the water." Or we might approach from the cosmopolitan suburbs of Kobe to the west and ride the Hankyū Railway, full of bourgeois charm, with its distinctive maroon cars and green-velvet benches. We would arrive at the grand terminal of Umeda, one of Osaka's commercial hubs, where a succession of retail developments, each one more immense than the last, continually alters the cityscape. Or perhaps we should approach from the capital, Tokyo. Disembarking from the bullet train at Shin-Osaka Station, we leave behind the bland efficiency of Japan Rail and step onto the platform and into the swirl of the colorful Osaka dialect. Riding the escalator, we recall (or are brusquely reminded) that here we must stand to the right, not the left as in Tokyo—a small manifestation of Osaka's obstinate contrariness. Each approach ushers us into a different city.

This book approaches Osaka through the literature and cinema of the transwar period, from the 1920s through the 1950s, and examines one persistent idea: of the city as treasonous. This idea echoes through the history of the city and the Japanese nation, but it takes on special resonance in the transwar period. Influential works of literature and cinema produced in this period imagined Osaka as a distinctly local order—of space, language, everyday life, gender, and more—alternative to the national order. Cultural production in modernity fosters national identity by promoting a narrative of the heterogeneous and fragmentary local incorporated within the unitary nation. This narrative presents the nation as an order that contains and transcends the local. Consider, for example, how a national language first codified at the turn of the century and based on the idiom of the capital became standardized, and how other local idioms were then redefined as "dialects" of this new "Japanese." Such processes of containment and transcendence are fundamental to Osaka's modernity, and many novels, films, songs, and other works set in the city uncritically illustrate and reiterate them. However, cultural production can also work to undermine that narrative. By thematizing the negotiation between local and national forms, certain works call attention to those processes of containment and transcendence, betraying the economic, political, and cultural interests that inform them. This is the treasonous potential of Osaka—a potential that the works examined in the following chapters variously exploit and constrain.

Osaka in History

The area around what is now called Osaka has been a destination and a transit point for immigration and trade since the beginning of Japan's recorded history. According to the ancient chronicles, Jimmu, the leader of the Yamato clan, sailed from Kyushu in the seventh century BCE to claim domain over the Japanese islands and first stepped ashore at the mouth of the Yodogawa, at a place he named Nami-haya, or Naniwa, meaning "swift waves." After vying with rival clans for several centuries, the Yamato eventually achieved dominance, and sometime around the turn of the fifth century CE their leader, Nintoku, established his headquarters at Naniwa and built his palace there.[4] Over the following century and a half,

Naniwa hosted envoys and delegations from the continent, representing the kingdoms of Kudara (Paekche), Shiragi (Silla), and Kōkuri (Koguryō) on the Korean peninsula, as well as Sui China. In 645, after one faction in the Yamato court asserted its hierarchy over the other clans in the Taika coup d'état and moved toward unification and centralization of governance, the new *tennō* (emperor), Kōtoku, located Japan's first "imperial" capital at what then became Naniwa-kyō. The capital was moved less than fifty years later, however, and Naniwa-kyō declined.

In the eleventh century, the nearby port of Watanabe no tsu emerged and gradually came to dominate shipping in central Japan.[5] Meanwhile, the nearby religious complexes of Sumiyoshi Taisha and Shitennōji, two of the oldest and most historically significant shrines in Japan, had become important pilgrimage sites, and market towns had grown up around them.[6] In the Muromachi period (1336–1573), the nearby city of Sakai, an autonomous trading port led by merchants, became one of the richest cities in the Japanese archipelago, its prosperity and independence attested by Catholic missionaries, who compared it with Venice.

The ruins of Naniwa-kyō were resettled at the beginning of the sixteenth century. The site was selected as a new center for the Jōdo Shinshū sect of Buddhism, whose temple in Shiga, near Kyoto, had been destroyed by a rival sect. Construction of this center, the Ishiyama Honganji, began in 1532, and the area around it developed into a sizable community. It was around this time that the name "Ōsaka" (great hill) gained currency. Eventually, Osaka's strategic location and its growing political power drew the attention of the warlord Oda Nobunaga, who had begun the process of unifying Japan's domains under his authority. Nobunaga led a campaign against the Ishiyama Honganji in 1570, eventually laying siege to it. Ten years later, he captured and destroyed the complex.

Osaka became the political capital of a newly unified Japan at the end of the sixteenth century. After Oda Nobunaga's suicide in 1582, Toyotomi Hideyoshi, who had risen from humble beginnings to become one of Nobunaga's top generals, took power. The next year, Hideyoshi began building Osaka Castle, by far the largest castle in the land. From his seat at Osaka, Hideyoshi completed the process of unification that Nobunaga had begun, bringing all the daimyō under his command. After Hideyoshi's death in 1598, however, Tokugawa Ieyasu moved to take power. In 1600, at the Battle of Sekigahara, Tokugawa forces defeated those loyal to Hideyoshi's son, Hideyori; and in 1603, the Tokugawa shogunate was established with Edo as its political capital. Lingering resistance was defeated in 1615, and Osaka Castle was burned down.[7]

The Tokugawa leadership recognized Osaka's usefulness to them even after this shift. They quickly rebuilt the castle and reorganized the city's merchant quarters. Governed by local representatives of the central government, the city became the shogunate's administrative center for western Japan.[8] The shogunate granted Osaka's great merchant houses a license to lend money and to oversee the shogunate's finances; these houses would become the foundation of the modern nation's banking industry. The shogunate permitted local merchants to repair and expand the city's canal system, which won Osaka the epithet "Capital on the Water." The products that these canals carried earned Osaka another epithet—"the Nation's Kitchen," or *tenka no daidokoro*—as it became the western hub for trade headed east to Kyoto and Edo. The merchant class thrived despite its low status within the strict social system enforced by the shogunate, and it underwrote a flourishing urban culture. At its height, Ihara Saikaku (1642–93), the most renowned prose author of the Edo period, and Chikamatsu Monzaemon (1653–1725), Japan's great playwright, both took as their subject the people and concerns of the city's merchant and licensed quarters, making Osaka the setting for some of the most popular and enduring literary expressions of early-modern urban life.

After the Meiji Restoration of 1868, Edo became Tokyo, the capital of the new nation-state, and Osaka was increasingly subordinated to state authority by the administrative centralization characteristic of modernity. This process was not entirely steady; at various times Osaka, along with Kyoto and other large cities, was granted some degree of political self-determination. However, as historian Kurt Steiner has noted, policing and education remained within the purview of national authorities, and local government was "entangled in a mesh of restrictive legislation, financial disability, and social inferiority."[9] Central control loosened somewhat in 1926, when city assemblies were granted power to elect their own mayor instead of having one appointed by the governor, and elected heads of towns and villages were no longer subject to ratification by the governor. The war, however, brought increased centralization and the disempowerment of local assemblies.

Despite its administrative subordination, Osaka remained Japan's preeminent city in other senses well into the modern era.[10] It ranked first among prefectures in industrial production through 1930, becoming known as the "Smoky Capital" (Kemuri no Miyako) and the "Manchester of the East" (Tōyō no Manchesutā). It remained a cultural capital, too. Many of the emblematic phenomena of Japan's modernity developed there first, before being exported to Tokyo. It was in Osaka that Japan's jazz scene first flourished and Japan's film culture first put down roots.[11] It was in Osaka that the Hanshin and Hankyū corporations pioneered a new mode of suburban life, perfecting in the Hanshin-kan area west of the city a model of development that would later be exported to the capital.[12] And it was in Osaka that the café was transformed into a critical space of modern life and the café waitress into its emissary.[13]

The city's preeminence peaked in the age of Dai-Ōsaka, or "Great Osaka." On April 1, 1925, under the leadership of a progressive new mayor, Seki Hajime, the city expanded to absorb several villages on its outskirts, increasing the city's area from 56 to 181 square kilometers and its population from 1,430,000 to 2,210,000 to become Japan's largest city—larger than Tokyo, and the sixth largest city in the world.[14] Meanwhile, Tokyo was struggling with the aftermath of the Great Kantō Earthquake of 1923, which had devastated the capital and surrounding areas, killing more than 100,000 people and driving many more from the city, along with much of its economic base (including the film industry). By 1932, however, Tokyo, having significantly recovered from the quake, reasserted its preeminence by expanding its own boundaries in turn, absorbing five counties and eighty-two towns to become Dai-Tōkyō, thus usurping Osaka's position.

The transwar period accelerated and confirmed Japan's political and economic centralization and cultural homogenization, as well as Osaka's concomitant subordination. Encompassing militarization, total war, occupation, and recovery, the term "transwar" calls attention to continuities from the prewar to the postwar; one such continuity was this centralization.[15] As the nation moved toward total war, the state government in Tokyo asserted its power over all aspects of life, appropriating political authority from other localities. A revision of basic laws in 1943 gave the home minister and the centrally appointed governor the power to dismiss municipal officials who were considered unfit for office, and local government was increasingly understood to serve as an organ of the state.[16] The wartime control economy seemed to deprive Japan's "merchant capital" of its raison d'être. After the war, U.S. occupation forces attempted to slow or reverse aspects of this centralization, but Japanese officials worked to frustrate those efforts and, once the occupation had ended, energetically pursued recentralization.

The Local City

Cities are both local and national. Our firsthand experience of a city calls on local knowledge and helps cultivate that knowledge as we navigate the city's spaces, observe its codes, and speak its languages. Media representations of our hometown, or of any town with which we claim a connection, may appeal to our distinctly local sensibilities and to our sense of identification with that locale and, at the same time, help produce them. On the other hand, cities have served as critical sites in the development of the modern nation-state and of national identity. The key factors in these developments—the rise of capitalism, industrialization, and the growth of mass culture—have played out in cities. As they did, literature and cinema of the city helped constitute the experience of a modern life that was, to a large degree (though not exclusively), perceived as national life (however far it might have been from lived reality in most corners of the nation-state). Inevitably, these two senses of the city—as local and national—diverge. The gap between them produces the resentment that locals may feel, for example, when we see our city's spaces chopped up and rearranged for a film, its culture caricatured, and its accent mangled. Voicing that resentment, we complain that the representation is "inauthentic." Often this sense of inauthenticity links to a deeper suspicion that the city, our city, is being oversimplified or distorted to serve the purposes of national media and to answer the needs of a national audience—an audience of outsiders.

Its combination of historical preeminence and growing subordination, together with its persistent cultural influence, make Osaka a privileged site for examining the tension between the idea of the city and that of the nation. Influential works produced during the transwar period responded to the war and its aftermath by celebrating Osaka as Japan's most recalcitrant locale. Some of these works imagine Osaka from the outside and for outsiders, in a manner that fits the city into a national narrative of modernization. Other works, however, imagine the city from the inside, observing it at ground level and close-up, rather than from above and at an observational distance. They record the spaces, the idioms, and the daily life of the city with geographic specificity. And they assume a degree of local knowledge on the part of their audience, rather than translating every custom, every expression, every neighborhood and landmark, into terms that a national audience might understand. Such works exploit Osaka's potential through their emphatic locality.

This sense of locality differs fundamentally from regionalism in the sense that some have characterized it as ethnic nationalism writ small. The region is typically understood to be rural, provincial, a protonational space not yet debased by industrialization; Raymond Williams, for one, noted the overlap between "regional" and "provincial" in contrast to "metropolitan."[17] Transwar literature and film, however, present a thoroughly industrial and metropolitan Osaka that remains indelibly local.[18] Williams further notes that the word "region" and its derivatives connote a sense of subordination that, I will argue, certain transwar works of Osaka resist.

This distinctly local—which is to say non-national—quality demands our attention. Tokyo has preoccupied scholarship on the Japanese city, particularly in English. Like Paris for France or Berlin for Germany, Tokyo became a metonym of the modern Japanese nation. But precisely because it is a capital, Tokyo cannot tell us everything we want to know about the city per se. In his seminal essay on the Japanese city, Henry D. Smith wrote that although he was choosing to focus on Tokyo as a "starting point," his underlying interest lay in the city more generally, adding, "I recognize that this bias [toward the capital] obscures the unique character of other large Japanese cities, particular Osaka, which both as a distinctive cultural tradition and as a major economic force was in certain ways critical in molding ideas of Tokyo."[19] In fact, many of the ideas of Tokyo that Smith identifies in his essay might be called, with at least as much validity, ideas of Osaka. As the preceding summary of its history suggests, Osaka signified "the city as power" well before Edo did. The idea of "the city as prosperity" certainly describes the merchant capital of Japan in the Tokugawa period. Osaka, like Tokyo, inspired concerns about "the city as problem" in the early modern era, and Osaka's interwar mayor, Seki Hajime, was prominent among the urban planners who pioneered the discourse of the "large city," or *daitoshi*, in response to those concerns, as Smith notes.

However, Osaka also differs fundamentally from Tokyo. One idea of Tokyo that Smith identifies in his essay is that of *miyako*. This word can signify a large city generally but more precisely connotes the seat of the imperial court: the capital. Smith suggests that while this idea attaches primarily to the premodern capitals Heijō-kyō (present-day Nara) and Heian-kyō (present-day Kyoto), some sense of *miyako* transferred to Edo when it became the seat of Tokugawa political power. Later, with the emperor's relocation from Kyoto at the time of the Meiji Restoration, Tokyo came to be styled the *teitō*, or "imperial capital." As noted, popular discourse has identified Osaka as a kind of capital, too: "the Capital on the Water" (Mizu no Miyako) and later "the Smoky Capital" (Kemuri no Miyako). Such epithets play on an awareness of what sort of capital Osaka is *not*: the official capital, the imperial capital. While brilliantly cataloging Tokyo as an object of intellectual inquiry, Smith's essay also points to Osaka's significance, both for what it is and for what it is not. As the capital, Tokyo is anomalous. Its image and its interests can hardly be separated from those of the state and nation. Tokyo's spaces become national spaces; its idiom becomes the national language; and stories set there become national stories, written about national subjects, addressed to a national reader. A fuller understanding of urban space and life as distinct from the national begins with Osaka.

The Treasonous City

Although we tend to imagine the local—local space, of course, but also local accents, local cuisines, local customs, and more—as a constituent part of the national, contained and transcended by it, literature, cinema, and other popular media have consistently associated Osaka with the excessive, the excluded, and the treasonous in a way that refuses such containment. The association with excess dates back at least as far as the Tokugawa period, when the expression "Ōsaka no kuidaore"—conveying the notion that Osakans will bankrupt themselves over food—marked the city as a space of excessive appetite and expenditure. Those particular excesses constitute an important trope in transwar fiction and cinema, and continue to define Osaka today. The city has also long been linked with comedic excess, including the narrative exaggeration and linguistic elaboration of traditional *rakugo* comic storytelling and *manzai* team comedy, and more recently the slapstick skit comedy of the Yoshimoto Shinkageki theater. Such has been the success of these forms—and of the corporate institutions that developed and marketed them—that (a stylized, show-business version of) Osaka's distinctive dialect has become the default language of Japanese comedy nationwide. The strength of that association is evident at the local level, too, in the success that comedians have enjoyed in Osaka politics: Yokoyama Knock, a former *manzai* comedian, was elected governor of Osaka Prefecture in 1995, and the comedian Nishikawa Kiyoshi served in the upper house of the Japanese Diet for eighteen years. Excess figures, too, in the stereotype of Osakans' taste for flashy fashion—a stereotype that the author Tanizaki Jun'ichirō repeatedly endorses, as we shall see. Finally, postwar popular culture has marked Osaka as a setting for violent criminal excess. One of the most sustained examples is the popular and long-running film series *Akumyō* (Bad reputation), produced by Daiei throughout the 1960s and based on a novel by Kon Tōkō, set among the criminal underworld in the Kawachi area of Osaka.[20] Later works reiterated the association, including Izutsu Kazuyuki's minor classics of gang life, *Gaki teikoku* (Empire of brats, 1981) and *Kishiwada shōnen gurentai* (Kishiwada young thugs, 1996), as well as Miike Takashi's early video and film productions.[21]

Osaka has also become identified in popular culture as a home to various groups marginalized in Japanese society. These include several significant immigrant communities. Of course, some works feature characters who are born-and-bred Osakans with deep roots in one of the old downtown neighborhoods; the Osaka equivalent of Tokyo's Edokko, or "children of Edo," they are heirs to the venerable "Kamigata" culture influenced by the ancient capital, Kyoto. Osaka is better known, though, for those who were not born but who made themselves Osakans. Since the 1920s, the largest community of *zainichi* (Japan-resident) Koreans has resided more specifically in Osaka; fully one-third of all *zainichi* Koreans lived there in the 1930s. The city is also home to the largest community of Ryukyuans outside Okinawa. In addition to such migrant communities, Osaka is home to the largest urban population of *hisabetsu burakumin*—ethnic Japanese whose ancestry links them to feudal-era outcaste groups. Osaka is particularly associated with economic outsiders, too. The largest population of marginally employed day laborers in Japan is found in the city's Kamagasaki neighborhood.

Excess and outsider status characterize cities generally, of course. What lends these tropes an edge in Osaka literature and cinema is the added idea of treason. I borrow this term (in a slightly motivated translation) from an essay by Sakaguchi Ango, one of the most representative writers of the immediate postwar era. Ango wrote the essay "Ōsaka no hangyaku" (Osaka's betrayal/treason) to honor his close friend, the writer

Oda Sakunosuke, after his untimely death.[22] Ango's title alludes to a strategy in the chess-like game of Go used by the Osaka master Sakata Sankichi, who challenged the Tokyo masters with his unconventional play. Oda himself opened his famous essay on "Kanōsei no bungaku" (The literature of potentiality) with a moving account of Sakata's career and his daring style of play. In Sakata, Oda found inspiration for his own challenge to the "lethargic orthodoxy" of the Tokyo literary establishment, manifested in the solipsism of the I-novel (*watakushi-shōsetsu/shi-shōsetsu*)—a form of prose narrative that purports to present the author's direct experience in a confessional mode and that preoccupied Japanese letters in the 1920s and after.[23] The idea of "Osaka's treason" also cites a local history of antagonism toward central authority dating back to 1600. "Treason" continues to frame popular images of Osaka, as demonstrated recently by the success of Makime Manabu's novel *Princess Toyotomi*—a *DaVinci Code*–style mystery that imagines an independent "Osaka Nation" and the plot to betray the secret of its existence.

The five chapters that follow examine several examples of the deployment of Osaka's locality and how it links to ideas of the city's betrayal—both how certain ideas of the city betray imperial discourses and how certain works betray the idea of the city. Each chapter focuses on a work of popular fiction, the fifth also including several film adaptations. The discussion takes in a variety of other cultural forms as well, including radio, television, popular music, and stand-up comedy. And each chapter introduces a key aspect of Osaka's locality as it operates in these works.

Tanizaki Jun'ichirō's novel *Manji* (1928–30), examined in chapter 1, stages a contest for control of the local voice. The first of Tanizaki's novels set in Kansai, written after he moved from his native Tokyo to escape the destruction caused by the earthquake of 1923, *Manji* concerns a treacherous love affair between Sonoko, a bourgeois housewife from the suburbs of Osaka, and a younger woman from the downtown merchant quarter, Senba. Organized as Sonoko's confession to a diegetic auditor whom she calls "Sensei," *Manji* tells its story through two competing narrations: one "spoken" in the first person, in Osaka's distinct dialect, and another "written" in the third person, in the national standard language. I read *Manji*'s doubled narration as dramatizing strategies of citation and containment—of oral performance by writing, of queer female desire by straight male desire, and of the local language by the national. I also discover within the narrative the potential subversion of this strategy. I then examine critiques of Tanizaki made by several Osaka writers, and weigh their assertions of local *authenticity* against his claim to an ethnographic *mastery* of the local.

Chapter 2 concerns an archetype of local Osaka masculinity, the *bonbon*, and his local practice of expenditure and play, as celebrated in Oda Sakunosuke's *Meoto zenzai* (Sweet beans for two, 1940). "Bonbon" refers to the spoiled, lazy, pleasure-seeking young man of Senba, who had been a fixture of the city's literature since the seventeenth century. The bonbon resurfaced in Oda's story as the Pacific War loomed. Oda grew up in the age of Great Osaka, but he pursued his brief career under militarization, wartime, and postwar occupation, as centralization subordinated his hometown to Tokyo. In that context, he produced stories of emphatic locality. This, his best-loved novel, tells the story of Chōko, a hardworking geisha with aspirations to respectability, and her irresponsible lover, Ryūkichi, who spends money faster than she can save it. While the state promoted "rational consumption" in support of a war that would demand the catastrophic and irrational expenditure of lives and material wealth, Oda's novel details a practice of gourmandise and play, presented not as irrational but as rational within a different order of logic: a local order.

In *Waga machi* (My town, 1942), Oda traces the flows that link his local Osaka to the far-flung corners of Japan's empire. After 1900, Japanese workers began migrating to the Philippines in growing numbers. At first, they went to work for the U.S. colonial authority alongside Chinese and Filipino workers, building the Benguet Road through the jungle to the new summer capital. Later, they found jobs in the booming Japantown of Davao. This population became one rationale for Japan's invasion of the Philippines in 1941. Oda's novel begins in the Philippines, where its protagonist, Takichi, joins a crew on the Benguet Road. After returning to Osaka, Takichi works pulling a rickshaw through the city's streets and dreams of returning to the Philippines. Chapter 3 details how *Waga machi* illustrates the allure of empire as a transcendent form that unites all locales: "the eight corners of the world under one roof," as one wartime slogan put it. At the same time, it argues that Oda's novel betrays the reality masked by this notion—of a hegemonic form that subordinates one locale to another—and offers as an alternative a vernacular cosmopolitanism rooted in Osaka and embodied in Takichi.

Chapter 4 maps local and national vectors of nostalgia and futurity, diseased and healthy bodies, in *Sasameyuki* (Fine snow, 1943–48). Tanizaki's great novel concerns the four daughters of a Senba merchant family in decline. Japan's imperial project interrupted the production of the novel and constantly intrudes at the edges of its story. I read *Sasameyuki* against the productivist and reproductivist ideology of imperialism. The bonbon appears here in the figures of the sisters' dead father, who destroyed the family business through his extravagance, and of the youngest daughter's lover, who draws her into inexorable decline. Tanizaki contrasts the bonbon with the two married sisters' husbands, who trade Senba and its merchant economy for the suburbs and the modern work of the white-collar executive. Like Oda, Tanizaki presents the bonbon as unproductive, but where Oda explores the potential of his inutile expenditure, Tanizaki mourns him as an anachronism unequal to the demands of imperial expansion. The bonbon becomes the fatal link between Osaka's old merchant quarter and the cosmopolitan suburb of Ashiya, imagined as a space of disease, filthiness, and failed reproductivity. Tanizaki's ironic presentation of this space serves as an excuse and a consolation for the impossibility of narrating his historical moment.

The 1950s produced a string of films set in Osaka that participated in the postwar reassessment of Japanese values and institutions and helped reconstruct Osaka's image for a postwar audience. Novels and stories by Tanizaki and Oda provided the source material for several of these films; another important source was a new literary voice, Yamasaki Toyoko. Chapter 5 examines this group of film adaptations, focusing on Yamasaki's 1957 novel *Noren* (The shop curtain) and Kawashima Yūzō's film adaptation, released the following year. Both novel and film recount the careers of a father and son as one builds and the other revives an Osaka family business, tracing historic shifts from merchant house to corporation, affiliative to filial succession, connoisseurship to consumerism, and regional market to national. This final chapter explains how film adaptations refit local stories into a conventional narrative of the city's decline. It then analyzes the performance of locality by the actors who regularly appeared in these Osaka films—most notably Morishige Hisaya—and details how, through gesture and voice, such performances haunt the conventional narrative, reminding the viewer and auditor of what has been lost.

Osaka Literature and Minor Literature

The three authors at the heart of this study—Tanizaki, Oda, and Yamasaki—produced some of the most influential stories of Osaka in the transwar period, stories that continue to shape the idea of the city in the Japanese imagination. They are very different writers, but all three are popular writers who fit awkwardly, if at all, within the Japanese literary establishment centered in Tokyo. Tanizaki is certainly the best known and the most "establishment" of the three. He enjoyed great success during his lifetime and maintains a reputation today as a giant of Japanese and world literature. Indisputably canonical and major, he is generally counted as a *junbungaku* author, on the side of "pure literature" and opposite mass literature in the division that defined the Japanese literary world through much of the modern era. This characterization, however, has more to do with Tanizaki's stature than the nature of his works; while he may be called a *junbungaku* author, it would be difficult to describe him as an author of *junbungaku*, and the novels discussed in this book hardly belong in that category. Tanizaki turned his back on Tokyo, the city of his birth, after the Great Kantō Earthquake of 1923, relocating to Kyoto and then to Kobe. Oda Sakunosuke, Osaka's favorite son, is also a canonical writer in Japan, but he is a stubbornly local one. For that reason, he remains minor in national terms, though no other figure is more important to modern Osaka letters. Oda moved to Tokyo at the beginning of his career but soon returned to his hometown. Before his death at the age of thirty-three, he was hailed as the heir to Saikaku and to the tradition established by that early modern author: that of a realism concerned with the lower classes and infused with earthy humor. Yamasaki Toyoko, another Osaka native, was until her death in 2013 one of Japan's best-selling and most widely adapted postwar authors. Despite, or perhaps in part because of, this success, she remains almost ignored by scholarship. A concern with the world of business and with broad social issues places her novels at the furthest remove from "pure literature." Nevertheless, she played a primary role in imagining Osaka for readers in the 1950s, as Tanizaki did from the 1920s through the early 1960s, and as Oda did in the 1940s.

Along with the physical distance they maintained from Tokyo and their stylistic distance from the "pure literature" of the Tokyo literary establishment, these three authors share a fascination with the speech of Osaka and a facility for rendering it on the page. More than any narrative description of local places, events, customs, or atmosphere, the written approximation of characters' local speech produces the idea of Osaka in literature (as the recorded voice does in cinema). Should we wish to catalog an Osaka literature, such use of local language would certainly be the primary criterion for identifying its constituent works (and its representative authors would include, in addition to Tanizaki, Oda, and Yamasaki, such predecessors and early contemporaries as Uno Kōji and Kamizukasa Shōken, and such successors as Miyamoto Teru and Tanabe Seiko). These authors inscribed the local idiom onto a "standard" Japanese that had been derived from the speech of Tokyo and had come to dominate prose narrative around the turn of the century.

This use of local language encourages us to consider these works as a minor literature in the sense that Gilles Deleuze and Felix Guattari have described it, as "that which a minority constructs within a major language." The use of local language, especially when conceived and deployed not as a substitute grammar but as a potentially infinite and ungrammatical variation, exploits the "internal tensions" of the national language to effect a deterritorialization of language.[24] While such a deterritorialization based on regional identity may often be immediately accompanied by a reterritorialization, certain texts indicate a line of flight out of national configurations of periphery and margin toward another, alternative configuration identified as immanent to the local. Osaka's treasonous potential is critical to understanding how these works might (or might not) constitute a minor literature, for although treason may often be committed in an attempt to substitute one authority for another, the term connotes at its root a betrayal or a breach, a violation of sovereignty, a surrender. It is therefore worth asking not so much whether a particular work is or is not "minor" but to what degree and in what ways it manages, while fostering a sense of the local as minor, to maintain a skepticism toward its institutionalization—a skepticism that guards against any easy reterritorialization of the city.

Chapter One

Mastering the Local

Narration in Tanizaki Jun'ichirō's *Manji*

Nakagawa-ke is the name of a very funny Japanese *manzai* comedy team made up of two brothers, Tsuyoshi and Reiji, whose work is, like so much effective comedy, perceptive ethnography as well. Some of their funniest bits exploit the comic potential of the tension between local Osaka dialect and the national standard language. In the brief bit of *monomane*, or mimicry, called "Okan ga denwa ni deru toki" (When Ma answers the phone), the younger brother, Reiji, playing a middle-aged housewife, first answers the telephone speaking polite, standard Japanese in a soft voice, then, realizing it is "her" son on the line, switches into loud, familiar, local speech: imagine a British mother shifting from the plummy tones of BBC English to the broadest Scouse. The humor lies not only in the comedian's skillful impersonation but also in the abruptness of the code-switching and the contrast in the two languages—one public and self-conscious, the other private and unrestrained.

In a longer skit, set in a cell-phone store, Reiji plays an increasingly frustrated customer with a broken cell phone. His agitated patter reveals him to be a parody of the Osaka small-business owner: he needs to get his phone to work before the arrival of a client from Nagoya, whom he is picking up at Shin-Osaka Station and bringing to a screw factory in East Osaka to look at screws for a new style of *takoyaki* pan—*takoyaki* being Osaka's most famous street food, and screws being the sort of low-tech, low-margin product with which East Osaka is historically associated. He grows frustrated with the polite but unhelpful clerk, played by the older (but smaller, more fastidious) brother, Tsuyoshi. The incommensurability of local and global economies symbolized by *takoyaki*-pan screws and cell phones is made audible in the gap between two languages: the coarse familiarity of the customer's local dialect and the corporate impassivity so eloquently communicated in the super-polite standard speech of chain-store service. The artificiality of that "standard" speech quickly becomes ludicrous in the context of *manzai* comedy, where the standard is, in fact, the Osaka dialect.

The gap between local and national languages, and how literature negotiates that gap, is the subject of this chapter. The modern state depends on a sense of community among its constituents. In Japan, a state that, before the modern era, had comprised numerous relatively independent territories, this sense of community depended on a narrative of the manifold and fragmentary local unified within the unitary nation—or, to put it another way, it depended on an idea of the nation as a form that contains and transcends the local. Language is one of the most powerful tools for fostering a sense of national identity, and after the Meiji Restoration, leaders of the modern Japanese state worked hard to establish a common national language. This, too, they promoted as the result of the unification—or, more precisely, the reunification—and transcendence of the myriad and often mutually incomprehensible local idioms spoken in the territories. In the process, they redefined those local idioms as corruptions of an original language and non- (which is to say, "sub-") standard "dialects" of the newly restored national language. In this sense, just as national language is basic to the construction of the nation, so, too, is local language basic to the construction of the local as supplemental to the nation.

Cultural production in modernity worked to promote this narrative of (re)unification and transcendence of the local. One of its most effective technologies for this purpose was the *shōsetsu*, the representative modern prose genre, narrated in a mode purported to approximate the new national colloquial language. But cultural production worked to undermine this narrative, too. In modern novels that make extensive use of dialect, the negotiation between a national language of narration and a local language of dialogue may not only record and support but also critique the broader political, economic, and cultural containment of the local by the national. The novel *Manji* (1928–30), written by Tanizaki Jun'ichirō just after he moved to the Kansai region to escape the destruction of the Great Kantō Earthquake of 1923, provides us with a particularly illustrative example of the negotiation between local and national languages. The production of Tanizaki's novel and the critical response to it manifest the struggle to narrate and characterize the local—a struggle that invokes competing claims to mastery and authenticity and turns on a strategy of citation.

The Nationalization of Language

I will begin by detailing how the dynamics of local and national play out in *Manji*, which I characterize as a struggle over the authority to narrate. I will then review criticisms of Tanizaki's novel lodged by several Osaka writers who asserted their local authority as they challenged his mastery of the local. I will also explore the notion of Osaka's essential *yayakoshisa* (complicatedness), which some of these critics employed to define the character of the city as essentially unmasterable. Finally, I will consider the question of mastery in the context of translation theory. First, however, a preliminary explanation of the terms "Osaka language" and "national language," and some history of their development, will provide background for the discussion that follows.

What I will here call "Osaka language" is usually termed in Japanese "*Ōsaka hōgen*," "*Ōsaka-ben*," or, more pejoratively, "*Ōsaka namari*." All of these might be translated as "Osaka dialect." Japanese scholarly discourse often refers to "*Ōsaka kotoba*" and "*Ōsaka-go*," or "the Osaka language," terms that mitigate against the sense of "substandard" that colors the other terms, as it colors the English word "dialect." Two related terms, "*Kamigata-kotoba*" and "*Kamigata-go*," refer, usually in a historical sense, to the common idiom of Kyoto and Osaka. It is also important to note that due to its past cultural dominance as well as its continued currency in entertainment media, the idiom of Osaka still enjoys a privileged status relative to other local languages or dialects.

The concept of a unitary "Osaka dialect" or language is a convenient imprecision, like "southern accent" or even "Boston accent." Many of the characteristics commonly identified with a specifically Osakan idiom—the use of the be-verb "*oru*" rather than "*iru*," for example, or the use of the negative suffix "*-hen*" rather than "*-nai*"—are not in fact limited to Osaka but are used throughout the Kansai region. On the other hand, the term elides the variety of idioms specific to neighborhoods such as Senba and Kawachi and to social groups such as the prewar merchant class. The term tends to efface as well changes in the dialect over time. With these caveats, I will use the term "Osaka language" here to refer generally to the collection of local idioms and their representation in fiction.[1]

Likewise, behind the term "national language" lies a collection of interrelated Japanese terms, including "*nihongo*," "*kokugo*," "*hyōjungo*," and "*kyōtsūgo*" (respectively, "Japanese language," "national language," "standard [spoken] language," and "common/mutual [spoken] language"). Both "*hyōjungo*," which has been used since the Meiji period, and "*kyōtsūgo*," which gained currency after the war, disregard the specifically national character and, in that sense, the historicity of the idiom they connote. As names for a modern national idiom, they also obscure the existence of earlier standard or common languages. Well before the institutionalization of an Edo idiom as *hyōjungo*, *Kamigata-kotoba* had constituted a "common language," and even a standard one, in the sense that it represented a widely acknowledged ideal, though it was not supposed to be an idiom that everyone should speak everywhere, at all times.[2] Furthermore, these terms obscure the existence of idioms that function even today as "standard" or "common" languages for communities defined in other terms than nation.

All these terms must be historicized within movements to reform language and literature that gained momentum around the beginning of the Meiji period and were pursued beyond the end of World War II. Language reform in Japan was championed as part of the construction of a modern nation-state by intellectuals and bureaucrats who had studied European languages and in many cases traveled to Europe on behalf of the Meiji government to master branches of Western science. These reformers recognized that economic and military modernization would require an educated workforce to master and disseminate imported technologies. Modernization would also require mobility and the exchangeability of people as units of labor, characteristics that were frustrated by a multiplicity of regional spoken languages so variant as to be in some cases mutually incomprehensible. In addition, the efficient administration of the state and its participation in a world order for which the nation was the basic unit were seen to require an officially sanctioned national language of governance and diplomacy. To these ends, reformers pursued several goals. They sought to identify an idiom that could serve as a national standard and promote its use in every aspect of public life. They sought to standardize and simplify orthography. And they sought to replace the collection of literary styles then in use with a style that more closely approximated colloquial speech.[3]

As debate over *genbun'itchi* (unification of writing and speech) flared in the late 1880s, one issue was the effect of colloquialization on the various established idioms spoken in regions other than Kantō. In his influential book, Mozume Takami noted with approval *genbun'itchi*'s potential homogenizing effect on speech across the nation.[4] Tatsumi Kojirō identified that same potential as an argument against *genbun'itchi*, noting that its establishment would require people to speak two languages, one local and the other national.[5] Both positions signaled a recognition that the new mode would not simply describe an existing colloquial language but would eventually prescribe a national grammar and, when combined with a new orthography, a national pronunciation.[6]

I do not want to exaggerate the efficacy of these top-down movements. In some ways, they were attempts by the state and the intellectual establishment to commandeer a process that had already begun from the bottom up.[7] Furthermore, reformers failed to fully realize key goals (notably script reform) until the end of World War II. Nevertheless, these collaborative movements represented the participation of educational and legislative discourses in an ideological struggle that produced what Mikhail Bakhtin calls a "common unitary language."[8] Although such a unitary language is "at every moment of its linguistic life . . . opposed to the realities of heteroglossia," Bakhtin asserts, it also requires heteroglossia in order to "make its real presence felt" through the imposition of limits. Here I would like to call attention to language reformers' production of dialect as one element of such heteroglossia.

Reformers recognized that the establishment of a standard language would further the hegemony of one locale over others. In a treatise written in 1890, in which the term "*hyōjungo*" appears for the first time, Okakura Yoshisaburō acknowledged the constructed nature of both standard language and dialect. He observed that the selection of one idiom as a standard language (*hyōjungo*) renders all other idioms used within the boundaries of the nation dialects (*hōgen*), and that such a selection is based not necessarily on the inherent suitability of a particular idiom to the free exchange of ideas but on considerations of political power.[9] While some advocated the adoption of Kamigata language as a standard and others proposed that an entirely new standard be invented, influential reformers campaigned for a standard based on the speech of the educated classes in the new capital.[10] This became the de facto standard in 1901, when the Ministry of Education declared it the language of instruction nationwide. The publication of *Kōgohō* (A grammar of the spoken language) in 1916 confirmed this, identifying as its model the language spoken by the educated classes in contemporary Tokyo.

This hegemonic move was, however, presented as a transcendence of local divisions and a return to a unified national order. Lee Yeounsuk notes that the concept of "*kokugo*" was advanced in early Meiji as though it were founded on a preexisting "one *nihongo*" spoken by all the people, when in fact the inverse was true: the "unobtrusive base" of *nihongo* was constructed only *after* the "glittering spire," *kokugo.* Lee further argues that the concept of diversity results from the projection of unity; that is, "variation depends upon a standard," and she continues: "Japan's 'linguistic modernity' starts from doubts about whether a linguistic unity called 'Japanese' truly exists in the first place. It can only be said that '*kokugo*' is a concept constructed in order to refute by force these doubts."[11]

In other words, in a process that Benedict Anderson, among others, has detailed, the idea of nation is validated by positing a linguistic unity prior to contemporary linguistic diversity. That diversity is a construct of nation: in the same way that the idea of nation encourages people to think of their discrete community or domain as one fragment of a greater whole, so the idea of a standard language encourages them to conceive of the language they have been speaking as a "dialect" that is variant and therefore nonstandard.[12] In the narrative Lee describes, the notion of *hyōjungo* serves as the principal tool by which this diversity is "retrained" to the unity of an original *nihongo*—a unity that becomes the justification for promoting *kokugo* as one key attribute of *kokka*, or nation.

The scholarly and political project of producing such linguistic diversity and relativizing it to the new national standard began under the leadership of Ueda Kazutoshi and the auspices of the Tokyo Imperial University National Language Research Committee, and gathered steam as Japan pursued its imperial ambitions. In 1927, Tōjō Misao, Ueda's student, published *Kokugo hōgen kukaku* (The division of the dialects of the national language), tracing the various idioms of the Japanese territories—including the Ryukyu Islands—back to an original *nihongo.* In the same year, Yanagita Kunio, the father of Japanese folklore studies, proposed the theory that variation from a standard language expands in concentric circles from a cultural center, and that elements of the ancient language survive at the margin.[13] Okura Shinpei, an instructor at Keijō Imperial University in colonial Seoul, applied these theories to the language of the Korean peninsula.[14]

This scholarly discourse fit neatly with the imperial government's expansionist ambitions, as Yasuda Toshiaki has argued. As the government redefined Japan's margin to include the Korean peninsula, the Korean language was relativized to the ancient language of Japan.[15] Indeed, some scholars of national language, such as Kanazawa Shōsaburō, theorized that Korean was a dialect of the Japanese language. Colonial officials put this idea into practice, promoting the use of Japanese in public life and Korean at home. Policing of language quickly grew stricter in both the colonies and the *naichi*, or "home islands," developing into a campaign for dialect eradication, led by the Movement for the Enforcement of General Language (*futsūgo reikō undō*), founded in 1931.[16]

I do not mean to equate the position of Osaka vis-à-vis the capital with that of Korea or, for that matter, the Ryukyus, where the imposition of standard Japanese was far more forceful and outrageous. Nor do I mean to suggest that the Korean language or the Ryukyuan language stands in the same relation to Japanese as does the language of Osaka or the Kansai region. I do, however, mean to trace a continuity in the intellectual justification for the language policies pursued in the colonies and in the provinces. The common element is the notion of a "national" standard that unifies and transcends local variants—a notion that obscures an actual process of subordination, if not always subjugation.

The *genbun'itchi* movement helped impose this notion of a transcendent national language on prose narrative. *Genbun'itchi* was ostensibly meant to bring written style closer to colloquial speech. Colloquial, however, meant the newly established national standard. Refinements made to that standard for the purposes of composition, such as the "*de aru*" copula and the use of the "*-ta*" form, further estranged it from the language used by most people in speech. The abstraction, neutrality, and self-reflexivity asserted by these innovations was the privilege of narration, while characters' discourse remained concrete, committed, and intersubjective; and that privilege was associated with the national form. In earlier literary styles, the interplay between the narrative ground and character-oriented words negotiated various relations, including those between writing and speech, figuration and transcription, and tradition and contemporaneity. If there was, as well, a geographic aspect to this negotiation, the nation as a linguistic entity was not a primary party to it. Just as the idea of the modern nation asserted its transcendence of the local through political and economic means, so it did through novelistic narration, too.

The novel's inherent polyphony, however, reveals these effects as merely asserted, rather than fully realized. In the process, it reveals the hegemonic strategies belied by that assertion of transcendence. I previously cited Bakhtin to the effect that a common unitary language such as reformers effectuated in Japan requires heteroglossia to "make its presence felt." Dialect constitutes one aspect of such heteroglossia, and in works that make extensive use of dialect, the relation between the narrative description and the characters' speech can highlight the limits that standard language imposes on dialect. At the same time, dialect in a novel can also relativize the unitary language in turn.

Manji

Tanizaki wrote *Manji* after moving to Kansai from his native Tokyo to escape the destruction caused by the Great Kantō Earthquake of 1923.[17] The move to Kansai would mark a watershed in Tanizaki's writing. He set several subsequent contemporary novels in the Kansai region, including *Tade kū mushi* (Some prefer nettles, 1929), *Neko to Shōzō to futari no onna* (A cat, a man, and two women, 1936), and *Sasameyuki* (Fine snow, 1943–48). Tanizaki also evinced a new interest in Japan's native literary and aesthetic traditions in his first modern-Japanese translation of *Genji monogatari* (The tale of Genji, 1939–41) and his exploration of classical themes in the novels *Ashikari* (The reedcutter, 1932) and *Shunkinshō* (A portrait of Shunkin, 1933).

Already in *Manji*, Tanizaki is exploring this nativist impulse. *Manji*'s initial publication as a serial in the literary journal *Kaizō* began about three decades after the public debate among intellectuals over *genbun'itchi*, by which time that mode had come to monopolize prose narrative. Tanizaki rued the foreign influence to which he thought *genbun'itchi* had exposed Japanese literature. In an article published in 1929, the same year that the serialization of *Manji* concluded, he complained, "As far as I am concerned, current colloquial style has absolutely killed the unique beauty and strength of our national language."[18] He criticized the western style of *genbun'itchi*'s syntax and urged a return to oral forms that, he believed, preserved native syntax. These concerns no doubt underlay his determination to produce, in *Manji*, a novel "in which both the dialogue and the narration were written uniformly in Osaka dialect."[19] It also likely dictated Tanizaki's choice of a woman to deliver that narration, for he claimed that the language of Kansai women retained more of its local character than that of the men.[20] The resulting novel is written in dialect from beginning to end, with some short but, as we shall see, significant passages in standard Japanese.

Manji tells the story of a treacherous *ménage à quatre*. The participants are a young bourgeois housewife named Kakiuchi Sonoko and her husband, Kōtarō; Tokumitsu Mitsuko, a younger woman whom Sonoko meets at the art school where they both take classes; and Watanuki Eijirō, a well-off, handsome, and dissolute young man with whom Mitsuko is involved. The married couple live near Kōroen Station on the Hanshin Line. Mitsuko lives near Ashiyagawa Station on the Hankyū Line. Both neighborhoods lie in the Hanshin-kan, the stretch of commuter suburbs between Osaka and Kobe developed by the two railway companies beginning around 1909, when pollution, fear of disease, and a new discourse of environmentalism prompted an exodus of merchant and middle-class families from inner Osaka.[21] Mitsuko's is one such merchant family, with roots in Senba. Watanuki lives in Senba still. Rumors, initially unfounded, of a romance between Sonoko and Mitsuko bring the two together, and soon the women become lovers in fact. This leads to an arrangement between Sonoko and Watanuki to share Mitsuko's affections. Eventually Sonoko's husband becomes infatuated with Mitsuko, too. The ensuing complications end with an attempted triple suicide, in which Mitsuko and Kōtarō die, and Sonoko survives.

The character Sonoko narrates this story not to an implied reader but to a diagetic auditor, addressed by Sonoko as "Sensei" and indirectly identified midway through the story as a well-known novelist. *Manji* is presented as Sensei's written record of Sonoko's account, interrupted by several "author's notes."[22] The novel therefore provides two narrations: an extensive one given by a woman in Osaka language and marked as oral (i.e., presented as a transcription of oral testimony and rendered in an approximation of the local spoken idiom), and a brief and intermittent one given in the national language and marked as written, by a self-identified "author" who has generally been presumed to be male. In this sense, Tanizaki stages a contest between Sonoko and Sensei over the authority to narrate. At stake in this contest is access to the transcendence that modern narration claims. In the course of this contest, *Manji* enlists several surrogate oppositions, including female and male, orality and writing, "traditional" genres and the novel, and queer and straight desire. Underwriting all these is the dynamic fundamental to Tanizaki's writings on Kansai: the local and the national.

Sonoko's narration emphasizes its own orality from the beginning. Her first word (the first word of the text) is a vocative "Sensei." The first sentence references being listened to, and in the passage that follows, Sonoko explicitly cedes literary authority to Sensei and at the same time alludes to the novel, written out by him, that her narrative will—or has—become:

> Sensei, I came here today intending to have you listen to the whole story, but I know you're busy; are you sure you don't mind? If I tell you every detail, it will take quite a long time. I keep thinking, if only I could write it all down from beginning to end, arrange it like a novel, and have you look at it. . . . The truth is, I tried to write it down the other day, but what happened is so *tangled up* I had no idea where to start and how to put it, so I thought I would just have to ask Sensei to listen to me.[23]

Note the repeated references in this brief opening passage to telling, listening, writing down, arranging, looking at. The style of direct address fundamentally calls attention to the *énonciation*, but these references both to her own telling and to Sensei's eventual retelling further highlight its special significance in this novel. Punctuating the rest of her narration are responses to unrecorded but implied questions and prompts that remind the reader to understand this narration as spoken (chapter 30, for instance, begins with the colloquial affirmative "*Haa*, . . ." [Yes, that's right], and the final passage in the novel begins with "*Haa?*" [What's that?]). Most of all, the fact that Sonoko's narration is phrased in heavy dialect throughout marks it as oral with each passing sentence. Much of Sonoko's local vocabulary and usage, especially the polite, humble, and honorific forms that do so much to distinguish Osaka language from national language (and from *genbun'itchi*), is possible because her narration is styled as direct oral address.

The dialect in which Sonoko speaks marks her background and gender. She uses not conventional Osaka language but (an approximation of) a suburban variant that was developing in the Hanshin-kan at the time. As Kōno Taeko, a writer and critic, has explained, the upper classes of Osaka who were abandoning the inner city had first moved to the Mikage area, between Osaka and Kobe, in the mid-Taishō period (around 1920) and there had maintained "standard" Osaka speech. By the early Shōwa period (from 1927), the same families were moving to the east, closer to Osaka, to the area around Ashiya, Shukugawa, and Kōroen, where, after mixing with families who had moved there from the Tokyo region, they began to speak a new, suburban variant of Osaka language.[24] Tanizaki's use of this suburban idiom identifies Sonoko very specifically—even before Sensei's "author's notes" describe her—as a suburban bourgeois daughter of the Osaka merchant class.

Sonoko employs this local, female voice to narrate her story. In doing so, she stakes a claim to the transcendent subjectivity characteristic of modern novelistic narration. Tomiko Yoda has demonstrated how first-person narration works to construct a modern subjectivity. With Mori Ōgai's *Maihime* (1890) as her example, Yoda describes a process enacted by the narrated *I* and the narrating *I*, one immanent to the story-world, the other transcendent, "situated in the *instance of discourse* primordial to objective time and space," the two both separated and linked by "the distance marked by the passage of biographical time and the subjective process of remembering one's past." Out of the self-referential apparatus emerges what Yoda calls "one of the most paradigmatic signifiers of the modern subjectivity," the first-person *I*.[25] The retrospective narration that takes up most of *Manji* presents Sonoko's attempt to work through the process Yoda describes and, by narrating herself, to transcend the story-world.

Sonoko narrates not only her own story, of course, but Mitsuko's as well, and as narrator, she further asserts her subject position by objectifying her lover. At several points in the story, Sonoko joins men in regarding Mitsuko's image and discussing her appearance with them in a proprietary tone. She relates to Sensei the story of how, early in her infatuation, her picture of the bodhisattva Kannon, drawn to resemble Mitsuko, caused a scene at the art school. The school director comes into her class, notices the resemblance, and, without mentioning Mitsuko by name, tries to force Sonoko to admit that the younger woman was her model. Unintimidated, Sonoko engages in prolonged, teasing repartee with the director, trying, for her part, to force him to say exactly whom he believes the painting resembles. They indulge in this sparring match while standing together before the drawing—that is, before the objectified Mitsuko. When the director finally backs down, Sonoko is thrilled to have won the "fight" ("*kenka ni katta yō na kii shite, erai tsūkai deshiten wa*").[26] Immediately after relating this story, Sonoko shares with Sensei a photo of herself and Mitsuko, boasting of her lover, "You won't find another such beauty among all the young girls around Senba."[27] Later, standing with her husband before the drawing in her home, Sonoko boasts again of her lover's beauty; eventually, she will come to share Mitsuko with him. Sonoko presumes to join in the objectifying gaze, just as she presumes to narrate her own story of desire.

Sonoko's narrative of her desire for Mitsuko marks the spatial distance between the inner city and the suburb, as well as the temporal distance between Osaka's merchant past and its bourgeois present. Mitsuko, though she lives now in the suburbs, is the daughter of a wholesale woolens merchant whose shop was in the Senba district. Her boyfriend, Watanuki, lives near Mitsuko's father's shop. They are revenants from the merchant economy of Osaka's past glory and the urban district where it flourished. In contrast, Sonoko and her husband live in the new suburban development around Kōroen Station on the Hanshin Line, built in 1907. Her husband studied German law, had "a splendid record as a student," thought of becoming a professor, and eventually opened a law practice. Sonoko claims the subject position to narrate the story of a daughter of the fading *chōnin* class, who can be only local and object. Her narration is the voice of the suburbs attempting to cite and transcend the city center. On a larger scale, it dramatizes Osaka's claim to narrate its own history in the face of its relativization to the Tokyo-centered nation.

Sensei counters these claims through his own strategy of citation. His narration appears in brief passages, labeled as "author's notes," that interrupt Sonoko's testimony several times in the early chapters, once later in the story, and again at the very end. The notes serve several purposes. Some of them introduce evidence—photos and documents—relevant to Sonoko's tale. With these notes, Sensei confirms what Sonoko tells him and asserts the disinterested authority to do so. Other notes confirm Sonoko's observations. In the second note, for instance, after Sonoko has described Mitsuko as a "dazzling beauty," the "author" interrupts to address the reader: "Certainly, there could be no doubt that she possessed beauty."[28] With these comments, Sensei attempts to usurp narrative neutrality, implying that Sonoko's own judgments are too interested, too local, to stand on their own. Finally, the notes display the "author's" knowledge of local ways—a knowledge shared with the reader in a superior tone. As he introduces the photo Sonoko has shown him of herself and Mitsuko in matching kimonos, Sensei tells us, "The 'matching kimonos' were the garishly colored sort ("*kebakebashii shikisai no*") popular in the

Kyoto-Osaka region."[29] He uses the word "*kebakebashii*" (garish) again later to describe the stationery the two women used for their passionate notes to each other, and he distinguishes this from tastes in the capital: Tokyo women would use something plainer, he insists, and Tokyo men would take a dislike to anyone who sent such a love letter. Here again, he describes the bad taste that Sonoko and Mitsuko display not as a personal failing but as a regional trait: "The taste for gaudy and loud things is, after all, [typical of] Osaka women." Sensei takes evident delight in detailing that bad taste, and comments, with a shiver of distaste, "This author was quite taken aback at the sight."[30] In this way, the notes assert an ethnographic mastery of the local. Sensei presents himself as the most effective of ethnographers, one who has won the trust of his research objects—a trust he betrays with his asides addressed to his audience in the capital.

Whereas Sonoko's narration is emphatically oral and local, Sensei's is literary and national. By labeling them "author's notes," his text claims the writerly prerogative that Sonoko's testimony cedes at the outset. By framing her narrative with these notes, however minimal, Sensei attempts to turn it into one long citation, framed within his own. Though Sonoko is the teller of her tale, Sensei is the author of the novel. In this way, *Manji* dramatizes the process of citation that Miyako Inoue describes in *Vicarious Language*. Inoue argues that national language cites and contains "women's language," in the process depriving the gendered other "of its semiotic capacity to provide itself with *metalanguage* (an authoritative representation of what the cited voice means)." She writes, "The epistemic violence of linguistic modernity lies, therefore, not so much in its erasure of what the other is saying but in the exclusion of what the other is saying about what he or she said."[31] Or, as Shibata Shōji puts it in his study of "the narrator who cannot 'tale'-tell," Sonoko "cannot occupy a metalevel in regard to the past experiences of the self [that narrates]."[32] In *Manji*, Tanizaki applies this strategy of citation to the local–national dynamic. By containing Sonoko's story within his own, Sensei attempts to exclude what the suburban Osaka of the present day is saying about its urban past.

Thus, *Manji* makes Kansai the locus for what Marilyn Ivy has called "the modern uncanny." Ivy explores this notion through an analysis of "the founding work of Japanese folklore studies," *Tōno monogatari* (Tales of Tōno), a collection of stories from rural Iwate Prefecture published in 1910—just twenty years before *Manji*—by Yanagita Kunio, who claimed to have transcribed the stories "as they were told" to him by his native informant, Sasaki Kizen. Just as Ivy suggests it was for Yanagita, so it seems that for Tanizaki, "thinking about that which evades representation—voices, dialects, margins, ghosts, deaths, monsters—was a way of thinking about literary writing: that writing which . . . writes what cannot be said."[33] In *Manji*, Tanizaki dramatizes a relationship between informant and ethnographer much like the one Ivy discovers in *Tōno*, in which "Sasaki's unskilled tales provided precisely the lack that Yanagita—as author and ethnographer—would supplement with his own literary skills."[34] By doing so, he calls our attention to the strategy whereby the ethnographer asserts his mastery and containment of the marginalized local.

Tanizaki offers us no one-sided contest, however. Sonoko effectively relativizes Sensei in turn. She hails him into the diagesis with her first word, that vocative "Sensei." She quickly identifies and particularizes him as a novelist and grounds his narrative act in the local space of the Hanshin-kan, denying him transcendence of the story-world. We might even argue that she uses Sensei to disseminate her story and her language, making him the host to her agent. Asserting narrative mastery, Sensei is (willingly?) mastered. Recall, from the first lines of her story, Sonoko's reference to the novel her narration will become: is it really unwitting? It rather suggests that Sonoko, at least, knows just what game they are playing.

This is the narratological drama of Tanizaki's novel—the struggle to assert and deny a transcendent position from which to narrate the local. Bakhtin writes, "When there is no access to one's own personal, 'ultimate' word, then every thought, feeling, experience must be refracted through the medium of someone else's discourse, someone else's style, someone else's manner, with which it cannot immediately be merged without reservation, without distance, without refraction."[35] In *Manji*, who is being refracted through whom? Is it Sonoko, in the context of Osaka's loss of primacy and its progressive containment and subordination to national forms, forced to refract her story through Sensei's national writing? Or is it Sensei, in the context of what Tanizaki perceived to be an increasingly homogenized and westernized Japan, forced to refract his story through Sonoko's local speech? In either instance, we must acknowledge the potential for the refracted voice to turn this process to its advantage. In the first instance, the national language becomes a channel, allowing the eccentric voice to infiltrate and potentially undermine those processes of containment and subordination. In the second, dialect becomes a refuge from the depredations of language's nationalization and perceived westernization. Or, finally, is it Mitsuko, the symbol of Senba, who is doubly refracted, first through Sonoko's oral narration and then through Sensei's written narration? And if so, how does she turn this process to her benefit?

GENDER IN *MANJI*

I have been using male pronouns to refer to Sensei, but in fact, as Atsuko Sakaki points out, *Manji* does not definitively identify Sensei as a man. The respectful title "sensei" does not indicate the gender of the addressee, nor does the grammar of direct address in Japanese. If Sensei's narration, like Sonoko's, were presented as (transcribed) speech, then the vocabulary, the sentence-ending particles, and other elements of the original Japanese would likely indicate the "speaker's" gender. However, because they are presented in the written national standard, the "author's notes" reveal little about the author's gender (or geographical origins or social position, for that matter). *Genbun'itchi* is precisely a technology for subsuming such particularities into a national subject. Nevertheless, Sensei has invariably been taken for a man. The revelation that Sensei is a well-known novelist living somewhere in the Hanshin-kan suggests an identification with Tanizaki himself, and as Sakaki notes, details about Sensei in the original serialized version of the novel encouraged that identification. Furthermore, the "author's notes" are filled with the sort of blithely judgmental ethnographic observations that Tanizaki himself made in essays published soon after his move there, such as "Hanshin kenbunroku" (Hanshin observations, 1925). The director Masumura Yasuzō cast a male actor, Mitsuda Ken, as Sensei in his 1964 film adaptation, a figure shown sitting in the shadows, silent, as Sonoko begins her narrative. Howard Hibbett, deprived of the Japanese language's potential for ambiguity, uses a male pronoun to refer to Sensei in his 1994 English translation ("'Really, you're a friend of his?' she said").[36]

While we may understand the character of Sensei to be male, however, it is important to recognize exactly *how* he is male. Sensei is unmarkedly male, nonspecifically male. The obscurity of Sensei's gender is critical to his participation in the narrative contest that *Manji* dramatizes. It buttresses Sensei's assertion of a disinterested transcendence that would give him the upper hand in that contest. We have already considered how Sensei's narration models a strategy of citation whereby written narration purports to transcend speech and a Tokyo-centric national sensibility purports to transcend the local. So, too, does it model an abstracted national masculinity that purports to transcend gender.

Manji defines this national masculinity against the other male characters in Sonoko's story. Sonoko's husband, Kōtarō, prefigures the characters Teinosuke and Tatsuo in *Sasameyuki* (who are discussed in detail in chapter 4); all three attempt, with mixed success, to join in a newly established petit bourgeois economic masculinity. Like Teinosuke the accountant and Tatsuo the banker, Kōtarō the lawyer has taken his place in a new white-collar, corporate economy. Like them, he lives in the suburbs. Like them again, however, he remains financially dependent on his wife and, through her, tied to an older economy that is mercantile and rooted in Senba.

Mitsuko's lover, Watanuki Eijirō, is a more compromised male figure. A Senba bonbon like Kei-bon in *Sasameyuki*, he enacts an anachronistic masculinity, irreconcilable and even menacing to modern marriage and productive sexuality. When Sonoko describes meeting him for the second time, she recalls thinking, "Oh, what a beautiful boy!" (Aa, binanshi [bidanshi] ya naa).[37] Later, she recounts hearing that Watanuki is "impotent and a sexual neuter" (Munōryoku-sha de chūsei no ningen) who has been taught by a lesbian how to pleasure himself, and that he is said to be a "man-woman" or "woman-man" ("Otoko-onna" ya toka "onna-otoko" ya toka iu yō ni natta non ya sō desu).[38] Sensei affirms Watanuki's queerness in an author's note, describing the young man's handwriting as "kosekose shita," suggesting with this and with other details a distasteful fussiness about Watanuki. The three significant male characters in *Manji* thus clearly mark the novel's three levels: Watanuki is irredeemably urban, local, and queer. Kōtarō is neither fully local nor fully national, living in the suburbs with one foot in the modern bourgeois economy and one back in Senba. Married but cuckolded and seduced by his wife's female lover, Kōtarō figures a sexuality that is apparently normative but in fact perverse. Neither constitutes a threat to the national authority that Sensei, the third male character, asserts.

With this authority, Sensei attempts to cite and thereby contain a story of queer desire. Noguchi Takehiko has discussed this theme in *Manji* with reference to the novel Tanizaki wrote just prior, *Chijin no ai* (A fool's love, 1924; published in English as *Naomi*). Noguchi suggests that Tanizaki presented the main character of the earlier novel, Naomi, as a sort of transcendent existence, a *kami* (god), but because Naomi exists within the context of Jōji's heterosexual desire, she can attain transcendence only within the male imagination. With *Manji*, Noguchi supposes, Tanizaki wanted to see if a woman could attain a similar transcendence outside the male imagination: "One subject of *Manji* is whether it is possible, in the world of lesbianism, which does not permit the participation of male consciousness, for woman to transcend herself."[39] The male imagination is by no means absent from *Manji*, however; it manifests in Sensei's role as auditor, narrator, and judge. In the earlier novel, Jōji's first-person narration requires no framing device. *Chijin no ai* begins with an "I" addressing the reader directly: "Watashi wa kore kara . . . " In contrast, Sonoko's narration in *Manji* begins with "Sensei," as she recounts her story for his delectation, guided by his implied interrogatives. His hand inscribes her voice and, in so doing, purports to contain her confession of queer desire within a transcendent male fantasy, consonant with the fantasy of linguistic transcendence imagined by the proponents of *hyōjungo* as well as the broader imperial-national fantasy of a political, economic, and cultural transcendence of the local.

Manji, then, presents us with three orders, each contained by the next, expressed in terms of space, of economy, of gender and sexuality, and of narrative authority. In the first order we have Watanuki and Mitsuko, envoys of Senba and of the merchant economy that thrived there. Fundamentally queer characters, they claim almost no authority to narrate their own tales. These two local characters are instead narrated by Sonoko, who together with Kōtarō occupies the second order. Bourgeois envoys of the suburbs, neither fully in nor fully outside the city, married but seduced by the queerness that emanates from the city's center, they perform a sexuality that is similarly ambivalent. Sonoko claims the authority to narrate Mitsuko's story but is in turn narrated by Sensei, who inhabits the third order. The author of novels, writing in the standard language, a man alone and inviolate, Sensei is an envoy from the would-be transcendent space of nation—"an empire of language that so privileges the male sex as to confuse it with the human race."[40]

These orders are not perfectly discrete, however, and containment is more asserted than accomplished. Mitsuko and Watanuki manage to author their own tales to some degree—she through her letters to Sonoko, and he through the contract he pens and forces Sonoko to sign, for Sonoko shows these documents to Sensei, who then records them as part of the transcript that ostensibly forms the text of *Manji*. The queerness of those documents bleeds through Sonoko's story and tints Sensei's entire manuscript.

GENRE IN *MANJI*

Manji deploys one more citational practice that participates in these dynamics of speech and writing and the local and the national, and in the theme of transcendence: the generic citation by the novel of older performance traditions. Several of Tanizaki's novels reference Japan's literary tradition in various ways. Critics have noted the elements of classic *monogatari*, or tales, in the style of his later works. Furthermore, Tanizaki, like many other novelists, borrowed themes and plot elements from classical works; Orikuchi Shinobu and Noguchi Takehiko have identified in *Sasameyuki*, for example, elements from *Taketori monogatari* (The reedcutter's tale) and *Genji monogatari* (The tale of Genji). Here, however, I want to draw attention to his citation of a later genre with close links to Osaka.

The plot of *Manji* alludes to a representative text of a performance genre closely associated with Osaka: Chikamatsu Monzaemon's *jōruri* drama *Shinjū: Ten no Amijima* (The love suicides at Amijima, 1721). In each work, a love triangle involving a husband and wife and another woman ends in the double suicide of the husband and the other woman, a double suicide that, as Eric Gangloff has explained, the wife "authors"—in *Amijima*, through Osan's decision to reveal that she sent a letter to her husband's lover, Koharu, and in *Manji*, through Sonoko's decision to bring together Mitsuko and her husband and to encourage their affair.[41] Both stories revolve around obligations and written pledges. *Manji* has the love letters that Sonoko and Mitsuko exchange and the sham contract that Watanuki cons Sonoko into signing (both of which Sensei transcribes, reiterating their written character, in long "author's notes"). These compare, in *Amijima*, to the written oaths that Jihei and Koharu have exchanged, the letter from Osan to Koharu that implies a debt Koharu tries to honor, the promise that Jihei's aunt requires him to write down on paper for Gozaemon, and the bill of divorcement that Gozaemon tries to force Jihei to write. Even the extended description in *Manji* of the two women's note paper reminds us of the numerous playful references to paper in Chikamatsu's drama.

Like the narrative negotiation previously detailed, this citation of Chikamatsu's play and of the *jōruri* tradition manifests the tension between local and national forms. Tanizaki's Kansai novels often reference regional artistic traditions. In *Tade kū mushi* (Some prefer nettles), the father's love of the puppet theater and a performance of the same Chikamatsu play, *Amijima*, galvanizes Tanizaki's theme of the tension between East and West, tradition and modernity. In *Sasameyuki*, Taeko's study of a local Osaka style of dance reveals the trace of tradition in the most modern of the four sisters; the death of her teacher, the last of that style, signals a broader passing of local tradition. In these works, Tanizaki cites a genre that is historically associated with pre-Meiji Osaka. He cites it in such a way as to relegate the genre—and, by extension, Osaka itself—to tradition and relativize it to the modern prose genre within which he is working. In *Manji*, Tanizaki cites Osaka tradition—Osaka *as* tradition—by borrowing elements of his plot from one of Chikamatsu's most famous plays and containing them within the written notes of a man diagetically identified as a *shōsetsu-ka* (novelist).

Here again, the local–national dynamic is linked to socioeconomic developments. The Osaka tradition that Tanizaki cites is the *sewamono*, which famously treated the concerns of the city's merchant class at the early stage of modernity in Japan. *Amijima* links merchant and "pleasure" quarters in a local economy mapped through a litany of shop names and street corners, and through a running account of money earned and owed. The play presents the periphery of the city as the limit of this economy, a place from which to access transcendence in the Pure Land through love suicide. The letter from Osan to Koharu, by which the former "authors" that love suicide, attests to a vow between the two women—one from the merchant quarter, one from the licensed quarter—a vow with implications for religious salvation. *Manji*, on the other hand, links the merchant quarter and that new feminine space of seduction, the suburbs.[42] Mitsuko belongs to the former space, Sonoko to the latter, and to the new middle class that settled the Hanshin-kan. The letters they exchange lead to a love suicide in the suburbs. But that suicide is farcified by Sonoko's participation, her survival, and her narration of the tale for Sensei's benefit. What Osan in *Amijima* calls "*onnadōshi no giri*" (obligation between women) becomes a sexual infatuation that descends into scenes of masochism retold for Sensei's benefit. In place of *Amijima*'s excession from Confucian immanence to Buddhist transcendence, *Manji* substitutes graduation from the urban merchant economy to white-collar work and concentrated capitalism in a progressive historical trajectory. Tanizaki rewrites Chikamatsu's merchant tragedy as bourgeois farce.

How should we account for Tanizaki's foregrounding of these citational practices and his treatment of the text he cites? We have seen already how *Manji* dramatizes the tension between spoken and written word, highlighting the act of *énonciation*. By presenting Sensei's "transcription" of the letters between Sonoko and Mitsuko and the contract between Sonoko and Watanuki, the novel draws attention to the act of citation. By framing the novel as Sensei's record of Sonoko's testimony, it references the broad historical transition from *jōruri* to novel, and the process by which narration was abstracted and disembodiment. Finally, by inviting a comparison between the lofty themes of Chikamatsu and its own mundane concerns, *Manji* seems to dispute either the quality of transcendence or the access to it.

Tanizaki provocatively signals ambivalence toward the notion of transcendence with his reference to the figure of Kannon (in a novel that he titled with the Buddhist symbol for "dharma"). Recall that love blooms between the two women in *Manji* after Sonoko portrays Mitsuko as the bodhisattva (or the bodhisattva as Mitsuko). As a bodhisattva, Kannon's existence is defined not by a completed transcendence but by transcendence held in abeyance. Kannon is a shape-shifter who takes on various appearances, male and female, to end suffering, willing to incarnate in whatever particularity is required by those who call her name.[43] For Sonoko, the petit bourgeois suburban housewife, she incarnates as the daughter of a merchant house in the old downtown, avatar of an earlier modernity that lifted Osaka to preeminence. The bodhisattva's name, Guanyin/Kannon or Guanshiyin/Kanzeon (觀音/觀世音), derives from the Sanskrit Avalokitasvara; means "perceiver of sound," "observing the cries [of the world]"; and refers to the practice of listening. Sonoko, who eschews writing and begs Sensei to listen to the story she narrates in her local language, idealizes her crush object as a goddess who abjures transcendence and manifests in particularity in order to listen to those who are mired in immanence. This would-be Kannon, however, completes her love suicide and thus—according to the conventions of the *jōruri* genre—achieves transcendence in the Pure Land. It is rather Sonoko who, like the bodhisattva, stays behind.

Authenticity and Mastery

The negotiations in *Manji* between speech and writing, and between local and national language, are complicated by questions of insider and outsider status and the values of authenticity and mastery. These questions not only run through the story itself; they also accompanied both the production of the novel and the critical reaction that it drew.

Tanizaki did not begin by writing *Manji* in dialect, and he was not solely responsible for the dialect in the final published version. *Manji* was originally published in installments from 1928 to 1930. In the first installment, Tanizaki rendered both Sensei's written narration and Sonoko's "spoken" narration in forms of the national standard language. He began to use Osaka language for Sonoko's narration only with the second installment. The author and critic Kōno Taeko, an Osaka native, notes that Tanizaki's attempts at dialect in the second installment are still awkward, nothing like the smooth dialect of the later book version. By the second half of the third installment, both the dialogue and Sonoko's narration are in dialect, but for the fourth installment, Tanizaki returned to standard Japanese for the narration. Kōno also notes that Tanizaki's rate of production fell off as he (presumably) struggled with the dialect; while the first two installments ran to five and five and a half pages respectively, the third fills only two and a half pages, and the fourth, only three. Tanizaki had lived in the Kansai region for only five years when he began writing *Manji*. Once he decided to use dialect for Sonoko's narration consistently throughout the novel, he employed two young women, students from the English department of an Osaka women's college, to help him. Kōno hypothesizes that Tanizaki must have prepared his manuscripts in standard Japanese, then given them to these two "dialect consultants" ("*hōgen no komon*"—Tanizaki's term, from his introduction to the 1931 *tankōbon* edition), who would translate them. Tanizaki's mastery of the local therefore required editorial submission to two local college students: an irony that perhaps appealed to a writer with a taste for reversals of power relations.

Tanizaki's attempts to render Kansai dialects in *Manji* and in later works elicited comment from several Osaka writers. Kōno's 1976 essay provides a particularly vivid example of the insider's reaction. She begins by identifying herself as "someone with connections to Osaka, including the Hanshin-kan." She first details Tanizaki's use of the language consultants.[44] She then reports that although one of Tanizaki's consultants was born and raised in Osaka, the other came from Okayama, where she would have heard and used a Kansai dialect but not an Osaka one. This, Kōno suggests, accounts for the peculiar quality of the dialect in the story, which she finds inelegant and inappropriate to Sonoko's age and situation.[45] After reviewing the history of the novel's production and before getting around to a discussion of its masochism, Kōno spends seven pages detailing Tanizaki's mistakes in dialect, even suggesting alternative translations.

Kōno's critique attempts to reverse the gaze from Tokyo, countering Tanizaki's mastery with an assertion of her own authenticity. But does she miss the point of mastery? We speak of actors "mastering" an accent. The appreciation of such mastery divides the audience into insiders and outsiders—or, in other words, a local audience and a national audience. A Boston native cannot watch a movie like *The Departed* without passing judgment on the actors' attempts at a local accent. That judgment, like Kōno's, is grounded in local authority. The performance of that mastery, on the other hand, depends on outsider status. The native can never master his or her own dialect; only the outsider can. Mastery involves a kind of citation: as filmgoers, we know that Leonardo DiCaprio is not from Boston, and this extradiagetic knowledge places his production of a local accent in quotation marks; it makes the production a performance. By writing *Manji* in dialect, Tanizaki made no claim to an *authentic* Kansai voice; indeed, the inauthenticity of his narration is the point, since authenticity is irreconcilable to mastery. Moreover, Kōno's critique presumes a "natural" *Ōsaka-ben*, against which she judges Tanizaki's, and claims this natural dialect for the native speaker. This denies her own performance of local language. Precisely because standard language is, by definition, a language to be mastered (by everyone) and, in this sense, no one's authentic language, it is rather in "dialect" (and locality generally) that mastery and authenticity must be performed. The nation produces the local as a site of performance—a performance that invokes these competing values of mastery and authenticity.

Decades earlier, Oda Sakunosuke offered a more ingenious critique of Tanizaki's Osaka idiom. Oda, an author closely associated with Osaka from his earliest works, included his detailed remarks on *Manji* in the essay "Ōsaka no kanōsei" (Osaka's potentiality, 1947), in which he comments on several writers' attempts to render Osaka dialect in literature. Oda writes, "I often think that there is no language more difficult than Osaka dialect to put into writing." The difficulty arises from the fact that Osaka dialect has no standard, he writes; variation is its defining characteristic. He criticizes Tanizaki for failing to grasp this, writing of *Manji*:

> The intention of the author to try to write this work entirely in *Ōsaka-ben* meets with success. Yet this novel's *Ōsaka-ben*, although not stereotypical [*monkirigata*] *Ōsaka-ben*, somehow feels like a standardized [*hyōjungata*] *Ōsaka-ben*. Ordinary Osakans use a more corrupted style of *Ōsaka-ben*, and almost no one chatters away in this sort of standard *Ōsaka-ben*. This is an

> aestheticized and idealized *Ōsaka-ben*, and the effort to be Osaka-like in every detail, on the contrary, erases the reality of *Ōsaka-ben*.[46]

For Oda, the potential of the Osaka language for literature lies in its richness of nuance and variety, its deviation from standards and expectations. He argues that, in this, the language reflects the broader character of the region and its people:

> It is not only language; there are many traditionally accepted opinions about the Osaka region and the characteristics common to Osakans. . . . [But] every time I see or hear such a fixed idea, I feel, "Ah, Osaka is not well understood." Actually, Osakans will show their tail only when they deviate from fixed stereotypes, and unless one catches that tail, one cannot understand Osaka. This is exactly what Osaka's potentiality is about.[47]

By insisting that its true nature resides in its variance and unpredictability, Oda defines Osaka in such a way as to make it unmasterable. Tanizaki's very mastery betrays his inauthenticity, and the more masterful, the less authentic.

Yayakoshii

Oda's critique of *Manji* and his characterization of Osaka evoke a notion that had been circulating among other Osaka literati: of Osaka as *yayakoshii* (complicated, confused). One of these was Koide Narashige (1887–1931), a well-known painter of *yoga*, or Western-style pictures, who was also an essayist and a native of Osaka. In his essay "Ōsaka-ben zatsudan" (Ramblings on Osaka dialect, 1930), Koide wrote of his discomfort in speaking standard Japanese, and the estrangement from language that results:

> Osaka people are born with *Ōsaka-ben*, Tokyo people are born with *Tōkyō-ben*. How wonderful, if the language you were born with by chance becomes your country's standard language! When someone like me, who speaks *Ōsaka-ben*, goes to say something correctly, it comes out sounding like lines from a play—and not very good lines! And because I'm conscious of the poor quality of my lines, I become hesitant about what I want to say, and I become angry at my inability to express myself. Like thinking

> about waltzing as you're fleeing an earthquake—it's that bad an estrangement. The unpleasant feeling that my heart, my words, and my intonation are unrelated—it's unbearable![48]

For Koide, standardization brings a consciousness of the performativity of speech. He goes on to express his regret at the effect of standardization on Osaka language, which has become but a shadow of itself, he writes, "clad in a robe of *hyōjungo*."[49] In another essay, "Mossari suru mandan" (An uncouth discourse), Koide identifies the word "*yayakoshii*" as one of several regional words that the people of Kansai use to express complicated ideas, and in yet another essay, "Yayakoshiki manpitsu" (Confused jottings/Jottings on "*yayakoshiki*"), he elaborates on this "valuable" word that expresses contradictions in one's heart: an ally that is also an enemy, someone you love but hate or hate but love. For Koide, "*yayakoshii*" captures the contradictory essence of Osaka, an essence inscrutable to outsiders.

This contradictory essence comes up again in a literary exchange prompted by Koide's death. Tanizaki mentioned the artist in his long essay "Watakushi no mita Ōsaka oyobi Ōsakajin" (Osaka and Osakans as I see them, 1932), citing Koide as "the most exemplary artist of Osaka." It is in some sense a backhanded compliment, based on what Tanizaki perceives to be Koide's provincialism and the commercial nature of his work. In the essay, Tanizaki condemns Osaka as a city preoccupied with moneymaking and unconducive to artistic production. He writes:

> If even one great novelist had lived in Osaka during the years of Meiji-Taishō, the city would have produced one or two works comparable to [Higuchi Ichiyō's] *Takekurabe* [Growing up] or [Nagai Kafū's] *Sumidagawa* [The river Sumida], but there is not even one such. This can safely be called a disgrace for such a large city. Broadly speaking, it should be considered a loss to Japanese literature that all novelists discard their hometown and set their minds on Tokyo.[50]

Asked by a newspaper for his reaction to Tanizaki's essay, the painter Nabei Katsuyuki wrote his own essay on "Ōsaka damashii" (The Osaka spirit, 1932). In it, after disputing Tanizaki's characterization of Koide as provincial and commercial, Nabei agrees with Tanizaki that Osaka's merchant spirit is inimical to artists. Next, however, he asserts that the struggle with this spirit is the essential quality of Osaka's artistic production:

> [Tanizaki] insists that, if there is no hometown author like Kubota Mantarō left in Osaka, it is to the great city's shame.[51] But this is the passing remark of an outsider, the superficial opinion of someone who doesn't know the inside story. Just as I have been saying, the "Osaka spirit" has become a heavy artistic burden for artists born in Osaka, and every one of the Osaka artists I know curses the "Osaka spirit" that resides within himself . . . [but] if one were to write "Osaka" only with the sort of pure hometown love that Kubota Mantarō holds for Tokyo, the spirit of true Osaka locality [*shin no Ōsaka kyōdo no tamashii*] would not emerge. It is difficult to write a sort of self-intoxicated Osaka while thinking, "To hell with that garbage!" And at the same time, if you are not thinking, "To hell with that!" then you're not a true Osaka artist.[52]

For Nabei, a literature proper to Osaka must be complicated and confused by the author's resentment of Osaka's merchant essence.

Uno Kōji (1891–1961), one of the greatest authors of modern Osaka, picks up on this idea in one in a series of essays on his childhood (Uno was born in Fukuoka but was sent to Osaka at the age of eight and grew up near the Dōtonbori, the center of nightlife in old Osaka). Uno begins by citing Tanizaki's essay, then quotes at length both Koide's "Yayakoshiki manpitsu" and Nabei's "Ōsaka damashii" (including the preceding passage). Uno then concludes, "These two excerpts from Koide and Nabei are really Osaka-ish. And borrowing their words makes this essay really '*yayakoshii*.' That being the case, it is not incorrect to see it as symbolizing Osaka and Osakans. Framing this as a conclusion, it becomes 'the *yayakoshii* capital and a *yayakoshii* people,' in other words, 'Osaka and Osakans.'"[53]

Oda managed to convey this quality of *yayakoshi-sa* in his own writing. Oda was an acquaintance of Uno's and was certainly influenced by the older writer's work; he referenced another of Uno's essay from the same series, "Ki no nai miyako" (City of no trees) in the title and opening passage of his own story, "Ki no miyako" (City of trees, 1944). Throughout his Osaka fiction, Oda fully exploits the potential of the Japanese writing system for what we might call "heterography"—ways of rendering words on the page that mark them as nonstandard. The most common of these is the katakana syllabary, used primarily to highlight language or to mark it as outside the everyday. Writers often use katakana to indicate local variations of "standard" pronunciation. Oda uses katakana in this way; for example, in *Zoku meoto zenzai*, we read the exclamation, "*aa shindō*" (Aah, I'm exhausted!), written "ああしんどオ."[54] "*Shindoi*" is a

Kansai word, used where a speaker of standard Japanese would probably say "*tsukareta*." Here, the "o" sound rendered in katakana indicates the Kansai practice of dropping the final "i" and lengthening the penultimate vowel sound. Oda also uses various forms of glossing to highlight differences between local and national language. For some *kanji* compounds, he supplies pronunciation glosses in *rubi* or parenthetical glosses for *Kansai-ben*—for example, where he glosses the Kansai word "*benchara*" (flattery) with the standard word "*o-sēji*."[55] Furthermore, in Oda, local words and forms are not strictly relegated to speech but occasionally infiltrate narrative description as well. Such devices not only render the pronunciation and vocabulary of Osaka but also illustrate in a small but insistent way the artificiality of the national grammar and orthography that has been imposed on the local—the attempt to standardize Osaka. Oda exploits the potential of the Osaka vernacular within *hyōjungo* to rediscover the plurilingualism in Japanese.

By comparison, in *Manji*, a novel composed almost entirely in dialect, Tanizaki takes almost no advantage of the potential for heterography. Tanizaki uses katakana in *Manji* mostly to indicate the longer final vowel sounds. For example, the word pronounced "*kii*" in Kansai and "*ki*" in standard Japanese (mind, disposition) is rendered with the Sino-Japanese character and the katakana "*i*"; likewise, the word "*ee/e*" (picture). But Tanizaki makes little use of the various forms of gloss in his Kansai novels and seldom if ever allows local words and forms to infiltrate the non-person narration (*Manji*, of course, has no such narration).

The standardization of grammar and orthography, together with the rise of *genbun'itchi*, asserted the transparency of the narration of national subjectivity and denied the same transparency to local speech, which was made nonstandard, to be rendered with *rubi*, katakana, and other opaque marks of aberrance. Oda exploits these marks, materializing the *yayakoshii* quality of local language. Oda's careful and, one might say, pointed discrimination between standard and nonstandard language constitutes, in and of itself, a statement about the relation of the local to the national, the particular to the universal, the frankly immanent to the would-be transcendent. As previously demonstrated, in *Manji*, Tanizaki addresses that relation in terms of space, economy, gender, and genre—and, most fundamentally, through the narrative structure of the novel. In all these ways, Tanizaki disputes the simplistic notion of the subordination of the immanent local to the transcendent nation. Oda's critique suggests, however, that Tanizaki betrays his own critique by reducing Osaka complex and contradictory local language to a different sort of simple standard. In recording it, Tanizaki has codified it, giving in to the same ethnological impulse that Ivy identifies in Yanagita's *Tōno monogatari*, in which "Yanagita not only wrote down the unwritten and changed the vernacular to the literary, but also produced a *dialectal* vernacular as the standard literary."[56]

Narration as Translation

The stakes of the negotiation recorded in *Manji* become clearer if we think of national and local languages in terms of translation, in the sense that Walter Benjamin and, later, Jacques Derrida theorize it. In the essays "On Language as Such and on the Language of Man" (1916) and "The Task of the Translator" (1923), Benjamin theorizes the relation between a plurality of immanent idioms (the languages of man) and a singular transcendent language. The translator's task, as Benjamin saw it, is not simply to represent or transmit accurately the information in a given text but to "liberate the language imprisoned in a work in his re-creation of that work."[57] Benjamin framed his practical prescriptions within a messianic concept of language that exalts translation as the means of access to "a higher and purer linguistic air" where we may gain some intimation of the nature of pure language. In *Monolingualism of the Other*, Jacques Derrida responds with evident sympathy to Benjamin's prescriptions. At the same time, he raises a concern at several points across his extended engagement with Benjamin. That concern focuses on the relation between the many languages and the one, and the distinction between an *invented* monolingualism that functions as a "prosthesis of origin" for the diverse idioms in which we write and speak, and an *imposed* monolingualism of the colonizer, "the language of the master."[58]

Benjamin develops the notion of a prelapsarian ideal language in "On Language as Such." He describes a language of pure name that Adam knew before the Fall and "the plurality of languages" that multiply afterward, as humankind "makes of language a means," a "mere sign."[59] In "Task," he elaborates on the relation between singularity and plurality, of pure language and idioms, with two key metaphors: the kinship of languages and the shattered vessel. Both metaphors emphasize the partial nature of those entities that make up the plurality, denying wholeness to any one of them alone; both prescribe an inevitable transcendence of this partial nature; and both describe this transcendence as a consolidation into totality. The whole vessel represents the full intention of pure language, which cannot be realized except in totality. Each fragment is one earthly idiom, which shares in that original intention but remains incomplete. The analogy denies wholeness and sufficiency to idiom; if the purpose of a vessel is to contain, then the individual shards remain useless until they are reassembled. The analogy therefore implies a necessary transformation from fragmentation to wholeness through a process of restoration.

The analogy of the vessel clarifies the terms of Benjamin's earlier metaphor, that of the kinship of languages. Benjamin describes the plural idioms as interdependent and insufficient, each on its own, by emphasizing that their relationship is filial. Their kinship is not based on "a vague alikeness," he specifies; rather, "All suprahistorical kinship of languages rests in the fact that in every one of them as a whole . . . one and the same is meant, which, however, is not reachable by any one of them, but only by the totality of their mutually supplementing intentions—pure language."[60] According to Derrida in "Des Tours de Babel," what connects the plural languages is "transmission of a family seed."[61] If the kinship of languages rests in intention, then that intention is like an inherited genetic code. Pure language, as the sum of these intentions, is realized through the reconsolidation of that disseminated code. Benjamin's account is of a singular pure language as the origin and end of idiom's plurality. Singularity is a promise within idiom's plurality, and translation reveals that promise to us.

In response to this conception of singularity and plurality, Derrida posits in *Monolingualism* the uncountability of language, between an invented monolingualism that can belong to no one and an infinity of idioms that must remain only promises. Derrida writes that the colonial subject possesses only languages of arrival (*langue d'arrivée*); denied a mother tongue, the colonial invents one in order to define an *I* in which to write in alienation to it. Having invented this monolingualism of the other, the subject marks on it "a language different enough to disallow its own reappropriation within the norms, the body, and the law of the given language." The result is an "untranslatable translation" of the monolanguage "that gives *a* language the uniqueness of idiom, but only by promising to give it."[62] This performance of linguistic invention makes testimony possible.

Manji presents us with a literary performance of this process. Sensei takes Sonoko's testimony, given in her uniquely local idiom, and marks it on the invented monolanguage of *hyōjungo*, just as Tanizaki submitted his own testimony, which he had written in that monolanguage, to translation by local women, his "language consultants." Where this performance fails, for Oda, is in the resulting idiom of testimony—too standard, too completely translated, not nuanced enough to "disallow its reappropriation within the . . . given language." Oda, in line with Koide, Nabei, and Uno, identifies the complicatedness, the contrariness, of Osaka language as the quality that makes it untranslatable and that disallows its reappropriation, and faults Tanizaki for ironing out those folds.

In Derrida's account, Benjamin's plurality of earthly languages becomes uncountable, like the infinite individual idioms written upon French. Likewise, monolingualism remains uncountable because it is retrojected into a "past that was never present" and therefore belongs to no one. This goes back to the antinomy with which he opens his essay: "1. We only ever speak one language—or rather one idiom only; 2. We never speak only one language—or rather, there is no pure idiom."[63] Derrida brandishes this antinomy against the threat of colonial violence, for he speaks of "the monolingualism of the other" in another sense: as that monolingualism imposed by an other, "through a sovereignty whose essence is always colonial, which tends, repressively and irrepressively, to reduce language to the One, that is, to the hegemony of the homogenous."[64] As the alien monolanguage upon which the writing *I* marks its idiomaticity, the monolanguage is always promised, never present. In this sense, it is a messianic promise. But he warns that in another sense, in a present sense, "the language of the other as the language of the master or colonist" also contains a threat of colonial violence: "in the eschatological or messianic horizon that this promise cannot deny—or that it can merely deny—the pre-originary language can always run the risk of becoming or wanting to be another language of the master, sometimes that of new masters."[65]

Although Benjamin clearly states that pure language cannot be experienced on earth, we can easily imagine the danger Derrida warns of, easily imagine how the implications of Benjamin's metaphors—the filial relationship, the denial of independence to any part, the narrative of reconsolidation into a transcendent totality—could be co-opted by an imperial project. This, indeed, is the story told by the ideology of *kokugo*—that a pure Japanese language existed prior to the corruption, the twisting, which results in "dialects" in both the home islands and "brother nations" beyond; and that the return to that pure language requires that the "corrupt" be purified and the "twisted" made straight.

Derrida is talking here specifically of a colonial experience, and although he argues that this experience is "exemplary of a universal structure" that "represents or reflects a type of originary 'alienation' that institutes every language as a language of the other,"[66] he insists that his alienation as a colonial is not only different but more complete than the alienation of the provincial: "For the child from Provence or Brittany, there is surely an analogous phenomenon. . . . But the other, in this case, no longer has the same transcendence of the *overthere*, the distancing of *being-elsewhere*, the inaccessible authority of a master who lives *overseas*. A sea is lacking there."[67] As we acknowledge the qualitative difference between these two experiences, however, we can again recognize continuities: the attempted containment of idiomatic diversity by grammatical law, in one instance located in the colony and the metropole with a sea between and, in the other, in the imagined spaces of city and nation separated by the gap between two imagined orders, urban and national. "Dialects" are among the multiplicity of languages of arrival aiming toward the "originary" monolanguage, and a speaking *I* characterized by locality is produced in that act of narration as translation.

Conclusion

Language reforms beginning in Meiji and continuing through postwar occupation presented the establishment of a national language (in spoken and written forms) as the reunification and transcendence of local idioms. At the same time, *genbun'itchi* and related innovations in prose narrative established a new narrative mode purported to transcend the story-world. Rendered in a variant of the new national language, this mode realigned the relation between narrative ground and a character's discourse in terms of a transcendent national sensibility and an immanent local sensibility.

Manji, written just after Tanizaki moved from Tokyo to Osaka and in direct response to the effects of *genbun'itchi*, explores the relation between national and local languages by staging a contest over the authority to narrate the local. This contest spills over into the arenas of gender and sexuality and genre. Key to this contest is a strategy of citation employed by both Sonoko, the voice of the local, and Sensei, the representative of national authority. But citation is not a perfect strategy; it cannot completely contain Mitsuko and her partner, Watanuki, in their queerness, their locality, their urbanity. *Manji* teases the reader with the threat—the promise—of the narratee turning the tables on the narrator, of the local exceeding the boundaries that the national order imposes. By foregrounding this practice of citation and entertaining the prospect of its failure, Tanizaki calls attention to the construction of a language and a mode that framed the citation of dialogue in terms of the nation containing the local.

Osakan critics, however, objected to Tanizaki's presumption in narrating the local. Responding to Tanizaki's displays of mastery, these critics opposed their claims of authenticity. They sought to define the character of the local in terms of an essentially unmasterable *yayakoshisa*. Oda in particular draws attention to Tanizaki's repression of difference, revealing an operation that is continuous with colonial domination. For while Tanizaki's story challenges the local's subordination, the language in which he writes it "standardizes" Osaka language, training it to national orthography. Oda, by stressing *Osaka-ben*'s *yayakoshisa* and by exploiting the potential of Japanese heterography to render it, makes it opaque and reveals its inscription as performance. Unlike Oda, who writes Osaka language back on to the monolanguage, Tanizaki cites Osaka language, effectively containing it within the monolanguage. Thus, while his plot and his narrative apparatus indicate a concern for the fate of the local within the nation-state, his grammar ends up confirming that fate.

In order to read the local in a way that does not contain it within an imperial framework of center and periphery, we must try to read it in a spirit of radical alienation, denying linguistic mastery to the unitary narration that structures the modern novel. The critical discussion of the *yayakoshii* quality fundamental to Osaka and its language highlights the changeable, contradictory nature of speech as a way to resist citation, containment, and mastery. Those Osakan critics claimed for the local something that exceeds definition and iterability, and they faulted Tanizaki for trying to make Osaka iterable. By performing the local, Tanizaki opens himself up to it and gives himself over to it. By foregrounding the performance of the local, he calls attention to its production in the process of its subordination to national authority, and he undercuts that authority—as instituted in national language and national literature. At the same time, the self-consciousness of his performance introduces an ironic quality (which Masumura Yasuzō elevates to camp in his film adaptation). And by seeking an iterable performance, Tanizaki retains authority over the scene, betraying his own mastery.

Chapter Two

A Local Practice of Play

Oda Sakunosuke's *Meoto zenzai*

In any culture, certain character types become closely associated with specific locales as they move to the fore of the national imagination. After the burst of the asset-price bubble in Japan, for example, the downtown Tokyo neighborhoods of Shibuya and Harajuku became closely identified with the various subspecies of young women—known as "*gyaru*" (gals)—that proliferated on the streets, in the shops, and in the media. Today, in the national memory, the *moga*, or "modern girl," of the interwar period seems always to have been stomping the Ginza, though of course she moved through other neighborhoods and cities, too. Osaka, on the other hand, has been considered the natural habitat of a certain breed of *obachan*, or "middle-aged woman": high-spirited, shameless, a bit vulgar, partial to gaudy clothes and jewelry, and obsessed with money matters (perhaps best represented in the mass media by the comedian and all-purpose "talent" Kaminuma Emiko). These local archetypes arise for a variety of reasons. Historical events and demographic factors certainly play a part, as do commercial interests. But they grow and spread through popular culture to the degree that they resonate with the interests and anxieties of regional, national, and even transnational audiences, and so they invite us to consider the purposes to which they are employed and the broad circumstances to which they seem to respond.

This chapter examines one of the most influential Osaka stories in modern literature, Oda Sakunosuke's novella *Meoto zenzai* (Hooray for marriage; or, Sweet beans for two), and an archetype of local Osaka masculinity, the *bonbon*, in his most memorable iteration.[1] *Meoto zenzai* describes the relationship between Chōko, an ambitious and hardworking geisha from a humble background, and Koreyasu Ryūkichi, the spoiled, ne'er-do-well son of an Osaka merchant house. After the two meet, Ryūkichi abandons his wife and child and risks disinheritance to move in with Chōko. Together, over roughly a decade, the couple try their hand at several business enterprises, but Ryūkichi's laziness and profligacy repeatedly defeat Chōko's ambition and discipline, until at last they find some success running a café. Chōko's other ambition is to win the acceptance of Ryūkichi's family, and in this, success eludes her. Throughout their struggles and the attendant recriminations, however, the love between Ryūkichi and Chōko seldom truly falters, and it persists—rather than "triumphs"—in the end.

Published in 1940 and set in the 1920s and 1930s, Oda's novella responds, in its insistent locality, to Osaka's gradual subordination within a national economy. More specifically, it responds to the system of values promoted by the wartime state. *Meoto zenzai* presents in Chōko a woman who at first aspires to propriety and productivity, and in Ryūkichi, a model of inappropriate and unproductive masculinity. Over the course of the story, as Ryūkichi undermines Chōko's efforts, the two shift into a queer domesticity.[2] The novella indexes that shift to two economies through a fiscal accounting of money earned, saved, and spent, and an affective accounting of emotional energies—attraction, affection, respect, disappointment, contempt—won, lost, given, and withheld. These accountings detail a practice of wasteful expenditure grounded in the local. United in this practice, the couple transcend the economies that link and divide them. After briefly reviewing Oda's career and his place in Japan's and Osaka's modern literary tradition, I consider the figure of the bonbon and his relevance to Georges Bataille's notion of expenditure. I then detail how Chōko and Ryūkichi together enact the tensions between both propriety and impropriety, and productivity and unproductivity, and how they finally resolve those tensions in a local, everyday practice of gourmandise. To clarify this, I read *Meoto zenzai* together with several works by the great early-modern playwright Chikamatsu Monzaemon. Finally, I consider how Oda extends these themes in a recently discovered sequel that went unpublished during his life.

Oda Sakunosuke

Oda produced some of the most acclaimed stories of Osaka in modern times. He set most of his fiction there and theorized the city in critical essays, writing self-consciously as an Osakan to Osakans. Born in present-day Tennōji Ward in 1913, Oda grew up as Osaka's star was ascending, but he became a writer as the city was being subordinated under militarization, total war, and occupation. After completing middle school, he moved to Kyoto to attend the prestigious Third Higher School in 1931, the year of the Mukden Incident. He had already contracted the tuberculosis that would contribute to his death. In 1936, one year before full-scale war with China, Oda left school to move to Tokyo and pursue his career as a writer. Both his parents were already dead. He returned to Osaka just three years later, in 1939, and made his debut as a writer on the national stage with his second novel, *Zokushū* (Vulgarity), which was short-listed for the Akutagawa Prize. He published *Meoto zenzai*, his best-loved work, the next year, just before the start of the Pacific War. With the war's end in 1945, Oda began to enjoy popular national success, but by that point he had just two years more to live. Still suffering from tuberculosis, his health further compromised by his use of methamphetamine, Oda died in 1947 at the age of thirty-four.

Japanese literary history has grouped Oda with his better-known colleagues Dazai Osamu, Sakaguchi Ango, and Ishikawa Jun in the Buraiha, or Decadent School, a term coined by Dazai (and also translated by scholars variously as the "hooligan school," "libertines," "outlaw school," "wastrel faction," and "Group of Ruffians").[3] However, this categorization has more to do with Oda, Dazai, and Ango's friendship; their drinking and drug use; and their antipathy for the Tokyo literary establishment than with any significant stylistic similarities. Oda himself preferred the categorization "*shin* [new] *gesaku*." "*Gesaku*," or "frivolous compositions," refers to several genres of light, often comic popular writing published from the late Edo period into the beginning of the Meiji period (i.e., during the latter half of the eighteenth century through the Restoration in 1868 and for a few decades after). *Gesaku* did not deal overtly with great political or moral questions, concerning itself instead with life in the pleasure quarters and an elaborate stylistics of referentiality and punning. However, it did use humor to register the frustrations of an increasingly powerful bourgeoisie with the Tokugawa authority's strict social control. Masao Miyoshi notes that *gesaku*, "often taken to be a literature of decadence, is at the same time an expression of resistance and criticism, however modest its scale and impact."[4] As a young writer, Oda considered Stendhal his model, but once *Meoto zenzai* drew comparisons to the work of Ihara Saikaku, the giant of Edo-period prose fiction, Oda undertook to read that author in earnest.[5] He soon came to identify himself with

Saikaku and later *gesaku* writers (who faced government censure, as Oda would) and their abject genre. In Oda's story "Sesō" (The state of the times, 1946), a first-person narrator whose circumstances closely match the author's own writes of drawing inspiration from the "writers of gesaku fiction in the Edo period" and of his delight in "thumb[ing] my nose at the world."[6] Oda's debt to Saikaku's innovations in prose is also suggested by another, more geographically specific term that the postwar critic Maeda Ai applies to Oda: "Osaka-style realism."[7]

However he may be categorized, Oda occupies an ambiguous position in the modern Japanese canon. Burton Watson notes in the introduction to his collection of translated short stories that Oda's work is included in the various multivolume editions of modern Japanese fiction, but most nonspecialists outside the Kansai region are unfamiliar with the author, and he is little read or studied in the United States.[8] In his hometown, on the other hand, Oda remains a household name; in conversation, one antiquarian bookseller advised me that Oda's significance to Osaka was second only to that of "Taikō-sama" (a term of respect for Toyotomi Hideyoshi); on hearing this, another Osaka native insisted that Oda eclipses even the Great Unifier. Oda's fame is inescapably local and therefore, in the order of national literature, minor. But this discrepancy between local and national orders is not a reason to dismiss Oda; rather, it is the key to his significance as a writer. Writing through a transwar period of increasing homogenization and centralization, during which Tokyo most forcefully asserted and then confirmed its dominance, Oda produced stories of emphatic locality.

Meoto zenzai

Meoto zenzai provided Oda Sakunosuke with his big break, and it remains his best-known and most influential work. First published in a local Osaka literary coterie magazine, *Kaifū*, the story was selected for republication in the national magazine *Bungei* (Literary arts), a distinction that brought Oda to the attention of the Tokyo literary establishment. *Meoto zenzai* continued to resonate throughout Japanese popular culture for decades after. It was adapted into a highly successful film released in 1955, directed by Toyoda Shirō and starring Morishige Hisaya and Awashima Chikage, which won the prestigious Blue Ribbon awards for best director, best actor (Morishige), and best actress (Awashima), and the Mainichi Concours award for best actor and best screenplay (Yasumi Toshio). The film (discussed in chapter 5) ranked second after Naruse Mikio's *Ukigumo* (Floating clouds) on the *Kinema junpō* top ten films for the year.[9] A sequel, *Shin meoto zenzai* (New sweet beans for two, 1963), reunited director and stars eight year later. The novella inspired at least two other films: *Chōchō, Yūji no* Meoto zenzai (Chōchō and Yūji's *Sweet beans for two*, 1965), starring the popular *manzai* comedy team of Miyako Chōchō and Nanto Yūji, and *Kigeki meoto zenzai* (Sweet beans for two: The comedy, 1968). Oda's novella was even adapted as an opera, composed by a native of Senba; advertised as "an opera in Osaka dialect"; and staged in Osaka, Kyoto, and Kobe in 1957.[10] In a more recent sign of the novel's enduring appeal, Japan's public television network, NHK, produced a new adaptation for 2013 to mark the hundredth anniversary of Oda's birth.

The year of the first film adaptation's release also saw the debut of a popular radio program that took its name from Oda's novella (this program would later appear on television as well). Miyako Chōchō and Nantō Yūji, who were for a time partners in life as well as comedy, hosted the show, combining advice for young couples with comic repartee delivered in Osaka dialect.[11] *Meoto zenzai* debuted on the Asahi Broadcasting Corporation (ABC) radio network in 1955 and ran there until 1970, enjoying sustained success (it ranked as the top program on Japanese radio in June 1959) and helping to earn ABC a reputation for comedy programming.[12] Chōchō and Yūji continued to host the show after secretly ending their marriage in 1958 (a development that no doubt added piquancy to their advice). In August 1963, the program began broadcasting on the TBS television network, too, where it continued until 1975, Chōchō hosting alone after Yūji passed away in 1973 at the age of forty-eight. In total, *Meoto zenzai* ran for 825 episodes on radio and 633 on television.[13]

This extended afterlife in adaptation indicates the powerful appeal of the novella's characters, its themes, and the very words "*meoto zenzai*." Oda took his title from a small shop in Osaka that sold (and indeed still sells) *zenzai*, a simple snack of soupy, sweetened *azuki* beans topped with cakes of pounded rice. This sense of the term is local to the Kansai region; in Kantō, *zenzai* refers to the same basic ingredients handled rather differently. The Osaka shop's twist was to serve *zenzai* divided into two bowls, for wife and husband (*me-oto*). Oda's title thus invokes a tight knot of associations. It first calls to mind the intimacy of a shared life, with its constant balancing of affections and responsibilities, as well as the love that transcends any such accounting. It invokes as well the luxury of eating not so much for sustenance as for pleasurable distraction. Finally, it conjures the locality of Osaka: its reputation as a place of good, cheap food and mass culture, as well as its literary legacy as the birthplace of the domestic drama. These same associations imbue Chōko's relationship with the bonbon.

The Bonbon

The term "bonbon" is native to Senba, the merchant quarter of Osaka, first established at the beginning of the seventeenth century. Strictly speaking, it is a form of address used by servants to sons in merchant households there: an honorific form when used to address someone older, and a familiar term of affection for someone younger.[14] "*Bonchi*" is a closely related term. Yamasaki Toyoko, who set many of her early stories in Senba, draws a distinction between the ordinary irresponsible bonbon and the bolder, more business-minded bonchi.[15] Others employ the two terms interchangeably.[16] More broadly, "bonbon" is used in the Kansai region to refer to a handsome, well-off, urbane young man, particularly one with a frivolous air. In one of her early novels, Yamasaki offers a neat sketch of the type: "He had a shop, he had cash, he was born handsome, and he wanted to try for himself everything interesting, everything pleasurable, everything good."[17]

Chōko's father hails Ryūkichi into this tradition early in *Meoto zenzai*. Ryūkichi lives on the Umeda Shinmichi road, between Senba and Umeda (not in Senba proper), where his family runs a well-known shop, a wholesaler of cosmetics. Soon after he and Chōko move in together, her mother learns of Ryūkichi's continued womanizing and complains to her husband, who responds matter-of-factly, "He's a bonbon, so it's no wonder."[18] This also hails Ryūkichi into a long literary tradition. The general type of the *dame-otoko*, or "no-good guy," would have been familiar to local and national audiences from as far back as the *sewamono* of Chikamatsu Monzaemon at the beginning of the eighteenth century. These domestic dramas, written for the puppet theater and set among the contemporary merchant class, were first staged in the merchant capital Osaka and were, many of them, based on local incidents. Although they are not called "bonbon" in the plays, such Chikamatsu protagonists as

Tokubei in *Sonezaki shinjū* (The love suicides at Sonezaki, 1703), Chūbei in *Meido no hikyaku* (Courier for hell, 1711), and Jihei in *Shinjū: Ten no Amijima* (The love suicides at Amijima, 1720) established the charming, indolent, extravagant son of the merchant quarter as an archetype of local masculinity.

In early modern prose-fiction, Iwano Hōmei's "Bonchi" (1913) and Ishimaru Gohei's *Senba no bonchi* (A Senba *bonchi*, 1919–21) both feature the type as protagonist. The former tells the dark story of Sada, the bonchi of the title (and addressed as such in the story), who sets out for the resort town of Takarazuka with companions on a lark and meets with a tragic end.[19] Hōmei, a native of Awaji island in the Kansai region, employs Osaka dialect throughout the story. He later wrote, "I wanted to try to write an 'Osaka work' [*Ōsaka-mono*] that was pure in terms of both the characters' daily lives and their idiom."[20] Ishimaru's popular novel follows the story of Nishida Tomijirō, known familiarly as "Tomi-bon," the second son of an important Senba merchant house, who wallows in dissipation, causing constant worry for his family, until he decides to take some money and run off to Tokyo.[21] Both works treat the bonchi as a representative contemporary Osaka type.

The terms "bonbon" and "bonchi" retained currency after the war, though they began to acquire a nostalgic cast. Tanizaki Jun'ichirō introduces the bonbon into his great novel of Kansai life, *Sasameyuki* (Fine snow, 1943–48, published in English as *The Makioka Sisters*), in the figure of Taeko's boyfriend, Okubata Keizaburō, known to the Makioka family as "Kei-bon." Begun during the war but published as a complete work only in 1948, Tanizaki's novel treats the bonbon as an anachronism.[22] Similarly, Yamasaki's *Bonchi* (1959) employs the archetype to elegize the imagined splendor of prewar life in the merchant quarter. This long literary legacy suggests the bonbon's distinction within the national imagination. Although Edo/Tokyo and Kyoto both had merchant districts and—no doubt—spoiled, spendthrift heirs, the Osaka bonbon holds a special significance.

Oda inserts the bonbon into the historical context of the Taishō and early Shōwa periods, which witnessed increasingly intrusive efforts to discipline the body and its impulses to the service of the expansionist state. Already in 1922, as Sheldon Garon has noted, the Home Ministry's Social Bureau had launched a campaign for "restraint in consumption" that criticized citizens' taste for "luxury and self-indulgence."[23] The following years would see more state-sponsored moral suasion campaigns to encourage frugality and rationalized consumption. Meanwhile, the state sought to extend control over the body itself. The Ministry of Health and Welfare (Kōsei-shō) was established in 1938, superseding the Bureau of Hygiene, and the National Physical-Strength Law (Kokumin tairyoku hō) was passed in 1940 to increase state control of male bodies and to encourage physical discipline—part of an ongoing effort to refashion the national body, as Sabine Frühstück has argued, to better serve Japan's expansionist aims.[24]

Such direct state interventions were accompanied by a broader social discourse of middle-class propriety. George Mosse has described how, in interwar Germany, the middle class distinguished itself from both the aristocracy and the lower classes through the idea of respectability, a way of life based on "frugality, devotion to duty, and restraint of the passions."[25] Among its effects were the differentiation of normal and abnormal sexualities and the valorization of the nuclear family. Respectability helped first to legitimize the middle class and then to insulate it from the vagaries of the modern age. Respectability became allied to the ideology of nationalism, and through the dissemination of these values, the state engendered in its autonomous subject-citizens an internalized self-control demonstrated by obedience to norms of behavior. Full citizenship and subjectivity were predicated on such self-control. The outlines of Mosse's argument bear as well on the interwar history of Japan, where the growth of nationalism paralleled the development of a small middle class and of a much wider discourse of middle-classness that was dispersed through the mass media. This discourse underpinned the demands made on men by the Japanese state during mobilization to postpone gratification, work hard, make homes, and raise children. *Meoto zenzai* presents the bonbon as inappropriate to those demands.

Expenditure

Around the same time that Oda was writing, the French intellectual Georges Bataille was developing his theory of "general economy," first outlined in the essay "The Notion of Expenditure" (La notion de dépense, 1933) and then expanded in *The Accursed Share* (La part maudite, 1949)—an economy in which "the 'expenditure' (the 'consumption') of wealth, rather than production, was the primary object."[26] In the latter work, Bataille describes how energy that exceeds the limits of growth builds pressure that must find release in either the extension of those limits or loss. Such loss takes various forms of "luxury" and "squander." Bataille identifies war as an extreme example of squander—a "catastrophic expenditure of excess energy."[27] The two world wars that he had just lived through (and that framed Oda's much shorter career), he writes, had "organized the greatest orgies of wealth—and of human beings—that history has recorded."[28] Bataille elaborates on Marcel Mauss's study of the concept of "the gift" and, in particular, the practice of potlatch, observing that such expenditures are often made with some expectation of return (in the form of increased social "rank," for example). However, he explains that other sorts of expenditure, made without such expectation, can bring an experience of "life beyond utility," which is "the domain of sovereignty."[29]

Bataille's general economy builds on his earlier efforts to theorize a new materialism. Asserting that existing materialisms elevated certain types of matter in a hierarchical order and therefore tended rather to idealism, Bataille focuses on the "base matter" that such idealism excludes, specifically "luxury, mourning, war, cults, the construction of sumptuary monuments, games, spectacles, arts, perverse sexual activity (i.e., deflected from genital finality)."[30] As the scholar Benjamin Noys explains it, for Bataille, "base matter is an external reminder, and remainder, of all that threatens to drag down and ruin the ideal."[31] Bataille's base materialism, in Noys's understanding, proposes neither a simple inversion of high and low nor a dialectical synthesis of the two; it is a "deconstructive third term" that makes the high–low duality possible only to destabilize it, a "thought of matter as difference."[32] In Bataille's own words, it is a "*non-logical difference* that represents in relation to the *economy* of the universe what *crime* represents in relation to the law."[33]

Bataille's notions of expenditure and sovereignty, together with his broader theorization of general economy and the function of base materialism within it, inform the analysis of *Meoto zenzai* that follows, clarifying Chōko's development as protagonist, and Ryūkichi's role as antagonist and model of an alternative local masculinity. This novella, published at the onset of a war that, as Bataille notes, "exuded" the excess of modern capitalist industry, presents a couple who continually negotiate between propriety and impropriety, productivity and unproductivity, until they destabilize that polarity through luxurious consumption, substituting for the catastrophic squander of war a more sovereign expenditure.[34]

Propriety/Impropriety

Chōko begins the story as a model of proper filiality. She first goes to work as a maid and later becomes a geisha in order to help her parents financially. She continues to send them money after she leaves home. By contrast, Ryūkichi is an irresponsible and unfilial son. Thirty-one years old when the story begins, he should be taking over the family business from his ailing father, but he leaves this to his brother-in-law. Even after his father has been confined to bed by a stroke, Ryūkichi continues to raid the coffers to pay for his amours and amusements, instead of helping with day-to-day operations. Later in the story, we see the effect that Chōko's attachment to Ryūkichi has on her behavior, when she stays beside him in the hospital, though he is in no danger, rather than visiting her mother's deathbed. The guilt Chōko feels after her mother's death testifies to her filial instincts, but her attraction to the bonbon is stronger.

Chōko also sacrifices her respect for the institutions of marriage and motherhood to Ryūkichi's impropriety. Ryūkichi leaves his wife and young daughter to live with Chōko. When his father first learns of the affair, he summons Ryūkichi and his wife to discuss the state of their marriage, and the ensuing scene emphasizes the bonbon's abandonment not just of his wife but of his responsibilities as a father as well.[35] Several scenes describe Chōko's solicitude toward Ryūkichi's daughter, an impulse made poignant by the daughter's supercilious rebuffs. And when Ryūkichi's wife dies of tuberculosis, he demonstrates no guilt or regret, not even proper piety; it is Chōko who has a memorial tablet made with the dead wife's name, sets it on the household altar, and places fresh flowers before it every morning, behaving, as the narration notes, faultlessly.[36]

An ulterior motive drives Chōko's punctiliousness, of course, but what is that motive? It is to win a proper place in Ryūkichi's family. Two memorable scenes surround moments when such a place is, in a small way, granted to Chōko and, in a more definitive way, denied her. The first comes toward the end of the novella, when Ryūkichi's sister visits him in the hospital. She addresses Chōko familiarly as her elder sister ("*nēhan*") and slips her some money from Ryūkichi's father. The money signifies the recognition Chōko has waited ten years for, but she almost returns it, so moved is she by the familiar address.[37] The second moment comes when Ryūkichi's father nears death. Ryūkichi heads home to be at his father's side, and Chōko urges him to convince the old man to acknowledge their relationship. She then rushes to have a formal kimono made for the funeral, anticipating that acknowledgment. She is all ready when Ryūkichi calls with word of his father's death, but he tells Chōko she had better not attend the funeral—a crushing rebuff that leads her to attempt suicide.

As an unmarried and childless couple living together, Ryūkichi and Chōko share a domesticity that lies outside the economy of reproductive intimacy increasingly promoted by state ideology. This domesticity is further marked by their unconventional gender-role behavior—his financial dependence on her, her physical domination of him. When Ryūkichi returns home from a bender one night and Chōko administers a particularly harsh beating, the narration emphasizes the unconventionality of their relationship through the observations of their landlord's wife, who considers Chōko's behavior unfeminine. When Chōko bursts into tears, this woman notes that it is the first time she has seen their tenant behave like a woman—if unintentionally. The same woman also sees Ryūkichi shaving his own dried fish flakes every morning and wonders what sort of wife would allow her husband to do such a thing.

The gradual slide into this state of queer domesticity represents Chōko's surrender to, and her embrace of, the bonbon's lack of self-discipline and his disregard for the proprieties of middle-class family life. The bonbon refuses—or is not allowed—to grow up. Long into adulthood, he remains a son, his fortune controlled by his father and then his lover. The narration has Chōko identify this essential immaturity and vow to alter it: "In her heart she felt like telling Ryūkichi's father, 'Don't worry about your boy—I'll show you I can make a man out of him!'"[38] But she fails. Ryūkichi never matures into his father's—or the modern Japanese state's—notion of a proper man. He has already abandoned that role to join Chōko in a relationship that remains childless and that seems to have no room for anyone else, a relationship unsanctioned by the state and unrecognized by his family.

Productivity/Unproductivity

The course of Chōko and Ryūkichi's household economy parallels this affective economy, as he repeatedly frustrates her attempts to establish financial security. Each new business enterprise that the couple undertakes becomes an economic and moral opposition between Chōko's exemplary work ethic—a caricature of the Meiji-period discourse of *risshin shusse* (advancement and success), pathetic in its futility—and Ryūkichi's indolence. As their first venture, the razor shop, fails to attract business, Ryūkichi absorbs himself in a new hobby: reciting *jōruri*, the chanted narrative that accompanies the bunraku puppet theater. Just when the couple can hardly afford it, he has started taking *jōruri* lessons "at five yen a month."[39] Their next venture, a restaurant serving the humble stew *Kanto-daki*, succeeds at first, but the proximity of alcohol is too much of a temptation for Ryūkichi, who starts to drink to excess. The description of the next venture, a fruit stall, likewise contrasts Chōko's efforts to charm customers with Ryūkichi's failure to do the same. Punctuating this history are a series of kindnesses shown to Chōko: the offer of a job, made by her friend O-Kin; her father's help with the fruit shop; the gift of one hundred yen from Ryūkichi's sister; and a generous loan from Kinpachi, a former geisha who has married well, that allows them to open the final business, a café. All these people assist Chōko in her attempt to rise to middle-class respectability and to lift the bonbon up with her. But instead, he drags her down.

This duality of productivity and unproductivity manifests most conspicuously in the voices of Ryūkichi and Chōko, and this roots the duality in the story's setting. As the center of the bunraku puppet theater, *rakugo* storytelling, and, more recently, *manzai* comedy, Osaka has long figured in the national imaginary as a space of excessive oral production—the excess of dialect, of sentimentality, of laughter. Here, Ryūkichi's excessiveness and unproductivity are made manifest in dialogue. There is, first of all, Oda's expert rendering of dialect, with its contravention of the standardization (i.e., the nationalization) of language that had been effected through writing and grammar in just the sixty years or so prior to 1940, when the novella was published. Ryūkichi's dialogue compounds this subversion of standards because, throughout the novella, he speaks with a pronounced stutter. Exacerbated by tension and excitement (when he defends himself against Chōko's upbraiding, for example, but also when he offers her something good to eat), this affliction underscores the grain of the voice, which is irreducible to grammar—the grounding of language in the individual, physical body. The stutter also implies Ryūkichi's unproductivity: first of all, it hampers his production of speech (again, doubling up on his dialect, which may be seen to hamper production of *grammatical* speech). Furthermore, a stutter seems particularly problematic in the line of work to which Ryūkichi was born, sales, with its dependence on the pitch. At the same time,

Ryūkichi's favorite pastime is *jōruri* recitation, so while his stutter ill-suits him to work, it presents no impediment to verbal play. In contrast, Chōko uses her voice effectively in her various lines of work, whether singing at parties during her time as a geisha or hawking goods for the various shops she and Ryūkichi later run. The narrative notes that she takes pride in her voice, mentions how strong it is and how pretty, and adds that customers respond to it.[40] Hers is a productive voice.

Chōko and Ryūkichi's last two business ventures associate them with spaces of nonreproductive sexuality, further illustrating their slide into queer domesticity. They open their *Kanto-daki* shop, Chōryū, in a dicey neighborhood next to the Tobita red-light district. Its eccentricity is marked on opening night when, we are told, "an androgynous strolling musician, commonly known as 'the fag,' came around and gave a spirited rendition of the tune 'Green Willows,' so business was good."[41] The name of the shop, combining the first character of each of their names, "butterfly" and "willow," emphasizes the personal association. Later, the couple open a café under the name Salon Chōryū, and despite Chōko's determination to run a respectable establishment, the waitresses soon begin slipping out with the customers for quickies at rooms around the corner. At the time the story was published, cafés carried strong associations of challenge to social norms. Abolitionists who had tried to eradicate licensed prostitution through the 1910s and 1920s turned their attention to the booming café culture in the 1930s and to the selfish individualism and unmanageable sexuality that they believed were developing within, and they looked to the militarist state to help realize their goals.[42] The media particularly linked this dangerous modern sexuality to Osaka's cabaret-style cafés.[43] By referencing this issue, *Meoto zenzai* further marks Chōko and Ryūkichi's relationship as inimical to middle-class and national values.

Meoto zenzai's narrative tracks the cycle of Chōko and Ryūkichi's moral and business failures through an assiduous accounting of household finances. So prominently do accounts figure in the narrative that *Meoto zenzai* reads at points like the dramatization of a household ledger. Sentence after sentence records credits for what Chōko has managed to save and debits for what Ryūkichi has begged or stolen from her to pay for his little luxuries and trips to the geisha quarter. Another set of credits and debits documents the vagaries of the businesses that the couple buy and sell. When their first venture, the razor shop, fails, for example, the narration tallies their loss: "The Grand Closing Sale that they held on the last two days—'Prices slashed!'—brought in a little over a hundred yen, and along with the 120 yen they got for the rights to the store, that made a total of 220 yen or more. But by the time they paid off what they owed the wholesaler and a few other debts here and there, there was less than ten yen left over."[44] In the following three years, through ruthless economizing, Chōko manages to save up 200 yen. She tries to consult with Ryūkichi about a new business venture, but he only replies, "'What can you do with a piddling sum like that' and took no interest in the proposal. Then one day he managed, in a matter of hours, to spend fifty of her two hundred yen in the Tobita licensed quarter."[45] In this way, the narration lends to the couple's moral struggle a *calculated* realism that befits the story's setting: Japan's merchant capital. It also points to a sovereignty that Ryūkichi finds outside such calculations by rejecting the investment required of capitalist subjectivity. For, as Bataille writes, "What is sovereign in fact is to enjoy the present time without having anything else in view but this present time."[46]

Gourmandise

Meoto zenzai's lovers escape the dualities of propriety/impropriety and productivity/unproductivity through a practice of expenditure and profitless play, the greatest part of which is gourmandise.[47] Some of the most memorable scenes detail those most everyday of activities: preparing or procuring food and eating it. One such scene comes at the beginning of the novella, as Ryūkichi is courting Chōko. He introduces her to his favorite places to eat in south Osaka, or "Minami," the area around Nanba and Shinsaibashi stations (he insists there is nothing good to eat on the north side, or "Kita," around Umeda Station). These are not "first-class restaurants," however, which Ryūkichi says are a waste of time:

> About the fanciest place they patronized was a shop in Kōzu that featured boiled bean curd. Even less elegant than that were the night stalls where they went for *doteyaki* and dumplings stuffed with sake lees, or the place called Shiru-ichi in the street alongside the Sogō Department Store in Ebisubashi that specialized in a soup made of loaches and another made of whale hide. Then they had eel [*mamushi*] at the Izumoya at the east end of Aioi Bridge in Dōtonbori, octopus at the Tako-ume in Nipponbashi, *Kantodaki* or vegetables in broth at the Shōbentango-tei in the grounds of Hōzen-ji temple, *tekkamaki* sushi and sea bream skin in vinegar and miso sauce at the Sushisute just in front of the Tokiwa Theater in Sennichi-mae,

> rice cooked with vegetables and soy sauce [*kayaku-meshi*] and soup with sake lees at the Darumaya across the street, etc., etc.,—one unglamorous dish [*getemono ryōri*] after another, all made from ingredients that were anything but expensive. And the places where these dishes were served were hardly the kind one would ordinarily take a geisha to, so that at first Chōko wondered why in the world Ryūkichi was bringing her to such restaurants.[48]

This early scene introduces gourmandise as a theme of the novella and establishes the specific nature of the bonbon's gourmandise. First of all, the scene establishes its locality. The very subject of gourmandise references Osaka's local history. In the Tokugawa period, Osaka was called the world's kitchen (*tenka no daidokoro*) because it served as a hub for the transport and storage of foodstuffs from all over western Japan. Ever since, gourmandise has helped define Osaka in the national imagination; even today, any discussion of the city's character is likely to cite the phenomenon of *kuidaore*—the popular notion that Osakans will spend all they have for the love of food.[49] Building on this reputation, the passage appeals to local knowledge by name-checking small shops and night stalls whose fame remains local. The passage underscores this locality by using regional terms for several dishes. "*Kanto-daki*" (literally, "Kantō stew") is what people in the rest of Japan call *oden*; the short "o" reflects local pronunciation, and the verb "*taku*" at the root of "*-daki*," which in Kantō refers only to the cooking of rice, in Kansai also refers to the act of stewing. "*Kayaku-meshi*" is the Kansai term for *takikomi-gohan*. The word used for "eel" is the local "*mamushi*."

In addition to this locality, the scene identifies *getemono* as the object of Ryūkichi's gourmandise. The word refers to the cheap, base, or strange dishes, made from such humble ingredients as sake lees and fish skin, that Ryūkichi prefers to the fare served at "high-class restaurants."[50] This taste is such a defining characteristic that Ryūkichi has been nicknamed "Doteyaki-san" after a favorite *getemono* dish—pork rinds simmered down in miso-enriched broth.[51] Ryūkichi pursues this taste with a high degree of connoisseurship: his *yudofu*, or simmered tofu, must come from the shop Kōzu, his octopus from Tako-ume, and his eel from Izumiya (more precisely, the branch at Aiaubashi). Because it is applied to *getemono*, this connoisseurship does not connote the status-conscious (and, in that sense, productive) consumption usually associated with the

English word (in this sense, the Japanese word *tsū*, free as it is of such associations, better describes the character of Ryūkichi's taste).

If this scene begins to suggest a fanaticism about Ryūkichi's gourmandise that is incompatible with the state's campaign for rational consumption, a later one depicts this more clearly. The couple are now living together, and Chōko supports them by working as a *yatona*, a part-time geisha who is called in as needed. She has taken the last train home after a long night's work to find Ryūkichi still cooking a batch of *sanshō konbu*—a dish of simmered kelp seasoned with *sanshō* pepper—that he started the day before: "Ryūkichi would buy absolutely the finest *konbu*, cut it into small squares, put it in the pot together with the *sanshō* berries and plenty of Kikkoman dark *shōyu*, and simmer it over a low fire of pinewood charcoal for two days and nights. Ryūkichi said it was as delicious as the *sanshō konbu* sold at Ogurayama in Ebisubashi."[52] There are many other scenes of Ryūkichi's profligacy (including one where he spends ten days' earnings on lunch and coffee while remarking to himself how cheap it is), but none better illuminates the connection between excessive expenditure and the "irrationality" of the bonbon's rarified tastes than this *sanshō konbu*.[53] This scene contrasts Chōko's productive use of time—working hard to make ends meet—with Ryūkichi's waste of time: an entire day spent on a dish that serves only as a relish, not a meal. And by taking care to note the quality of the *konbu* and the quantity of the *shōyu*, the narrative implies a waste of money that the couple can hardly afford. In just this way, it illustrates the "true luxury" that Bataille would define a few years later:

> The true luxury and the real potlatch of our times falls to the poverty-stricken, that is, to the individual who lies down and scoffs. A genuine luxury requires the complete contempt for riches, the somber indifference of the individual who refuses work and makes his life on the one hand an infinitely ruined splendor and, on the other, a silent insult to the laborious life of the rich. Beyond a military exploitation, a religious mystification and a capitalist misappropriation, henceforth no one can rediscover the meaning of wealth, the explosiveness that it heralds, unless it is in the splendor of rags and the somber challenge of indifference.[54]

The dish of *sanshō konbu* is precisely Ryūkichi's "somber challenge," issued amid such "military exploitation" and "capitalist misappropriation."

Chōko answers that challenge, accepts Ryūkichi's gift, and surrenders to base luxury. In the earlier scene, going out on the town, she is initially disappointed that Ryūkichi keeps taking her to places unfit for a geisha. This suggests her recognition that the luxury available at such places is not, in Bataille's terms, productive of "rank." But the taste quickly wins her over: "As she listened to him explain, 'Wha-wha-what do you think? Good, isn't it? You c-c-can't eat such good stuff anywhere else!' Chōko would taste it and, sure enough, it was delicious."[55] Her moral sensibility of what seems proper concedes to the physical sensation of what tastes good, an ebullition manifested in Ryūkichi's stutter. The defeat of Chōko's sensibilities is reiterated in the scene of Ryūkichi making *sanshō konbu*, as her initial indignation quickly melts away. The narration describes Ryūkichi offering her a taste of the finished product and then tells us that "at such moments Chōko would be overwhelmed by a great torrent of affection for Ryūkichi."[56] These scenes describe a seduction through food, the overcoming not of sexual restraint by desire but of rational consumerism by connoisseurship.

Just as Ryūkichi's extravagance illustrates the incompatibility of connoisseurship and fiscal discipline, Chōko's thrill of affection, her acceptance of Ryūkichi's invitation, represents fiscal discipline's defeat. Her determination to earn, to spend rationally, and to save cannot compete with the exuberance of Ryūkichi's connoisseurship—the impulse to expend money, time, and effort in a pursuit of gustatory pleasure that must be considered improper and irrational within the contemporary militarized order. Bataille writes, "The world of *intimacy* is antithetical to the real world, as immoderation is to moderation, madness to reason, drunkenness to lucidity."[57] Chōko's concerns with propriety, with earning and saving, are real-world concerns. By inviting her to share his immoderate gourmandise, to join his profitless expenditure, Ryūkichi asks Chōko to abandon that world for the world of intimacy—to be concerned, as Bataille writes, not about "what will be" but about "what is." And this helps us understand the odd, timeless quality of *Meoto zenzai's* Osaka—not so much an Osaka viewed with nostalgia but a constant urban present conjured by Oda against the specter of Japan's imperial futurity. Could readers in 1940 already foresee the futility of any investment in the future? Did they also respond to Ryūkichi's invitation to consume it all now? "If I thus consume immoderately, I reveal to my fellow beings that which I am *intimately*," Bataille concludes. "Everything shows through, everything is open and intimate between those who consume intensely."[58] This intimacy animates the relationship at the center of *Meoto zenzai.*

Chikamatsu

At this point, a detour into the love suicides of Chikamatsu Monzaemon, the great Edo-period dramatist, will help clarify the dynamics at work in Oda's engagement with the political context of wartime Japan and with imperial claims to transcendence of the local. *Meoto zenzai* encourages such a reading; references to *jōruri* fill its pages. The narration notes that the shop from which the novel takes its title was started by a teacher of *jōruri.* The novella ends with the couple taking second place in an amateur *jōruri* contest. When drunk, Ryūkichi is inclined to recite passages from the puppet plays in a weepy voice. In one such instance, after an unexplained three-day absence, Ryūkichi returns home late at night declaiming a passage from the play *Hade sugata onna maiginu* (A stylish woman's dance robes, 1773), a *sewamono* by Takemoto Saburobei and others about a merchant's son who, like Ryūkichi, leaves his wife and young daughter to live with a lowly geisha, leading his father to disown him. Shindō Masahiro points out that the scene in Oda's novella amounts to a parody of the scene in the play, among the most famous scenes in all *jōruri*: Osono's soliloquy from the "Sakaya no dan." In it, the abandoned wife assumes the blame for her husband's behavior, whereas Chōko berates Ryūkichi. Shindō observes, "Through repetition, [Oda's] tale of the young master of a merchant house and a former geisha as a couple transforms the tragedy of, for example, a Chikamatsu love suicide into comedy, making it possible to attain a modern *jōruri.*"[59] Here I would like to pursue the significance of this repetition—or what I might rather call layering—with reference to the three Chikamatsu plays previously mentioned, all set in Osaka and first performed there: *Sonezaki shinjū* (1703); *Meido no hikyaku* (1711); and *Shinjū: Ten no Amijima* (1720).

The first point of commonality between Oda's novella and Chikamatsu's *sewamono* is the link between household and affective economies. Steven Heine notes that while some scholars have tended to view the suicides that end these plays, and the Amidist imagery that attends them, as awkward, tacked-on resolutions of the conflict between *giri* (social obligation) and *ninjō* (individual emotion), we can understand love suicide instead as the climax of a conflict between Confucian ethics and Amidist notions of salvation.[60] Amidism teaches that people can attain rebirth in the Pure Land simply by professing faith, without the assistance of institutions or devotional practices. Heine argues that these plays reflect the millenarian strain in medieval Amidism born of frustration with the Tokugawa social system (centered in Edo), which strictly defined social caste, prescribed behavior, and prevented social mobility. The dynamic informing the plays, he insists, is one of opposition not between *giri* and *ninjō* but between the condition of the outcast in the mundane world of *giri-ninjō* on the one hand and Buddhist transcendence on the other. *Giri* and *ninjō* are two poles of the same system, structure and anti-structure, the latter located in the *ukiyo*, or "floating world" (浮き世), of the pleasure quarters (but also commonly understood in the medieval period as 憂き世, the world of lamentation), and the former located in the world outside it. Successful merchants have a place in the *ukiyo*, where their money buys them the social standing that the Tokugawa social hierarchy denied them in the wider world; but unsuccessful "outcasts" who lack the resources to cut a figure in the *ukiyo*—like Tokubei, the protagonist of *Sonezaki*—seek escape through love suicide and rebirth in the Pure Land. Heine writes: "From the millenarian standpoint, the key issue is not a matter of asserting the priority of *ninjō* over *giri*, or vice versa, but of seeing how Amidism seeks to overcome this finite polarity; that is, the issue is a matter of *ninjō/giri* vs. a transcendental Amidist option that relativizes and surpasses both finite realms."[61]

The dynamic at the heart of *Meoto zenzai* becomes clearer in the light of this interpretation. Like Chikamatsu, Oda articulates the mundane sphere of the everyday by tracing the circulations of material value and emotional energy that constitute household and affective economies, as well as the circulation between these two economies. Indeed, "*giri-ninjō*" can be understood as another way of talking about these two economies. Again like Chikamatsu, Oda sets these economies against the backdrop of a national political authority centered in Tokyo. The strictures of the Tokugawa social system render Chikamatsu's lovers outcasts. The increasing productivism of the Japanese state in the interwar period renders Oda's lovers improper and irrational.

The second point of commonality I would like to explore is the authors' use of figures to index that circulation of value and emotional energy. Oda's heavy use of figures in *Meoto zenzai* first calls to mind Osaka's other early-modern literary giant, Saikaku. As previously noted,

Oda's early work drew comparisons with Saikaku, and Oda fostered the association. His critical essay "Saikaku shinron" (A new theory of Saikaku, 1948) begins with an emphatic assertion of his predecessor's locality: "Saikaku is a man of Osaka: he was born in Osaka and raised in Osaka, he wrote in Osaka and died in Osaka. And his grave is in Osaka, too." One aspect of their shared locality is a brand of realism grounded in quantification. Oda notes that "Saikaku was a writer who loved numbers," adding, "In this love of numbers I see the personality of a realist with a regard for Osakans, and I detect Osakans' knack for figures."[62] That "knack," of course, grows out of Osaka's merchant history.

However, Saikaku's contemporary Chikamatsu also shared this love of numbers. The dramatist's love suicides, set as they are among the Osaka merchant class, are full of numbers, and a comparison with Chikamatsu bears more directly on the significance of figures in Oda's novella. Key scenes in the love suicides dramatize the most fundamental of merchant activities—accounting—and these scenes draw a contrast between earnest accounting and parody. Early in *Meido no hikyaku*, for example, the merchant Chūbei and his friend and customer Hachiemon parody accounting and contractual obligations in order to deceive Chūbei's foster mother. When she insists that Chūbei give Hachiemon his remittance immediately, Chūbei, who does not have the money, substitutes a jar of pomade. Then, to satisfy his foster mother, who cannot read, he enlists Hachiemon to write out a fake receipt. On a slip of paper, Hachiemon writes the following:

> Item. I am not in receipt of fifty *ryō* of gold. The above is positive guarantee that this evening, as previously promised, I will go drinking in the Quarter, and will accompany you as your clown. I engage always to be present whenever there is merrymaking. In witness whereof, I accept this pomade jar as token of my intention to appear on all festive days.[63]

Later, as Chūbei prepares to run away with Umegawa, he tallies his debts to Umegawa's geisha house with sincerity and desperate generosity:

> The other day I gave you a deposit of fifty *ryō*. Here are 110 *ryō* more. That makes a total of 160 *ryō*, the money needed to ransom Umegawa. These forty-five *ryō* are what I owe you on account—you worked it out the other day. Five *ryō* are for the Chaser. I believe that Umegawa's fees since October come to about fifteen *ryō* altogether, but I can't be bothered with petty

> calculations. Here're twenty *ryō*, and now please clear my account. These ten *ryō* are a present for you, by way of thanks for your trouble. One *ryō* each goes to Rin, Tama, and Gohei.[64]

We see a similar use of accounting in *Amijima*. When the merchant Jihei's aunt and brother drop by to make certain that he has abandoned plans to ransom the prostitute Koharu, Jihei tries to impress them with his industry by ostentatiously running through some bogus "urgent calculations" aloud:

> Two into ten goes five, three into nine goes three, three into six goes two, seven times eight is fifty-six. . . . Magoemon, Aunt. How good of you. Please come in. I was in the midst of some urgent calculations. Four nines makes thirty-six *momme*. Three sixes make eighteen *fun*. That's two *momme* less two *fun*. Kantarō! Osue! Granny and Uncle have come! Bring the tobacco tray! One times three makes three. Osan, serve the tea![65]

Later, in the third and final act, as Jihei prepares to run away with Koharu to commit suicide together, he earnestly settles his accounts with the owner of the Yamatoya teahouse:

> Please use the money I gave you earlier this evening to clear my account. I'd like you also to send 150 *me* of Old Silver to Kawasho for the moon-viewing party last month. Please get a receipt. Give Saietsubo from Fukushima one piece of silver as a contribution to the Buddhist altar he's bought, and tell him to use it for a memorial service. Wasn't there something else? Oh yes—give Isoichi a tip of four silver coins.[66]

In both instances, money binds the lovers and their dilemma to the circulation of mundane economies. In both plays, the later, earnest accounting is a necessary step before the lovers can break from the mundane and journey toward transcendence. And in *Amijima*, Jihei's sham accounting convinces his family that he has renounced transcendence and embraced the mundane. The licensed quarters are often considered to exist outside the everyday, but these scenes emphasize how money links the merchant and licensed quarters of the imagined Osaka, suggesting an interpenetrant network. As well, in each case the sham accounting occurs in the merchant quarter, whereas the genuine accounting, which we might have expected there, occurs in the licensed quarter, underscoring the interpenetration of affective and household economies and belying the notion of the "floating world" as a refuge from real-world concerns.

Chikamatsu's plays set these mundane economies against the backdrop of the ideological system that animates the economic, fiscal, and legal policies of the Tokugawa central authorities. *Amijima*'s plot, for instance, hinges on several written contracts and promises, and whether they will be honored—that is, whether they are worth the paper they are written on. When Jihei's rival, the obnoxious Tahei, boasts of his financial resources, he mentions the "glitter of the great amounts of 'New Silver'" at his home (67)—an allusion to a severe currency debasement carried out in 1711. It was in the context of this currency debasement, as Tetsuo Najita notes, that Kusama Naokata wrote his history of money as "a merchant critique of politics."[67] Kusama, a merchant intellectual affiliated with the Kaitokudō academy in Osaka, argued that trade depended on trust in the currency, and that the shogunate's debasement of silver therefore constituted a breach of trust and threatened social stability.[68]

The plot of *Sonezaki shinjū* alludes to another contemporary violation of trust: the cancellation of debts owed by daimyō to merchants. The play was written and first performed in 1703. The bakufu had canceled debts in 1685 and 1702, and had refused to hear cases brought against members of the samurai class by rice brokers.[69] In 1705, the shogun Yoshimune would institute a policy denying merchants the right to bring litigation against members of the samurai classes over unpaid loans. *Sonezaki*'s plot is driven by the failure to honor such personal debts. When Tokubei refuses an arranged marriage, the girl's father demands that he return the dowry money, but Tokubei has lent it to a friend. That friend denies borrowing the money and cancels the stamp with which he notarized the debt agreement, leaving Tokubei without legal recourse. It is not difficult to discern in this plot, originally performed before an audience of merchants in a city far from Edo, an appeal to local resentment over bakufu policies.

In Chikamatsu's time, the Tokugawa bakufu provoked merchants' resentment with its debasement of the currency and cancellation of debts; in Oda's time, the military state did the same with the establishment of a control economy. Both writers address those resentments with stories full of figures, which appeal to a merchant ethic of strict accounting. Just as Chikamatsu's thematization of cash, debts, and contracts highlights the interpenetration of merchant and "pleasure" quarters, *giri* and *ninjō*, so, too, do Chōko and Ryūkichi's accounts highlight the interpenetration of household and affective economies. Propriety and impropriety function in Oda's novel in the same way that, Heine suggests, *giri* and *ninjō* do in Chikamatsu's plays: not as opposed ethics, each asserting priority, but as two sides of the same system, policed by a mundane authority that asserts a spurious ideological transcendence.

And here is the difference between the two authors and their ages. Chikamatsu's lovers slip the limits of the mundane through love suicide and rebirth in the Pure Land. Their tale promotes the potential of Amidist millenarianism to trump Tokugawa social strictures grounded in Confucianism. Oda's lovers, on the other hand, cannot escape. Instead, they give in to the mundane or, to return to Bataille, the base materiality of the local. Identifying in Bataille's theory a "prototype for what Derrida calls the '*general strategy of deconstruction*,'" Noys points us to the essay "The Big Toe," which, he asserts, "shows the process whereby the high or ideal denies its dependence on base matter by constructing it as disgusting and vile." In this way, Noys continues, "base matter is what makes the very structure of the high/low opposition possible in the first place *and* what ruins it."[70] By giving in to the mundane, Chōko and Ryūkichi destabilize the purportedly transcendent space—the would-be ideal—of empire.

This leads us to the third point of commonality: the use of locality. Like *Meoto zenzai*, Chikamatsu's love suicides bristle with Osaka place-names. The names of neighborhoods and particular streets of the merchant quarters and "pleasure" quarters, individual shops and teahouses, temples and bridges, crop up on every page of these plays, tracing trajectories through the early-modern city and lending specificity to the depiction of commoners' lives there. *Sonezaki*, for instance, locates the protagonist, Tokubei, even before it names him: he works for Hirano in Uchihonmachi. Tokubei himself then specifies several more stops on a merchant's itinerary of Osaka as he gives orders to an apprentice: "Go around to Kuhonji and Chūkuji in Teramachi and the mansions in Uemachi, then back to the shop. . . . Don't forget to call on the dyer in Azuchimachi and collect the money. Stay away from Dōtonbori."[71] In *Amijima*, the second act tours another corner of the city's economy as the opening narrative passage locates Jihei's paper shop on the street called Miya-no-mae machi, near the Tenjin-bashi bridge, and informs us that the housemaid has gone off to Ichinokawa on errands.[72]

With equal detail, these plays explore the spatial economy of the licensed quarter, Shinmachi, and the unlicensed quarters, Shimanouchi in the south and Dōjima and Sonezaki in the north. *Amijima* begins in the Sonezaki Quarter, with an introduction that locates it in reference to Shijimigawa, Umedabashi, and Sakurabashi. The narrative introduction to *Meido no hikyaku* similarly begins with references to Sado and Echigo, streets in the Shinmachi Quarter. Later, the prostitute Umegawa describes her day's itinerary, noting that she bought hair oil at Takemoto Tanomo's shop, then visited the Fan House Ōgiya, both actual shops. These names lend a geographic specificity—a locality—to the fundamental tension of the plays; as Heine describes it: the finite polarity of *giri-ninjō*, structure and anti-structure. This locality grounds the everyday that is constituted by the circulation within and between household and affective economies.

These place-names also play to a local audience, encouraging their identification with the city and confirming their urbanity. Underscoring this, each of the plays alludes to the countryside (*inaka*) and its bumpkins (*inakamon*) as outside threats. When Tokubei encounters Ohatsu at the beginning of *Sonezaki*, for instance, she is in the company of a "customer from the countryside" (*inaka no kyaku*).[73] Ohatsu warns Tokubei that her customer may cause trouble if he sees them together. Soon, *inaka* presents a greater threat to their relationship: we learn that Tokubei's master has threatened to exile him from the city. Tokubei then calls on the local urban audience to witness his good intentions: "I . . . will make amends by showing all Osaka the purity at the bottom of my heart."[74] In *Amijima*, another *inaka no kyaku* imperils the relationship between Jihei and Koharu. When reminded that if this *inakamon* ransoms her, she will have to move away from Osaka to the village of Itami, Koharu puns feelingly on the word for pain, a homonym (*itami*), as she cries, "Oh please don't say 'Itami, Itami!"[75] And again in *Meido no hikyaku*, an *inaka no kyaku* is attempting to buy out Umegawa's contract. At the beginning of the second act, she calls him an "oaf" from the country (*inaka no utezu*) and complains that if she allowed herself to be ransomed by such a man, she could never salvage her reputation.[76]

Oda's use of local place-names and shop names, like Chikamatsu's, grounds his characters' expenditures and hails a local audience. But Chikamatsu was writing for an Osaka stage and an Osaka audience at a time when the city was the center of *chōnin* culture and the reader's/auditor's familiarity with it could be assumed—a situation in which Osaka did not require explanation. Any allusion by Oda to that tradition can only highlight the very different circumstances of 1940, by which point Osaka's subordination to a national authority centered in Tokyo was well underway. By refusing to provide the explanation that a (Tokyo-centric) national audience now requires, Oda produces Osaka as an urban space resistant to the generality of nation; establishes the bonbon's local authority (and his own) over that space; and invites local readers, to the extent that they recognize those place-names, to share in that authority. It is now a dual address: to Osakans, who recognize the names as places they know or ought to know, and to national readers, for whom the encounter with place-names that they are expected *not* to know is alienating—if pleasantly so, in the manner of travelogues.

The most elaborate local citations in Chikamatsu's love suicides come in extended narrative passages filled with elaborate wordplay, listing local landmarks. *Sonezaki* opens with one such passage, which enumerates the thirty-three shrines in Osaka that venerate the goddess Kannon, punning on each shrine's name in turn. This itinerary described for its original audience a familiar Osaka, from Tenma through Tennōji to Teramachi. It also introduced the theme of Amidism and the promise of Buddhist transcendence through rebirth in the Pure Land, which is central to the play. More than a catalog, it is a textual pilgrimage that follows the order prescribed for actual pilgrims (at the same time publicizing the order and confirming it as knowledge shared by the local audience). As such, it foreshadows the less conventional pilgrimage the lovers will take to their death at the end of the play, the *michiyuki*, likewise narrated in a passage rife with wordplay.

If the first passage tours the city, the *michiyuki* delimits it, tracing Osaka's periphery, from Dōjima, past the Umeda embankment, to the Sonezaki shrine, where the lovers end their lives "in the wood of Tenjin."[77] Tenjin is the deified Sugawara no Michizane, and the shrine where Ohatsu and Tokubei die stands on the site where, according to legend, Michizane stopped and shed tears on his way into exile.[78] Robert Borgen notes that from early on, Michizane was regarded by commoners "as a divine ally in their protest against the established order in the capital."[79] By Chikamatsu's time, Tenjin was considered by the people of Osaka to be their city's guardian.[80] He was also associated with the bodhisattva Kannon. In this sense, the choice of his shrine as the site of the double suicide both grounds access to transcendence in the local and reiterates the sense of protest against a central authority.

Amijima, too, plays on the local associations of Tenjin. The protagonist, Jihei, lives in the neighborhood of Tenma Tenjin shrine, and the passage that announces his first appearance links him to Tenjin through an elaborate pun. (It is worth noting here that the unpublished sequel to *Meoto zenzai*, discussed at the end of this chapter, identifies Ryūkichi as a parishioner of the same shrine.)[81] And in this play, as in *Sonezaki*, the lovers make their final journey amid an extravagance of local references, the "*hashi-zukushi*" passage that enumerates the twelve bridges they cross on the way to their deaths. In this way, *Amijima*, too, grounds access to transcendence in locality.

Would it be ludicrous—not to say impious—to read the litany of *getemono* shops and food stalls at the beginning of *Meoto zenzai* as a similar sort of *tsukushi*? Oda's itinerary leads us through the southern hub of Osaka, describing a secular, sensuous pilgrimage of gastronomic pleasures as an escape from the massification of culture and the rationalization of consumption. And like *Sonezaki*, Oda's novella circles back, in its final scene, to the theme introduced in that early passage. After his father's death, Ryūkichi stays away from Chōko for a month, hoping to gain a share in his father's estate. When at last he does return to her, he explains his absence, then says, "Let's go get something g-g-good to eat. What do you say?" And the two head to the shop called Meoto zenzai—Sweet Beans for Two—in the compound of Hōzen-ji, a temple of the Pure Land sect near Dōtonbori.[82] There they indulge once more in the sort of humble local gastronomic pleasure, hardly fit for a geisha, that first seduced Chōko and bound her to Ryūkichi, against all propriety.

I previously quoted Shindō Masahiro's observation that by repeating aspects of Chikamatsu's love suicides, *Meoto zenzai* realizes a modern *jōruri*. What change is required to make the *jōruri* modern? Shindō suggests that it is the transformation of tragedy to comedy. And it requires an additional transformation: whereas in Chikamatsu the lovers seek to escape the space of the everyday, in Oda they inhabit it to enact a local practice of exuberant and profitless expenditure and play.

A Local Everyday

Chōko and Ryūkichi effect this expenditure through the pursuit of everyday life. In the early 1920s, the period in which *Meoto zenzai*'s story begins, a discourse of *nichijō seikatsu*, or "everyday life," was supplanting an earlier discourse of *bunmei kaika*, or "civilization and enlightenment."[83] The attention of government authorities, social critics and reformers, and the mass media shifted from the public-spirited and collective program of producing a national civilization in the Meiji period, to popular play (*minshū goraku*) and the individual consumption of cosmopolitan culture in the Taishō period. Oda's novella engages with this discourse of everyday life through its close attention to, and careful accounting of, Ryūkichi's consumer choices, particularly in relation to those most everyday of activities, the preparation and consumption of food.

But Ryūkichi's practice differs from the dominant discourse of everyday life in significant ways. First, it is hardly cosmopolitan. As we have seen, Ryūkichi is a local sort of bon vivant, an archetype rooted in Osaka's merchant history and literary tradition. His favorite pastime is not the moving pictures but the *jōruri*. The foods he consumes are Japanese, and the places he goes to consume them are marked as local. Just how local becomes clear if we compare *Meoto zenzai*'s gastro-geography of Osaka's Minami area with, for instance, the variety of international cuisines on offer in Tokyo's Asakusa neighborhood as imagined in Kawabata Yasunari's *Asakusa kurenaidan* (The crimson gang of Asakusa, 1929–30). Even the café Ryūkichi and Chōko open is emphatically Japanese. Although abolitionists at the time perceived the café as a Trojan horse of malign Western influence, Salon Chōryū features Japanese food, Japanese music, and waitresses dressed in the Japanese style. The narration notes, "Everything was arranged to the Japanese taste, and so it was more interesting, and appealed to a better clientele."[84]

Furthermore, the consumption *Meoto zenzai* describes is not massified. Everyday life is the process of constructing identity through choices about consumption. A hegemonic power such as the state exerts its influence over that consumption—and over the construction of identity—by ordering the production of goods and the development of markets. The pursuit of efficiency as part of such a strategy will lead to greater systematization, in the form of mass production and the homogenization of taste. "Everyday life" therefore tends toward mass markets and national life. The description in *Meoto zenzai* of a life that is lived locally (in the sense that it is lived, as far as possible, without reference to the nation—or even in resistance to the nation) constitutes a critique of the massification of consumption on a national order. The food stalls that Ryūkichi prefers to more glamorous restaurants, and the *getemono* sold there, appeal not only because they are good but because they are idiosyncratic and unknown to the developing mass market.

This concern with the locality of everyday life responds both to the historical moment into which *Meoto zenzai* was published, near the high point of Japan's imperial adventure, and to the period in which the novella is set. The discourse of everyday life arose at a moment of intense rivalry between Tokyo and Osaka. Jeffrey Hanes has described how this rivalry developed in the 1910s, as an economic boom buoyed Osaka and "the newfound wealth and *nouveau* ways of the infamous *narikin* (nouveaux riche) and their hangers-on was met with a mixture of envy, dismissiveness, and resentment by Tokyoites."[85] This rivalry deepened after the Great Kantō Earthquake of 1923, as Osaka financial capital flooded into the ruined, rebuilding city; meanwhile, Osaka superseded Tokyo as Japan's largest city. Influential social critic Ōya Sōichi, who was born in Osaka but moved to Tokyo to attend university, marveled at the modernity of Osaka's consumer lifestyle on a return visit in 1929, calling it "Japan's America." Six months later, Ōya was writing more ominously of "the conquest of Japan by Osakan culture."[86] But the 1923 earthquake that devastated the capital would come to be recognized as a turning point for Tokyo, a cataclysm that wiped the slate clean, allowing the city to be reconstructed for a new economy supported by mass consumption and entertainment.[87] Tokyo became ground zero of Japan's modernity, and Osaka, so recently perceived as the source of a dangerous new consumerism, was gradually relegated to tradition.

As Ōya's comments suggest, the rivalry between Osaka and Tokyo informed the discourse of "modern life." Critics compared practices in the two cities, asserting Tokyo's sovereign modernity and casting Osaka as Tokyo's foil. In the 1922 essay "Gin-bura to Dō-bura: Santo jōshu" (Ginza-cruising and Dōtonbori-cruising: The mood in three capitals), for example, preeminent critic of popular entertainment Gonda Yasunosuke considers the common Tokyo practice of aimlessly hanging out on the city's premier promenade and wonders at the absence of a similar practice on Osaka's Dōtonbori. He observes that "on the Ginza, walking itself has meaning, while on Dōtonbori, walking has meaning [only] as a means to some other end." He concludes that "to emphasize the goal, and for that reason to place value on the course toward it, is utilitarianism, and that is the glory of Kamigata pleasure."[88] Tokyo, Gonda suggests, is the natural environment of that modern creature, the flaneur. As noted by Jeffrey

Hanes, however, Gonda ignores the term *Shin-bura*, used in Osaka from the 1920s to describe the act of strolling Shinsaibashi, the shopping street adjacent to Dōtonbori.[89] In "Minshū goraku" (Popular entertainment, 1923), Gonda contrasts the "unpleasantly modest and gloomy" appearance of Tokyo's shops with the "extreme cheerfulness" of Osaka's, but goes on to assert that in Tokyo, "show windows have of necessity been modernized," while Osaka still lacks that modern appurtenance so characteristic of the flaneur's Paris arcades.[90]

Although Oda sets *Meoto zenzai* in this historical moment at which the discovery of everyday life overlaps with modern Osaka's economic and cultural ascendency, he publishes it in 1940, by which point the government had coopted the discourse of popular play into national play (*kokumin goraku*). Everyday life was drafted into military leaders' program of imperial aggression—a program that would effect the "catastrophic expenditure" of war.[91] Miriam Silverberg has argued that the "daily practice" detailed by Gonda and the other Tokyo-based "ethnographers of modernity" offered refuge from a productivist imperial ideology through a transnational "code-switching" between East and West. The daily practice Oda imagines for his readers likewise offers refuge from a productivist ideology that had only grown more powerful by 1940. To the "profound awareness of the ongoing construction of a new culture shared by all but at the same time differentiated by gender and class" evidenced by Gonda and his Tokyo cohorts, however, Oda adds a differentiation by locality, conscious (as he could not help but be) of the fate of the city within imperial modernity.[92]

The nation-state's assertion of a totality that subsumes the local, suspected in Chikamatsu, is by Oda's time undeniable—indeed, Oda's career is overshadowed by the project to amplify that totality across East Asia. Meanwhile, the religious transcendence that Chikamatsu's lovers imagine for themselves in the Pure Land was no longer available to the lovers in Oda's secular world. Against that asserted totality, Ryūkichi instead seeks, through everyday epiphany, a transcendence grounded in the local. By modeling an individual morality and a household economy that is patently irrational within the order of the wartime nation-state, the novella proposes another order, an urban and local order, citing local precedents and relying on local authority. By 1940, Osaka's cultural, economic, and political subordination was confirmed, but Oda's bonbon exploits his local authority to reclaim at the individual level an Osaka that the imperial nation has already managed, and models a sovereignty resistant to the homogenization and centralization of culture under national imperialism.

Epilogue: *Meoto zenzai*: The Sequel

In 1999, Japan's national newspapers carried reports that a manuscript written by Oda around the same time as *Meoto zenzai* and titled as its sequel, *Zoku meoto zenzai*, had been discovered among a collection of manuscripts donated to the city of Sendai in Kagoshima, on the island of Kyushu, by the family of Yamamoto Sanehiko, one-time president of the Tokyo *Mainichi* newspaper and founder of the important intellectual journal *Kaizō*.[93] A letter written by Oda around the same time as both stories attests to his concern over wartime censorship, suggesting that this may have prevented the manuscript's publication. As Hidaka Shōji notes, no publisher would likely have been interested in a sequel even less aligned than the original story with the propagandistic aims of the military government.[94]

The sequel picks up the story in 1937, one year after the close of the published novella. Ryūkichi is forty-five and Chōko is thirty-three. They are still living in Osaka and running their café, Salon Chōryū. An unsettled atmosphere hangs over the opening pages, however. Amid preparations for the summer festival at nearby Ikutama shrine, Chōko's father, Tanekichi, turns up unexpectedly and spends an evening getting drunk and singing songs, before staggering off. Two days later, he dies on the way home from a visit to Chōko's brother, Shin'ichi, in Kyoto. Meanwhile, Ryūkichi is spending more evenings away from home. Chōko slips into a funk. One night, unable to sleep, she prowls the Sennichimae entertainment district, searching for distraction. The narrative slips out of the everyday, following along as Chōko drifts through a catalog of *shomin* amusement—a women's jazz band, miniature cars, a shooting gallery, rocking horses, *shōgi* (Japanese chess), mah-jongg, table tennis—until she runs into Ryūkichi. Soon, however, Ryūkichi disappears again. After twenty days, he turns up to announce that he has sold the title to their café for a thousand yen, bet the money at the track in Kyoto, and used his winnings to buy the deed to a cosmetics shop in Beppu, a hot springs resort on the distant island of Kyushu. Three days later, they leave Osaka behind.

After this rupture, the rest of the sequel relates episodes from their new life. Through hard work, they make a success of their shop until the war intervenes. At the same time, they make a life for themselves in Beppu. They take up *jōruri* lessons with a local teacher. Chōko becomes mother hen to a group of local geisha. Their move reverses a common migration that brought people from Kyushu to Osaka in search of work. It also allows us to view Osaka from the outside, not from the capital but from a western periphery for which it constitutes the metropolis. In Kyushu, Osaka is a source of economic capital, supplying the goods Chōko and Ryūkichi sell in their shop. It is a source of cultural capital, too: they rename the shop "Osaka-ya" to draw attention from tourists, and on her sales rounds, Chōko uses her dialect to charm clients. Their *jōruri* teacher comes from Osaka, too, and together they reminisce about life in the big city.

What can we make of this abrupt change of setting, in the sequel to what has become the representative story of modern Osaka? One effect is that, with the sequel, Chōko and Ryūkichi's story enters national time. The year in which the story opens, 1937, marks the beginning of Japan's total war with China, instigated by the Marco Polo Bridge Incident of July 7. The operations of the Japanese state were ignored in the published novella, but the war intrudes on the sequel in several ways.

The first reference to the war comes when Chōko, along with her new geisha friends in Beppu, joins the Ladies' Association for National Defense, or Kokubō fujinkai (which developed out of a group founded in Osaka in 1932). Oda treats this episode with a parodic touch that makes it easy to understand why the sequel went unpublished. As she and her geisha friends see off a group of soldiers departing for the front, Chōko calls out to them, "Once you go off to the battlefield, you probably won't be shaving, but please, once in a while, remember the razors at Osaka-ya on Nagaregawa Road!" Oda renders the line with his characteristic flair for dialect: "*Senchi i ikihattara, hige mo soriharahen yaro kedo, tama ni wa Nagaregawa no Ōsaka-ya no kamisori mo omoidashito kure yassha.*"[95] Self-interest overwhelms patriotism; humor undermines militaristic piety; and a ludicrous sales pitch, delivered in the patois of the merchant capital, drowns out the language of national service and sacrifice expected on such an occasion.

The war intrudes more directly in the character of Chōko's brother, Shin'ichi. As Chōko sees off the recruits in Beppu, the narration notes, "Chōko thought to herself, 'soon my little brother will be conscripted, too,' and she took pride in that."[96] Again, the narration suggests properly patriotic sentiment, and again it undermines this sentiment:

Shin'ichi is indeed conscripted, but he is found to be sick with pleurisy, rejected as unfit to serve, and sent home. He then comes to live with Chōko and Ryūkichi. This episode plays on a contemporary stereotype of the Osaka man as particularly unfit for military service. The Imperial Army's Eighth Regiment, ostensibly the Osaka regiment (though its members were actually recruited from various locales), suffered an undeserved reputation for weakness and cowardliness.[97] A popular refrain at the time ran, "Have they lost again, the Eighth Regiment? In that case, they don't get any medals!" ("*Mata mo maketa ka, hachirentai? Sore de wa kunshō kurentai!*" with the final word, "*kurentai*," also serving as a pun on the Ninth, or Kyoto, Regiment). This reputation, disseminated through the popular media at the time, played on the perception that young men from Osaka were raised with more concern for business acumen than for bravery or physical strength.

The conscripted army is a primary technology of the nation. It is generally supposed to be one of the most efficient institutions for producing a modern national identity. Unlike the caste-based militaries of premodern times, the conscripted army draws men from all regions and classes and encourages them to suppress individual differences to become a uniform body, operating with one mind. The wry humor of the aforementioned refrain and the media commentary it inspired betray anxiety over Osaka's stubborn difference: the locality that will not dissolve into national identity. The stereotype of the Eighth Regiment pits self-interest against selfless sacrifice and local character against national identity. The figure of Chōko's sickly brother, Shin'ichi, in the sequel cites this anxiety. Once again, the Osaka man proves inutile to national interests.

This helps clarify the significance of the sequel's change of setting. As the war enters the story, the story enters history and progressive national time. In the original novella, Oda wrote Osaka as a constant urban present. In the sequel, that Osaka has become uninhabitable. The unavoidable fact of the Japanese state's imperial ambitions has pulled the story out of the constant present and pulled its protagonists out of Osaka.

We see this reflected as well in the sequel's shift away from play and toward work. After they move to Kyushu, Chōko, as ever, throws herself into sales. Now, however, Ryūkichi also takes to his work, and within a short time, the couple find success. They relocate their shop to the upscale neighborhood of Nagaregawa-michi. The tally of debits and credits that runs through the original story continues in the sequel, but it now tells a story of increasing success and security. As the shop flourishes, Chōko and Ryūkichi become successful enough to hire a maid and an apprentice. Gradually, the wartime control economy makes business more difficult; the shops around them are bankrupted by inflation. The tourist economy remains strong, however, and as the story ends, the couple are making plans to open their house to lodgers. The change in Ryūkichi, from irresponsible playboy to capable helpmeet, suggests that the bonbon cannot exist outside Osaka. Chōko's proper impulse—to work hard and save as an investment in the future—has won out over Ryūkichi's impulse to excessive expenditure.

The locality of its daily life, together with the narration's eschewal of historical and geographical context, lends the published novella *Meoto zenzai* an air that might be mistaken for simple nostalgia. Indeed, Oda himself later acknowledged the nostalgia of his early works. In the essay *Kanōsei no bungaku* (The literature of potentiality, 1946), he complains that the Japanese novel has long since sunken into a "lethargic orthodoxy." With the rigorous self-examination and confessional sincerity of the I-novel as its ideal, he charges, the literary establishment has come to value "profundity within strict limits" over a wider-ranging exploration of the potential of fiction. In his early attempts to escape this orthodoxy, Oda writes, he "fell into the dilemma of seeing through eyes tinted by nostalgia," and with this essay he resolves to confront the orthodoxy of Japanese prose fiction more directly. In *Meoto zenzai*, however, Oda's nostalgia, if we can call it that, is tactically effective in its own way. First, by coating his story in nostalgia, Oda made it palatable to government censors. By comparison, the sequel, which deals more candidly with Japan's imperialism, went unpublished. More than this, in its conservatism, this nostalgia, or rather anti-futurism, resists a revolutionary modernity that was being commandeered by empire. In this sense, Japan's militarization, and the capital from which it was directed, provide the essential anti-context to *Meoto zenzai*, a novella that is informed at every turn by the fate of the local within the time and space of imperial Japan.

Chapter Three

City, Empire, and Flow

Osaka and the Philippines in Oda Sakunosuke's *Waga machi*

In chapter 2, we saw how Oda Sakunosuke's best-loved work addressed the domestic aspect of Japan's imperial project, deploying an archetype of urban local masculinity and his practice of expenditure and play to destabilize state discourses of economy and propriety. Next, we turn to another influential work by Oda that links his local Osaka to sites of imperial ambition overseas. The 1942 novella *Waga machi* (My town) takes place largely in the author's hometown, but it is prefaced by two chapters set in various locales in the Philippines, which was a U.S. colony at the turn of the century, when the story begins, and which was invaded by Japan in 1941, when the story ends and a year before Oda published the novella. In the migrations of its poor, laboring protagonist, *Waga machi* imagines a distinctive cosmopolitanism that links city, nation, and empire.

Waga machi must be read against national and imperial discourses of universality and transcendence, both because the novella was published at the height of Japan's imperial expansion and because its deployment of events and images encourages us to do so. As stages in the centralization of authority, both nation and empire posit new unities that subordinate diverse spaces, populations, institutions, and phenomena, redefining them as particular, fragmentary, and constitutive of the new order. Just as the nation is purported to transcend localities, so, too, the empire is purported to transcend nations. But this notion of transcendence dissimulates the process by which one locale exerts hegemonic power over others. This is not limited to understandings of political authority per se; chapter 1 traced the same operation in the development of national language, whereby a universal standard redefined older idioms as "dialects," and native speakers of those older, local idioms came to think of them as transcended by and subordinated to a new (but retrojected) national language—an operation that was then extended to the Korean language. Similar operations attend the progressive centralization of nation and empire in myriad other aspects.

Waga machi engages these notions of universality and transcendence by tracing the networks and flows that link the city of Osaka to Benguet, Davao, and Manila in the Philippines. Osaka is a "provincial" space over which the nation has already asserted its transcendence; the Philippines locales are "colonial" spaces over which the empire will do the same. However, *Waga machi*'s description of those networks and flows contradicts the notion of separate orders—local, national, and imperial—each transcended by the next. The story calls our attention to the continuities among these stages in hegemonic domination. Oda's engagement with the discourse of imperialism does not amount to resistance; indeed, the author can be said to have practiced a strategic complicity with the censorship under which he wrote. By the end of *Waga machi*, he has dramatized the irresistible allure of imperial transcendence and the futility of resistance to it. At the same time, though, he has offered a competing vision of the cosmopolitan and illustrated Osaka's potential—as the locus of that alternative cosmopolitanism—to decenter our understanding of Japan.

Waga machi

Waga machi first appeared in the 1942 New Year's edition of the journal *Bungei* (Literary arts), near the height of Japan's imperial expansion and under the strictest censorship. A year earlier, Oda's novel *Seishun no gyakusetsu* (The paradox of youth) had been banned. Accordingly, *Waga machi* displays a carefully calibrated jingoism and anti-American resentment. Kawamura Minato has categorized the novella as *goyō bungaku*—that is, literature produced in support of Japan's militarist policies.[1] At the same time, he agrees with the writer (and Oda associate) Aoyama Kōji that the story's militarism goes no further than "strapping on gaiters."[2] Kawamura concludes that "such a *local* story, which preaches the Naniwa gutsiness (*konjō*) of Osaka and Osakans more than the unity of the nation or 'Yamato spirit,' could not avail as *national literature*, meant to awaken the spirit of 'One hundred million people, one mind.'"[3] While the story's jingoism was emphatic enough to satisfy government censors and wartime audiences, it was not so strong as to preclude an extended postwar afterlife in adaptation. Oda's story was staged as *Bengetto no hoshi* (Star of Benguet) in August 1943 and as *Waga machi* in October of that year and again as *Bengetto no hoshi* the following year. In 1956, Nikkatsu released a film adaptation directed by Kawashima Yūzō and featuring Tatsumi Ryūtarō, a star of the Shinkokugeki (New National Theater) in the lead role. In 1961, the story was once again revived for the stage as *Sadojima Takichi no shōgai* (The life of Sadojima Takichi), starring Morishige Hisaya in one of his best-known stage roles.

Waga machi recounts the life of Sadojima Takichi and his family as a cycle of poverty, death, and migration, leavened by the comic genius of their hometown. The story is set almost entirely in downtown Osaka, but it opens in Benguet in the Philippines. Takichi is in the Philippines working first on a crew constructing a road and later on an abaca (hemp) plantation. After a few years, he makes his way home to Osaka, where he pulls a rickshaw to earn money. He dreams of returning to the Philippines, but various events conspire to prevent him. First, his wife dies, leaving him to raise their daughter, Hatsue, alone. He intends to return once she is married, but Hatsue's husband, Shintarō, heads off to the Philippines himself to find work, leaving Takichi behind to help look after Hatsue. Shintarō dies of cholera, and Hatsue dies soon after, leaving Takichi to raise another child—his granddaughter, Kimie. Once she is married, Takichi, now an old man, prepares to return to the Philippines at last, but this time he is prevented by the escalating war. He dies without returning.

The novella's title points to two "towns": on the one hand, the locales familiar to Takichi from his time in the Philippines, where the story begins (at one point in the story, Takichi boasts, "Manila is my town!" [Manira wa wai no machi ya]);[4] and on the other hand, Osaka—specifically the environs of Gataro Alley, where most of the story takes place.[5] The Philippine locales are broadly sketched, the place-names taken from a map. In the early chapters set there, the narration cites a number of historical figures and events. By contrast, Osaka is more closely observed and geographically intimate, and the later chapters set there are studded with the names of shops, subway stations, and other local landmarks. Though the alley at the heart of this local city is fictional, Oda modeled it after the Osaka neighborhood where he grew up, Hinomaru yoko-roji (literally, "Rising Sun side-alley").[6] Oda mapped Gataro Alley across several works: the stories "Risshiden" (Record of success, 1941) and "Konki hazure" (Beyond marriageable age, 1940), as well as *Meoto zenzai* (Sweet beans for two, 1940), are all set there. Takichi's granddaughter in *Waga machi*, Kimie, is the protagonist of "Risshiden"; and the protagonists of *Meoto zenzai*, Chōko and Ryūkichi, make several appearances in *Waga machi*, which reprises much of their story. Oda himself wrote in a postscript to the original published version of *Waga machi* that the alley had become almost real to him.[7]

In the pages that follow, I explore these two "towns." First, I detail how the opening of the novella, set in the Philippines, alludes to the history of Japanese migration and to official and popular discourses of colonialism, imperialism, and Pan-Asianism. I then analyze how the remainder of the novella, set in Osaka, maps a "city of flows"—streets and roads and the flow of traffic through them; water and the flow of goods and labor over it; the flow of speech; and the migrant flow traced by the protagonist—and how these flows link the local and immanent to the cosmopolitan and (would-be) transcendent. To finish, I describe the spatial and temporal axes at the intersection of which *Waga machi* locates its protagonist.

The Philippines and Migrant Flows

The early chapters of *Waga machi* trace migrant flows that embed the story in contemporary discourses of race, nation, and empire. In particular, these chapters reference two historical episodes in Japanese immigration to the Philippines: the building of the Benguet Road and the settlement of Davao. In Benguet, Takichi is working for the U.S. colonial authorities, who are building a road from Rosario up to the new summer capital, Baguio. Benguet is located in the mountainous area of northern Luzon, the largest island of the Philippines, which is also home to the capital, Manila. Because of the rugged terrain, few expeditions by Spanish military or missionaries reached Benguet until the nineteenth century. In 1846, a series of expeditions established the city of La Trinidad, which would become the capital of the state of Benguet. Thinking that the area's temperate climate would be ideal for recuperating troops, Spanish colonial authorities commissioned a plan to establish a sanitarium high in the mountains, at Baguio, where cool temperatures could provide relief from the tropical heat.[8] After colonial authority changed hands, a member of the U.S.-appointed Philippine Commission, Dean Worcester, got hold of the Spanish commission's plans and went to Baguio to investigate.[9] The Philippine Commission subsequently developed plans to establish a "health resort" at Baguio, anticipating that a settlement there, amid pine trees and grassland, would attract Americans to the colonial civil service.[10] The commission's report describes the climate as "very similar to that of Northern New England in the late spring or early summer."[11] In his own book, Worcester likened Baguio to the Adirondacks: "Roses, violets, azaleas, 'jacks-in-the-pulpit,' and several kinds of raspberries and huckleberries, all growing wild, make one feel as if back in America."[12] American officials formally established a settlement at Baguio in 1900.

In December of that year, the Philippine Commission authorized the construction of a road connecting Baguio to Rosario. The difficulty of the terrain and the climate, ignorance about the local geology and geography, and a shortage of labor plagued the project, which wildly overran estimates of total cost and time.[13] This changed in 1903, when Colonel Lyman Kennon of the U.S. Army Corps of Engineers took over supervision of the construction. Kennon assembled a crew of three thousand, consisting mostly of Filipino workers and migrant workers from Japan, especially Okinawa, and China. After slow progress under the first two general supervisors, the road was completed within eighteen months of Kennon's taking control. In recognition, the governor-general of the Philippines in 1922 named the road in Kennon's honor. Influenced by anthropological notions of national work ethic, Kennon favored Japanese laborers; and by recruiting them for the road, he initiated the flow of migrant labor from Japan to the Philippines. The Japanese presence in the Philippines was negligible before the turn of the century. When the Japanese consulate in Manila reopened in 1896, only 16 Japanese residents registered; by 1903, that number had surged to 1,215, most of them, like the fictional Takichi, there to work on the Benguet Road.[14]

The beginning of *Waga machi* memorializes Kennon's role in the construction of the Benguet Road. It describes how the colonel, aware of the work ethic demonstrated by Japanese in California and mindful of Japan's recent victory over the Manchu state, visits the Japanese consulate to request a contingent of laborers.[15] A secretary there sends him to the procurement agent of the Kobe Emigrant Corporation (Kōbe Tokō Gōshi Kaisha, a historical business), who finds a way around a law prohibiting migrant labor. Among the laborers who arrive in this group is the protagonist, Takichi. The work is dangerous, often deadly, but Takichi and the other Japanese take pride in completing a job that American and Filipino crews could not. By thus referencing Kennon, the narration ties Takichi's story to a figure and an episode that would have been familiar to contemporary readers from news accounts. And by noting the colonel's anthropological privileging of the Japanese, it appeals to readers' notions of Japanese racial and cultural superiority in Asia.

At the same time, the narration reciprocates the American's regard, calling the colonel, in the first sentence of the novella, a "samurai." In this way, the narrative reflects a historical interlude of mutual regard, when the Japanese state hoped it would be welcomed into the community of modern nations and colonial powers, and those nations and powers still trusted Japan not to claim full membership. U.S. officials and observers were praising the Japanese for having "an aptitude for acquiring the civilization of the West to which no other Oriental race can lay claim," as *Harper's Monthly* put it as early as 1860.[16] Meanwhile, Japanese diplomats and legislators were supporting U.S. domination in the Philippines, with such observers as Nitobe Inazō and Tsurumi Yūsuke praising the colonizers' efforts to improve health, education, and infrastructure.[17] The first lines of *Waga machi* echo this sense of affiliation between the Japanese and the Americans, even though Japan is not in fact a colonial power when the story opens but a source of labor for the U.S. authority.

In *Waga machi*, this sense of affiliation does not last long. When U.S. personnel begin using the Benguet Road in a manner that seems to underscore unequal colonial relations, the Japanese laborers—Takichi in particular—become indignant. The Philippine Commission initially intended that the settlement at Baguio should serve as a sanitarium for Filipinos as well as U.S. personnel, and in fact, in the early years, wealthy Filipinos made up the majority of patients there. Soon, however, more and more people were coming to Baguio primarily for vacation.[18] In 1905, U.S. Secretary of War (and future president) William H. Taft commissioned a plan for the new city, which called for a complex of national government buildings, an expansive army post, a large public common, two public parks, and a country club. In 1906, the commission leased out the main building of the sanitarium to a developer who converted it into a first-class hotel, later to become the landmark Pines Hotel. Baguio thus became as much resort as health facility and increasingly served U.S. personnel.

Briefly alluded to, these developments inspire an anticolonial outrage among Takichi and his mates. Hearing reports that the Benguet Road is being used "as a driveway for Americans going out to dance," they think to themselves, "Is this what we sweat and bled for?!" Takichi heads to Manila, where he walks the streets in a rage, accosting an American and taunting him: "Hey! The blood of six hundred men runs in the Benguet Road! And you're going to take it to go dancing, without a care in the world? Just try it!"[19] The specter that inspires Takichi's outrage—of American occupiers taking the road to go dancing in Baguio—underscores the reality of racial hierarchy.

If the early reference to Kennon's preference for, and privileging of, Japanese labor appeals to a sense (in the narration, among the fictional Japanese laborers, and among a wartime Japanese readership) of Japan's superiority over other Asians and an identification with the United States as fellow imperialists, Takichi's reaction to the Benguet Road's repurposing suggests an identification with Filipinos in their colonial abjection. Japanese laborers like Takichi working on the road would have found this combination of identification and superiority confirmed by U.S. authorities' employment policies. Responsibilities, pay, and food rations for laborers on the Benguet Road were determined by a complicated calculus of race and nationality. Americans and European Caucasians could become foremen, while Filipino, Japanese, and Chinese laborers could rise only as high as *capataz* (overseer), responsible for twenty to twenty-five men of the same race. Filipinos were paid far less than Japanese, however, whose base rate was the same as Americans' (though of course Americans were eligible for positions with a much higher pay rate). Europeans and Americans (including African Americans, who were grouped with Caucasians for the purpose of food rationing) received more generous rations than did Asians. Japanese received the same rations as Filipino laborers, but these were supplemented with staples of the Japanese diet, provided by Japanese merchants in Davao. Overseers of the construction crew compiled statistics measuring the average output of laborers by race and ethnicity to support their anthropological approach to management and compensation—though one historian notes that productivity differentials might more reasonably be explained by "disparities in food intake."[20]

The flow of Japanese migrant labor to the Philippines initiated by Kennon and the construction of the Benguet Road was encouraged by another historical figure and episode that are woven into the opening chapters of *Waga machi*: Ōta Kyōsaburō and the development of Davao. A seaside town on the island of Mindanao, Davao became home to the largest community of Japanese migrants in Southeast Asia, and Ōta's corporation was its largest landowner. Ōta was born in 1876, north of the city of Himeji in Hyōgo Prefecture. At the age of ten he was adopted by an uncle in Osaka, and he graduated middle school there before moving to Tokyo for high school. Ōta left Japan in 1901, going first to Hong Kong and then to Thursday Island in the Torres Straits off Australia, where the pearl industry was attracting Japanese workers. In July of the same year, he moved on to Manila, having heard the economy there was improving under the U.S. authority. In 1903, Ōta received permission from U.S. authorities to establish plantations on Mindanao to grow coconut and abaca, a source of hemp.[21] Abaca came to dominate the local economy. Poor Japanese flocked to Davao, establishing a "Japan town" there, with schools, newspapers, and a consular annex, and helping to kindle Japanese economic interest and colonial ambitions.[22]

Ōta's name appears in the second chapter of *Waga machi*. After the completion of the Benguet Road, Takichi and other Japanese without enough savings to return home are left to wander the streets of Manila, facing destitution. Ōta comes to Manila to recruit workers for his plantation in Davao, a "barbaric place," plagued by malaria, where only the Moro and Bagobo tribes live.[23] He promises the workers decent pay, a proper diet, and a Japanese doctor in residence. In fact, Ōta did supply Japanese foodstuffs to supplement the rations of Japanese workers on the Benguet Road from 1903. When construction on the road ended in 1905, about five hundred Japanese laborers remained in the Philippines, and many of these indeed went to Davao to find work, as Takichi does in *Waga machi*.[24]

Like the reference to Kennon, the mention of Ōta early in the story points the reader to an important historical context for Japan's invasion of the Philippines at the novella's end. World War I brought a boom in demand for hemp (most of which, in accordance with trade regulations, was exported to the United States). Meanwhile, the amicable relations between the United States and Japan following the Lansing-Ishii Agreement of 1917, a diplomatic note ostensibly resolving the dispute over the two nations' interests in China, encouraged Japanese immigration to the U.S.-controlled Philippines. By 1919, the number of Japanese there had reached 9,874.[25] Following this, another industry developed that would make the Philippines critically important to Japan's military plans: mining. In 1934, 7,240 tons of iron ore were shipped to Japan from the Philippines; five years later, with the involvement of such major corporate interests as Mitsui, Mitsubishi, and Ishikawa San'gyō, production exceeded one million tons, of which all but twenty tons went to Japan. This boom encouraged ancillary business activity: a beer brewery; a fishery; companies producing candies, liquor, cement, bicycles, and more. By 1939, Japanese in the Philippines outnumbered Chinese, with 17,888 in Davao and another 4,730 in the main city, Manila.[26]

This immigration raised U.S. concerns in the context of Japan's increasingly open imperialism in East Asia and Filipinos' anticipation of independence. In 1916, the Jones Law officially stated for the first time the U.S. government's intention to grant the Philippines autonomy "as soon as a stable government can be established," the fulfillment of that condition to be determined by the United States, which would also retain certain economic privileges after autonomy. The same law established a senate to replace the U.S.-appointed Philippine Commission as upper house, thus creating an all-Filipino legislature. The next major legislative step came in 1935, when the Philippines became a commonwealth of the United States, a status envisioned as a transition to fuller autonomy in 1946. In the meantime, the Japanese military and government had unmistakably signaled its imperialist ambitions. Japan's withdrawal from the League of Nations in March 1933 put into question the legitimacy of Japan's authority in Micronesia, which the Japanese government nevertheless refused to relinquish. In 1938, the American high commissioner to the Philippines, Paul McNutt, proposed that the United States postpone Philippine autonomy beyond 1946, alluding to the danger of an influx of immigrants who threatened the Filipinos with "racial extinction."[27] The Manila Chamber of Commerce also advised postponing autonomy (which officials rejected). The growing sense of both national sovereignty and vulnerability found expression in a variety of protectionist measures, which were seen to target Japanese as the largest and most economically influential immigrant group.

Ōta's name would have been familiar to readers of *Waga machi* from newspaper reports on these developments. A full page of articles in the *Ōsaka Asahi Shimbun* of November 19, 1935, was grouped under the heading "Japanese in Davao." One article relates Ōta's entrepreneurial accomplishments under the title "Behind Dominance of an Industry: A Romance of Blood and Sweat."[28] Like the construction of the Benguet Road, the development of Davao became a source of national pride in Japan, the story included in a textbook on ethics published in 1943 (a year after Oda's novella appeared) by the Education Ministry for use in elementary schools. That textbook presented Ōta as a "public-spirited" pioneer, who educates the Filipinos in proper farming practices and turns "desolate" Davao into a thriving community, surprising the Americans and Spaniards who had looked down on him.[29] Ōta's success would have been linked in many readers' minds to the issue of protectionist legislation and, specifically, what became known as the "Davao land problem" (*Dabao tochi mondai*). The reaction in Japan is suggested by the headline of another article that ran in the same edition of the *Ōsaka Asahi Shimbun*, next to the one on Ōta: "Nagging Land Problem: Pressing Forward, Indomitable Japanese Exploit Limitless Bounty."[30]

By the time *Waga machi* was published, Japan's leaders were promoting the Greater East Asia Co-Prosperity Sphere as an alternative to a purportedly universal Western modernity. Overcoming that Western modernity was said to require the transcendence of national divisions within East Asia. So, while Filipinos in the press, the government, and organized labor framed the issues of land rights and immigration control in terms of national sovereignty, some Japanese discussed those issues in terms of supernational solidarity against a white, Western, Christian threat. Furukawa Gizō, for example—Ōta's colleague and rival in developing Davao—linked the push for land reform to anti-Asian popular movements and legislation in the United States. (The Asiatic Exclusion League formed in San Francisco in May 1905, and the California Alien Land Law of 1913 prohibited from owning land or property those aliens "ineligible for citizenship"—effectively, all Asian immigrants.) Another Japanese observer, Masaki Kichiemon—a director of the Ōta Development Corporation and president of the Japanese club in Davao—stressed the pro-Japanese sentiments among the indigenous population there and suggested that fear of domination by Christian Filipinos motivated opposition among Mindanao's Muslim Moro community to Philippine independence, as well as the community's cooperation with the Japanese.[31] Both men spoke in terms that transcended national divisions. Their contention that race was an important determinant in these policies (including the imbrication of race with imperialist competition between the United States and Japan in the Philippines) should not obscure the nationalistic motivations of Japanese colonizers, politicians, and military planners. Pan-Asianism's language of transcendence masked a program of domination and subordination, later revealed in contradictory rationales that combined declarations of "brotherly amity" among the nations of East Asia with a conception of racial hierarchy that reserved authority to the Japanese.[32] The first chapters thus set Oda's story of the local city within the context of colonial development, racial competition, and transnational labor.

Osaka and Urban Flows

The remainder of the novel, set in Osaka, describes a city of flows, which link it to the Philippines and to the discourses of race, nation, and empire introduced in the early chapters. To be sure, the first detailed description of Gataro Alley, at the beginning of the novella's second section, suggests stagnancy:

> It was a poor, squalid neighborhood, and strangely unchanging; as lifeless as an old hand towel. The fruit shop on the corner had been a fruit shop for generations, the signboard so worn that not even the proprietor could read the shop's name. The *sake* shop hadn't moved in decades. The bathhouse hadn't changed hands. The druggist hadn't changed either: the same doddering old man was still measuring out doses in a shop hung with decades-old certificates from drug companies.[33]

In contrast to the Philippine locales, the alley seems here changeless and ahistorical. Progressive, national time, so clearly operative in the opening chapters, now seems held in abeyance. But as it continues, the story pulls the alley into the currents of history and empire.[34]

The most significant of these is the flow of water. Water, and the flow of goods and people it bears, has always defined Osaka. Located on a natural bay at the mouth of the Yodogawa, the area around what is now called Osaka has been a destination and a transit point for overseas travel, migration, and trade since Nintoku, the leader of the Yamato clan, established his headquarters at Naniwa, or "swift waves," and built his palace there around the turn of the fifth century. In early modern times, Toyotomi Hideyoshi's castle town was delineated by a canal, the Higashiyokobori, completed in 1585, which separated the merchant quarter, Senba, from the samurai quarter to the east. After Tokugawa Ieyasu's forces defeated those loyal to Hideyoshi's son and successor, Hideyori, Ieyasu appointed Matsudaira Tadaakira to rebuild the ruined city. Tadaakira permitted wealthy local merchants to construct new canals to carry goods and people throughout the city, an elaborate network that earned

Osaka the epithet "Capital on the Water." Among these was the Minamihorikawa (southern canal), begun by the entrepreneur Dōton Yasui in 1612 and completed three years later, when it was renamed the Dōtonbori (Dōton canal), despite its namesake's having fought for Toyotomi loyalists and against the victorious Tokugawa. The area around the Dōtonbori was designated an entertainment district in 1621 by the Tokugawa shogunate and remains one of the city's main commercial centers.[35]

These canals framed Osaka's landscape for centuries, and they survived until Oda's time, though they would soon be covered over, filled in, and otherwise obscured. *Waga machi* locates the imaginary Gataro Alley by the banks of the Dōtonbori, suggesting the significance that the story attaches to the flow of water. It underscores that significance by placing a public bathhouse at the center of the alley and giving that bathhouse a role in the plot. It further emphasizes the importance of water with the alley's name; "Gatarō" is a local expression for *kappa*, a creature of folklore that lives in streams and canals, making mischief.[36] In fact, Oda writes the name of the alley with the kanji for "*kappa*," giving "gataro" in hiragana as a gloss.[37] The term was also used to refer to poor people who would sieve the mud of Osaka's canals searching for lost valuables.

Jinnai Hidenobu has written eloquently of Edo's *shitamachi* (low city) as a "city of water," but much of what he describes applies at least as well (and perhaps more definitively) to Osaka.[38] For example, we can trace in Osaka—as Jinnai traces in Edo/Tokyo—the role of water in the city's economic development and the shift in modernity to a city on land, a shift effected by the development of rail networks and roadways to carry traffic that previously flowed through waterways. From the beginning, Osaka's canals shaped its development, too. Along their sides, common landings provided public access to the flow of goods and storage space for nearby businesses.[39] Rail began to usurp the canal system's role around the time of the First World War, and highways followed. The Nagahori was filled in and turned into a roadbed in 1961, and the elevated Hanshin Expressway was constructed over the Higashi-yokobori in 1965. At the beginning of *Waga machi*, however, canals still define the city and channel its economic flow.

Jinnai describes the significance of the waterside as an extraordinary space, removed from the everyday.[40] In early Edo, he writes, the location of shrines and temples on the city's periphery, either in the hills or along the water's edge, gave those peripheral spaces "a character of sanctuary."[41] As the Tokugawa period progresses, the sense of liberation from the strictures of the everyday endures even as those locales transform into pleasure quarters and entertainment districts, and sacred space becomes ludic. The hybrid nature of the water's edge, the shifting boundary between water and land, contributes to its extraordinary quality, as does its status as a place of departure and arrival for travelers in an age when travel itself was extraordinary. Here again, Jinnai's reading applies equally to Osaka and particularly to the Dōtonbori, where, he notes, "the essence of this Edo-period theater district persists" even today.[42] In *City of Flows*, Maria Kaika discovers a similar phenomenon in the flow of water through the modern (Western) city. She describes the modern project to separate nature, city, and home into "neatly and tightly sealed, autonomous 'space envelopes,'" making of nature an uncanny other to the city, and how the permeability of the city defeats this project.[43] In *Waga machi*, the waterside marks another sort of permeable border—between local and imperial, domestic and to-be-domesticated. It alludes to the ethnic hybridity of Osaka, and it suggests the tug of extraordinary adventure across the South Seas.

Nan'yō, or the South Seas, held a fascination for expansionists in Japan from the 1880s, who were inspired by the sense, in Japan as in the United States, of an approaching global conflict between Eastern and Western civilizations, and of the need to check Western expansionism in the region, as well as to shift population from Japan's crowded archipelago to overseas settlements and colonies.[44] The army and navy developed competing plans for expansion, the former advocating a northern continental expansion and the latter a southward Pacific expansion, the first anticipated to be a struggle against Russia, the second against the United States. The southward expansion was to be accomplished through some strategic combination of aggressive economic activity and colonial subjugation. Along with a strong navy and the opening of trade routes, emigration was critical to this strategy. With Japan's acquisition of its first colony, Taiwan, in 1895, at the end of the First Sino-Japanese War, expansionists turned their attention to the Philippines, then under the control of a relatively weak Spain. But outright seizure was frustrated by the United States' acquisition of the territory. Later, even as continental expansion proceeded with the invasion of Manchuria, proponents of the southern expansion renewed their insistence on the strategic importance of the *Nan'yō* to Japan's security and prosperity and, with immigration to the Philippines increasing, included those islands in their plans.[45] By the end of the 1930s, faced with the prospect of Philippine independence and the rise of Philippine protectionism, militarists stressed the importance of the islands as a "stepping stone." Eventually, the term *Nan'yō* fell out of favor, to be replaced by the Greater East Asia Co-Prosperity Sphere. When Foreign Minister Matsuoka announced the sphere as official policy in August 1940, he did not specifically mention the Philippines, perhaps due to the state of relations with the United States, but they were understood to be included in it.

The bathhouse that dominates tiny Gataro Alley illustrates this link. Key scenes are set in it: Kimie takes her first job there. From the entrance, she watches Jirō, her future husband, pass by. Jirō, who will become a salvage diver pulling up lost cargo from the bottom of Osaka's waterways—a modern-day *gataro*—learns there how to hold his breath underwater, instructed by Takichi. The name of the bathhouse, the Hinomaru-yu, may recall the neighborhood where Oda grew up, Hinomaru yoko-roji (side alley), but it alludes as well to the imperial context of the novella's publication and its story. Named after the "rising sun" image on the Japanese flag, the bathhouse is a bad neighbor. The owner (whom we never meet, in a story crowded with characters) is also the landlord of Gataro Alley, described by the narrative as "*gorigan*," a local word for "pushy" (given as a gloss for the kanji compound usually read as "*yokoguruma*").[46] The bathhouse's chimney spews soot across the alley, interfering with the other residents' daily lives, preventing them from hanging their washing out to dry. The setting of *Waga machi* thus suggests colonial relations in microcosm, and links the alley to locales across the South Seas in the context of Japan's imperial expansion.

Another flow—that of traffic through the city streets—marks the characters' days and years. Shintarō, the young man who will marry Takichi's daughter, runs through the streets in a marathon; his victory is Takichi's enduring memory of his son-in-law, and a photograph taken to commemorate it is Kimie's only memento of her father. Young Jirō runs through the streets delivering newspapers. As a child, Kimie runs through these streets, too, a lonely orphan chasing after her grandfather's rickshaw. As an adult, she takes a series of jobs that involve her in traffic. She first works as a telephone disinfectant girl, traveling throughout the city, selling contracts. A narrative passage takes us along with Kimie on her commute, as she boards the city bus at Dōbutsuen-mae, walks down Daimon-dōri to Haginochaya Station, and transfers to the Nankai Line. In her next job, she dispatches taxis from Namba Station through the same streets. Later she cycles through those streets and beyond, making deliveries. As they join the flow of traffic, these characters map Osaka as a network and describe the city in vectors of rapid movement through it.

Above all there is Takichi, who pulls his rickshaw through the streets. Even when that rickshaw is stolen and he is forced to find other work, he ends up roaming the streets again, this time pulling an udon noodle cart. He parades through the same streets annually in a ceremonial procession (*watari*) for the summer festival of the famous local shrine, Ikutama-jinja.[47] As he travels these streets, insinuating himself into a built cityscape and an established circuit, Takichi, in his old Manila vest, clings to the memory of building a road accessing a to-be-developed colonial city: clearing land, dynamiting, and paving—imposing himself on the unbuilt, disordered junglescape of Benguet.

One more flow establishes the locality of Oda's Osaka and, at the same time, alludes to relations of national and imperial hegemony: the flow of speech. Among the neighbors we meet in Gataro Alley, one, Gyokudō, works as a *benshi*, providing live narration for films. Another, Shimedanji, or "Shime," is a *rakugo* raconteur. Together, their presence alludes to the historical association of Osaka and the broader Kamigata region with oral performance. Concomitant with this, illiteracy figures prominently in the story, treated with Oda's trademark bathos. One early scene in which Takichi learns of the death of his son-in-law, Shintarō, in Manila, features an extended gag that turns on Takichi's inability to read the official death notice. Takichi has to ask someone at the local barbershop to explain the notice to him, leading to a broad pun on the homonyms for "letter/character" and "hemorrhoid."[48] Elsewhere, Shime recalls a *rakugo* skit called "Muhitsu no katabō" (Accomplices in illiteracy), about a group of people passing around a flier and making up ludicrous excuses for not reading it. In these episodes, we hear "the heteroglossia of the clown sound[ing] forth," in Bakhtin's words; a locally inflected orality noncompliant with "the unifying, centralizing, centripetal forces of verbal-ideological life."[49]

As discussed in chapter 1, Osaka's local idiom had by Oda's time been subordinated by an academic and political discourse of "standardization" to a national idiom adapted from the speech of Tokyo. *Waga machi*'s dialogue, presented against a narrative ground written in (not quite pure) standard Japanese, highlights the linguistic politics of nation and empire. The precision with which Oda records Osaka's mutable local speech calls attention to its status within institutionalized *kokugo.* In one representative passage, Takichi asks Kimie why she does not play at home ("Donai shiten? Uchi de asondorin kai na") and scolds her, first for putting her hands in her armpits ("Sonna toko e tē ireru mon ya arahen") and then for smelling her fingertips ("Babachii koto shitara ikan. Aho!"). Each line employs local vocabulary and constructions ("*donai*" for the interrogative pronoun "*nani,*" or "what?"; "*arahen*" for the negative "be" verb "*nai*"; "*aho*" as a light insult). The character [*te*], for "hand," is followed by a katakana [*e*], indicating the lengthened vowel sound typical of Kansai speech, and the gloss "*babachi,*" a Kansai word, is given for the root character in the standard Japanese word "*kitanai*" (filthy).[50] Earlier, in the Benguet chapters, an unnamed member of the work crew boasts in a rough dialect of the job they've completed:

> 「そうとものし、俺（うら）らはアメジカ人やヘリピン人や、ドシア人の出来なかった工事（こうり）を、立派（じっぱ）にやって見せちゃるんじゃ」
>
> "Sō tomo no shi, urara wa, Amejika-jin ya, Heripin-jin ya, Doshiya-jin no dekinakatta kōri wo, jippa ni yatte misecharun ja."
>
> "Even so, we really showed them we could complete a job that the Americans, Filipinos, and Russians couldn't."[51]

Here, the character for the plural personal pronoun "*orera*" is glossed as "*urara,*" "*kōji*" (construction work) as "*kōri,*" and "*rippa*" (splendid) as "*jippa.*" "*Doshiyajin*" for "*Roshiyajin*" (Russian [person]) may reflect the practice among some Osakans of saying "*da,*" "*di,*" and so on, where standard Japanese prescribes "*ra,*" "*ri,*" and so on. Oda's treatment of Takichi's first lines of dialogue subtly underscores the issue. In Benguet, urging the crew to bear up under horrible conditions, Takichi cries, "Waira wa shōshin-shōmei no Nihon-jin ya ze" (We're real, true Japanese!)[52] This speech is followed by the narrative observation, "he said in Osaka dialect." Uncharacteristic for Oda, who seldom marks dialect in this way, the narrative comment undercuts Takichi's assertion of his national identity by pointing to the linguistic evidence of his locality. Finally, Oda allows local language to infiltrate even the narrative ground, at several points, using the Kansai forms "*kōte*" (on p. 269, for example), "*tadayōte*" (p. 287), "*ōta*" (pp. 303, 329, and 338), and so on, instead of their standard equivalents: "*katte,*" "*tadayotte,*" and "*atta.*"[53] With these tactics, Oda inscribes the flow of local speech on the monolinguistic ideological system of *kokugo.*

Local Cosmopolitanism

The flows that define *Waga machi*'s Osaka—flows of traffic, of water, and of speech—carry the story to far-flung locales and into the context of colonial development and domination. In this sense, we may call them cosmopolitan flows. At the same time, these flows originate in the extreme geographical specificity—the locality—of Osaka's streets, its canals, and its idiom. Over the past two decades, scholars have attempted to recuperate the term "cosmopolitanism" from its associations with elite consumption in national capitals. Homi Bhabha has suggested the possibility of a vernacular cosmopolitanism, a "cosmopolitan community envisaged in *marginality*."[54] Pnina Werbner has reviewed other seemingly oxymoronic redefinitions, such as "cosmopolitan patriotism, rooted cosmopolitanism, cosmopolitan ethnicity, working-class cosmopolitanism, [and] discrepant cosmopolitanism," which "pose the question whether the local, parochial, rooted, culturally specific and demotic may co-exist with the translocal, transnational, transcendent, elitist, enlightened, universalist and modernist."[55] And R. Radhakrishnan has proposed the idea of "an 'ec-centric or ex-orbitant cosmopolitanism'—that is, a cosmopolitanism without the authority of a center."[56] *Waga machi* offers a provocative historical example of how such a cosmopolitanism was imagined.

Oda's novella—produced as Japan was attempting to draft neighboring nations into its conception of an Asian universal, the Greater East Asia Co-Prosperity Sphere—presents us with a cosmopolitanism firmly rooted in an ec-centric and vernacular, local, working-class Osaka, a cosmopolitanism without Tokyo, that stands in uneasy relation to the nationalism and colonialism of its moment. As Oda traces these flows with extreme specificity, he appeals to readers' local knowledge even as he establishes his own local authority and bona fides. In this way, *Waga machi* presents Osaka as the site of a local cosmopolitanism. Viewed from the perspective of Tokyo and within the discourse of a transcendent imperial cosmopolitanism, such a formation may seem paradoxical. Viewed from the eccentric perspective of Osaka, however, this local cosmopolitanism presents an alternative to empire by imagining the city not as subsumed to a larger unity but as linked with other particular locales by the long networks of modernity.

In this way, *Waga machi* proposes Osaka's local cosmopolitanism as what Pheng Cheah has called "an alternative vehicle of universalism." Cheah has traced fundamental changes in the understanding of the cosmopolitan and its "unstable" opposition to nationalism, arguing that it has not always been understood as antithetical to national attachment and that "the secondary understanding of cosmopolitanism that opposes it to nationalism and sometimes equates it with exilic migrancy only makes sense after the nation has been bonded to the territorial state, which then naturalizes its boundaries through official nationalism." Citing Naoki Sakai in his introduction to *Cosmopolitics*, Cheah notes that "Japan's imperial nationalism actively modulated into a violent institutional cosmopolitanism" in World War II.[57] Oda's novella reveals this development as it offers an alternative that must end in futility.

The locality of Oda's city is critical to the potential of its alternative cosmopolitanism. This is not the Osaka essentialism or "Osaka-ism" (*Ōsaka-shugi*) that Jeffrey Hanes has astutely identified in the work of later "Osakaologists" such as Ōtani Kōichi. Ōtani's attempt to locate "the auratic identity of place," Hanes writes, is a mere symptom of Osaka's subordination to a "national cultural hegemony" centered on Tokyo, rather than a challenge to it.[58] Such Osaka-ism is related to "the defense of marginality" that Bruno Latour views with suspicion. He writes, "The defense of marginality presupposes the existence of a totalitarian center. But if the center and its totality are illusions, acclaim for the margins is somewhat ridiculous."[59] Hanes's and Latour's critiques point to the primary danger in the writing of Osaka (and the study of it). *Waga machi* evades that danger, evincing if not an unconsciousness of Tokyo and the totality of nation for which it serves as metonym, then a willful disregard for the capital and a determination to write Osaka for itself. Oda presents the city without explanations addressed to a national audience and without comparisons to the capital.

Neither is this locality quite the same as regionalism. Certainly, "region" can serve as a useful category for the analysis of literary production. In his study of Osaka as a site of literary production to 1940, Richard Torrance persuasively defends the study of regional literature, disputing Roberto Maria Dainotto's charge that the revived interest in regional literature, though it uses the language of postcolonialism and describes itself as an attempt to recover some of the diversity annihilated by nationalism, is in fact part of the nostalgic search for ethnic purity. Dainotto argues that "the region is not so much the other for the nation; it is, rather, an unadulturated version of it."[60] Torrance, however, demonstrates that "in its specificity, regional literature can create alternative narratives of modern Japan that implicitly contradict the stereotypes of the national discourse."[61] Nevertheless, regionalism does not accurately describe the imagined Osaka of *Waga machi.* One reason is simply the extreme geographic specificity of Gataro Alley. Another is its urbanity. For Dainotto, the region is rural; he insists that "industrialization, in itself, *does* debase the place."[62] This, however, hardly describes Oda's local city, which stands for industrialization in the national imagination throughout Japan's early modern age yet equally maintains a stubborn placeness.

Regionalism also raises the specter of nostalgia. Dainotto argues that nostalgia for a lost national origin characterizes regionalism generally. While there is certainly a distinctly nostalgic cast to the Osaka of Oda's fiction, however (and this will deepen in postwar popular literature by such authors as Yamasaki Toyoko), it is not for a preindustrial moment when the nation was not yet polluted by the cosmopolitanism of the city. Rather, it is nostalgia for a modern moment when the cosmopolitan city was not yet subsumed by a national bureaucracy centered elsewhere. It invokes an alternative modernity that dates from the Tokugawa period and the rise of the merchant houses of Senba, that is based on trade and light industry, and that underwrote a culture local in nature, the product of a "scattered power."[63] The eclipse of this modernity by another, dating from the Meiji period, based on heavy industry, fostered by a national bureaucracy, and centered in Tokyo, is the context for Oda's locality.

More fundamentally, David Harvey has identified the renewed interest in locality and place as one aspect of postmodernity—in part a manifestation of the postmodern distrust of grand narratives—and has critiqued it as a limited and potentially misguided response to time–space compression. Harvey ties locality to a search for place-based identity and thereby to tradition and reactionary politics.[64] He also cautions that the "fetishism" of locality is likely to lead to fragmentation, which saps the power to understand and counter the workings of mobile, global capital.[65] But Doreen Massey responds by defending the interest in the local. She disputes that this interest is a new phenomenon responding to time–space compression: "Why should the construction of places out of things from everywhere be so unsettling?" she asks. "Who is it who is yearning after the seamless whole and the settled place?"[66] She rejects the fear of fragmentation, and she counters that "'local' in locality is not opposed to 'meta' as in 'metatheory.'" She writes, "There is a potential confusion between the question of level in terms of geographical scale and level of abstraction in thought."[67] Oda's work precisely demonstrates the usefulness of geographic specificity to an interrogation of grand narratives.

We must also recognize what this local Osaka leaves out: the city's significant migrant communities. Osaka at the time of Oda's novel was already home to the largest community of ethnic Koreans in Japan, as it remains today. By 1936, there were 224,749 Koreans living in Osaka Prefecture, 32.5 percent of all those living in Japan. That number continued to rise even as the percentage declined due to forcible relocation; by 1942, the year *Waga machi* was published, 412,748 Koreans were living in Osaka, still one-quarter of all those living in Japan. In that year, ethnic Koreans accounted for 10.4 percent of the population of Osaka city, and as much as 25.6 percent in Higashinari-ku, not far from the imaginary Gataro Alley.[68] In his essay "Ōsaka to iu shokuminchi" (The colony called Osaka), Kawamura Minato reviews Osaka's history as a destination for migrant workers, especially from Korea and the Ryukyus, as both a "homeland" and a "foreign land," and faults Oda for excluding these communities from the Osaka of *Waga machi*.[69] This "exclusion," if we consider it such, may constitute a nostalgic response to a crisis in civic identity prompted by that influx.

Without dismissing this reading, I would like to suggest another way of understanding the absence of migrant communities in *Waga machi*. First, we should note that this absence is not total; the narrative mentions that Takichi's neighbor, the *benshi* Gyokudō, is from Hiroshima and speaks in awkward Osaka dialect ("heta na Ōsaka namari"), which Oda reproduces.[70] More important, migrant groups are absent not only from *Waga machi*'s Osaka but from the Philippines of the early chapters, too. Although a majority of the Japanese laborers on the historical Benguet Road were Okinawan, as were a majority of the Japanese in Davao, they are absent from the story. So are the large number of Chinese who worked on the Benguet Road. For that matter, Filipinos are invisible; *Waga machi* includes none of the interactions with local people that we might expect in a more conventional "colonial" story. One figure dominates, Takichi, who synthesizes a moment in global capitalism, not in a racialized or ethnic body but in an urban body. As that body hustles through the city's streets, it traces a geographical, economic, and political relationship, not so much between the colonizing nation and the colonized as between Osaka and the Philippine locales of Benguet, Davao, and Manila as nodes in a network of subsistence-level labor over which the United States and Japan struggle for control. The allusions in the early chapters to colony, race, and nation serve as the backdrop to this urban figure.

Protagonist in Parallax

Takichi is produced as a cosmopolitan figure in the flow between these locales. In the Philippines, he proudly identifies himself as Japanese. Once he has returned to Osaka, however, he wears a vest made of Manila hemp and styles himself "Taayan of Benguet." One constant between these locales is the precarity that characterizes Takichi's existence. He returns from the Philippines no richer than when he left Osaka (and though Takichi's reminiscences inspire his son-in-law to travel to the Philippines himself in search of some livelihood, all the younger man finds there is death). Back in Osaka, his livelihood as a rickshaw man is threatened first when new river cruisers poach his passengers and again when his rickshaw is stolen. This precarity is expressed in the dissatisfaction—vague rather than defiant or transformative—that registers in his anger toward U.S. authorities in the Philippines and in Japan, where he once dumps an American passenger from his rickshaw. It registers, too, in his dissonance within his circle of neighbors, the circuit of the Osaka streets, and the routine of the everyday. It registers in his constant longing to return south.

Takichi's nickname marks him as a product of cosmopolitan flows, while his proper name alludes to an earlier stage in Japan's centralization and to Osaka's pivotal role as a nodal point in the networks that underwrote that process. In his nickname, Taayan of Benguet, the Philippine province—a destination for poor migrant laborers departing, like Takichi, from the Kobe port—replaces another place-name that serves as Sadojima Takichi's proper family name: Sadogashima (written with the same characters as "Sadojima"), the large island off the coast of Niigata.[71] In the first half of the Tokugawa period, gold and later silver mines there produced the wealth that financed the development of early modern Japan. In the process, the fishing village of Aikawa became a boomtown, as Davao later would. Some of Sadogashima's gold and silver would have flowed to Osaka, home to the nascent banking industry. The mine was taken over by the Mitsubishi Corporation in 1918, which employed Korean migrant laborers there. These became forced laborers in 1944, mining copper for the war effort—copper that would have presumably found its way to Mitsubishi's Osaka refinery. The protagonist's double naming thus invokes the flow of resources and migrant labor that underwrote forms—first national, then imperial—purported to transcend the local.

In the figure of Takichi, then, two axes intersect. His two hometowns define a spatial axis in the geography of empire, connecting Osaka and the Philippines. His two names define a temporal axis in the history of nation, linking the development of Sadogashima and of Benguet. The resulting cruciform mirrors the image that dominates the novella's close.

The Southern Cross

As *Waga machi* enters the Shōwa period, the militarization of Japanese society and international relations in the Pacific redirects the story's flows. Jirō, the modern-day *gataro*, is now salvaging metal for the war effort: the water has become a medium for patriotic work ("kokkateki na shigoto").[72] The story dramatizes the effect of this militarization when Jirō grows reluctant to continue the work. Jirō tells his boss that he worries about the danger of salvage diving. The narration pointedly notes, however, that rather than fearing the work, Jirō has come to hate it.[73] The migrant flow between Osaka and the Philippines has been militarized, too. After hearing a radio report of the Japanese landing at Lingayen Gulf, Takichi volunteers for military service but is told he is too old to serve. Heartbroken, he collapses and ends up in the hospital. Visiting him there, Shime, the *rakugo-ka*, announces that he himself is being sent by the military on a tour of the southern islands to entertain the troops—a trip that will enlist a local genre of spoken performance in imperial expansion. Military concerns have commandeered even the raconteur's flow.

Amid these references to empire, *Waga machi* presents a final image of cosmopolitanism that binds together Takichi's two hometowns and thematizes the relation between the local and the universal: the projected image of the Southern Cross. The constellation, visible only in the Southern Hemisphere, carried special symbolism for the Japanese empire's expansion. For instance, the cover of *Hoshi to heitai* (Stars and soldiers), a gazetteer for soldiers published in 1943, shows the Southern Cross looming above a soldier, who gazes up at the constellation as he marches toward it, his back toward us. The Southern Cross orbits into Oda's story just after Jirō, now an adult, returns to Osaka from Tokyo. Meeting Kimie for the first time since childhood, he invites her to a show at the new planetarium titled "Hoshi no tabi, sekai isshū" (Journey of the stars: A circuit of the world). In the darkened planetarium, Kimie hears the announcer say, "Now, everyone, the Southern Cross appears, and we have reached the southern sky. It is one a.m. Manila time, the middle of the night. The stars of this beautiful Southern Cross are quietly watching over the town, the fields, the mountains, and the palm fronds of Manila."[74]

She cries out, moved to see the same constellation her grandfather and father saw, the sky under which her father died. Kimie returns to Gataro Alley declaring that she has seen the Southern Cross. Several chapters later, after he has been hospitalized, Takichi leaves his hospital bed and goes to the planetarium himself to watch the show Kimie described. When the lights come up, he is dead in his seat, still wearing his old Manila vest. From here, the story winds down. When a neighbor drops by to offer condolences, Kimie speaks her father's eulogy: "He died watching the Southern Cross—the Southern Cross he was always saying he wanted to see once more. He's gone to Manila—the Manila he was always saying he wanted to visit once more. His spirit has gotten there before Shime-san."[75]

Though unnamed in the text, the planetarium where Takichi goes to die was in fact the centerpiece of the Osaka Civic Electric Science Museum (Ōsaka-shiritsu denki-kagakukan), known colloquially as the "Denkan," which opened in Yotsubashi in March 1937 and entertained visitors for over fifty years. The Denkan was the first science museum and the first modern planetarium in Asia. The Osaka city government, which had begun supplying electricity as a public utility in 1923, built the museum to commemorate that event. The projection system was purchased from the Carl Zeiss company in Jena, Germany, which had developed the first such system in 1924. The six-story planetarium cost 468,000 yen to construct, and an additional 30,000 yen was spent to transport the projector system and to bring a pair of engineers from Germany to oversee its installation and train operators.[76] The pride Osakans took in the planetarium may well be imagined. The art historian Hashizume Setsuya notes that the newly opened Denkan appears in a film made the same year, *Dai-Ōsaka kankō* (Sightseeing in Great Osaka), which took audiences on a tour of the modern industrial metropolis.[77] The planetarium made a lasting impression on another great Osaka writer, the "god of manga," Tezuka Osamu, who recalled his boyhood visits:

> I loved astrology as much as I loved the theater. In Yotsubashi in Osaka stood the Electric Science Museum, and inside was the first Zeiss planetarium in the East. Of course, I was a daily visitor. The majesty [of the

> projector], like a monstrous iron dumbbell, stirred my diverse fantasies, that cold mechanism intensifying my awe in machine civilization.[78]

The figure of the Southern Cross projected on the ceiling of the planetarium gathers together a constellation of associations. First, it signifies science and, with it, modernity and Japan's pursuit of it; it also signifies technology, including Japan's importation of it and tutorship in its use. The origin of this particular technology is Jena, a city of primary significance to modern thought and to the history of Prussia, Japan's model for so many of the technologies of the modern state. In the context of both this story, with its background of race competition and industrial development, and the historical moment into which Oda published it, we can also connect this sign of (imported German) science to broader Enlightenment notions of progress and developmental history—notions that Japanese expansionists embraced even as they argued that those same Western notions relegated Asian nations to subordinate status. Astronomy and the stars projected on the planetarium's ceiling gather in the idea of the cosmos, for what else could have motivated the Osaka city government to build this museum but an intention to encourage among its citizens a cosmopolitan view of the world?

Cosmopolitanism was, of course, also put into the service of imperial ambitions. The illusory transcendence of time and space, the fantasy of ultimate mobility that the planetarium projects, is also a fantasy of industrial development and the unimpeded flow of labor, capital, and technology across national borders. Under the slogan "*hakkō ichiu*" (the eight corners of the world under one roof), ultranationalist Kita Ikki theorized Japan's divine right to power, and prime minister Konoe Fumimaro in 1940 expounded a new order in East Asia, pursued through a strategy of Japanese hegemony masquerading as a transcendence of national borders and excession to a new universal order. That southern sky, mirrored in the *Nan'yō*, suggests the wartime discourse that argued the need for an Asian universality to challenge the West.

Such aspirations to transcendence seduced Osaka, too. And in *Waga machi*'s mapping of Osaka vis-à-vis locales in the Philippines, we can certainly trace the mutually reinforcing "oscillation . . . between universalism and particularism" by which, Naoki Sakai argues, both are "closed off to the singular."[79] The Denkan projects the stubborn civic pride of Osaka—still, as late as 1937, collecting "firsts," making claims for cultural primacy in Japan and East Asia. Produced in the flow that linked his two "hometowns" but now prevented from rejoining that flow, Takichi is finally enthralled by the image of the Southern Cross, an illusion of transcendence. Takichi himself does not model resistance to that illusion; rather, he manifests its fatal allure. He manifests, too, the futility of Osaka's aspirations—the irreversibility of Tokyo's hegemony, by the time of *Waga machi*'s publication, certainly evident to so astute an observer as Oda. In Oda's novel, the illusion of the cosmos contained within the Denkan enthralls Takichi, and he succumbs to it.

At the same time, the Denkan materializes, if not an oppositional cosmopolitanism then an alternative one. By rooting the vision of the Southern Cross in his imagined local Osaka, Oda decenters associations of nation and empire. He grounds the cosmopolitan in the city but not the capital—a metropole, certainly, but a secondary and subordinated metropole left to contain the influx of labor from which Tokyo was effectively shielded. He grounds it in a city long associated with defiance of authority centered in Edo/Tokyo, a city whose subordination within the national order resulted from Japan's pursuit of modern statehood. Osaka and Benguet bookend a critical stage in imperialist "transcendence": the successful absorption of the city into a national system, Japan, and the attempted absorption of the nations and Western possessions of East Asia into an imperial system, the Co-Prosperity Sphere. Therefore, while the projection of the Southern Cross manifests the illusion and allure of imperial transcendence—an illusion and allure to which Takichi succumbs—it also at least suggests the alternative of a cosmopolitanism without Tokyo.

Conclusion

Oda Sakunosuke wrote the city at a key moment in history, when the nation had already subordinated localities and the empire was pursuing the subordination of nations—both hegemonic processes wrapped in the language of transcendence. I have endeavored to chart the flows by which, in *Waga machi*, Oda links his hometown (a locale critical to the earlier process) with the Philippines (a locale critical to the later process). It is a testament to Oda's empathetic realism and his appreciation of paradox that, even as he dramatizes the allure of the Greater East Asia Co-Prosperity Sphere's ostensible universalism, he presents us with an alternative: a cosmopolitanism rooted in a local and eccentric Osaka and embodied in a laboring and precarious protagonist who comes to life in the exchange between two hometowns, provincial and colonial. The latter vision is not innocent of imperial ambitions, but it does demonstrate the potential to betray a misconception fundamental to empire. By locating that vision in Osaka, Oda suggests that city's unique potential.

Bruno Latour writes, "The moderns . . . mistook length or connection for differences in level. They thought there really were such things as people, ideas, situations that were local and organizations, laws, rules that were global."[80] Like their counterparts in the West, those responsible for justifying Japan's modern imperial ambitions mistook or misrepresented the networks and flows that link the local spaces of *naichi* and empire as a shift in level. By tracing those networks and flows, by demonstrating the permeability of the local spaces they connect, and by highlighting the hybridity produced in the oscillation between—in the intermundia of the South Seas—Oda's *Waga machi* underscores this "mistake."

Chapter Four

Diseased Dream

Nostalgia and Futurity in Tanizaki Jun'ichirō's *Sasameyuki*

A casual visitor to the neighborhood of Senba, in Osaka, would find little today to suggest the district's past glory. However, throughout the Tokugawa period, Senba served as the commercial heart not only of Osaka and western Honshu but of a trade network connecting Edo, the samurai domains, and foreign lands. Senba began to take shape in 1598. In that year, as Toyotomi Hideyoshi initiated an expansion of Osaka Castle and its grounds, displaced townspeople were relocated to the west onto former wetlands that had been filled during the dredging of the Higashi-yokobori, or "east-side canal," in 1583. Bounded by that canal on the east and the Nishi-yokobori on the west, the Ōkawa river on the north, and the Nagahori, or "long canal," on the south, Senba flourished as Hideyoshi built the city into the political and economic capital of the newly unified domains.

Even after political power shifted from Osaka to Edo in the East, economic power remained concentrated in Senba, the center of trade in rice, medicines, copper, and other commodities. In 1670, the Tokugawa shogunate authorized the formation of a privileged association of ten money-exchange houses to keep its accounts and oversee the other money changers in Osaka; these would become progenitors of Japan's banking industry. Over time, the greatest merchant houses of Senba accumulated wealth to rival the most powerful daimyō, wealth that made them the object of resentment among the samurai and the target of Tokugawa sumptuary laws.

Firms headquartered in Senba lost their preferences with the overthrow of the shogunate and the Meiji Restoration in 1868, and the neighborhood declined. However, Japan's first securities exchange was established in Senba in 1878, the same year that a bond market was established in Tokyo. Meanwhile, new firms were moving into the neighborhood and helping revive Senba's commercial significance. The economic boom that Japan enjoyed during World War I gave a boost to this revival, but as the war ended, so did the revival. Senba slipped back into decline, and this time, it would not rebound.[1] The increasing state control and centralization of the economy in the 1930s extended this decline as part of a broader subordination of Osaka and the Kansai region. Although Tokyo had long since become the political center of the nation, Osaka now relinquished economic primacy as well. With militarization and the control economy, Japan's economic output shifted from light to heavy industry, driving a geographic shift from the Osaka-Kobe region to Tokyo-Yokohama.[2] Government control over bank lending beginning in 1937 and comprehensive price controls after 1939 devastated Osaka's core economic sectors.

In *Sasameyuki* (Fine snow, 1943–48, published in English as *The Makioka Sisters*), Tanizaki Jun'ichirō produced the great novel of Senba's merchant culture and its decline. Very little of the story is in fact set in Senba; as in Tanizaki's earlier novel, *Manji*, discussed in chapter 1, the neighborhood figures indirectly and at the margins. The Makioka family sell their Senba shop and close up the main house in nearby Uehonmachi early in the story, when the eldest daughter and her family relocate to Tokyo. The rest of the novel plays out largely in the suburb of Ashiya, to the west of Osaka, and in Tokyo. Senba nevertheless is central to the novel. *Sasameyuki* imagines Kansai—and, more specifically, the Hanshin-kan region between Osaka and Kobe to the west—as the locale of a culture rooted in the merchant society of Senba. The novel tells how one family with roots in Senba negotiates the economic shift brought about by Japan's imperialism and militarization, describing that process as a movement out from the local onto a national and international stage, and out from anachronism into contemporaneity. That avatar of Senba society, the bonbon, whom we have already met in chapter 1 (in the character of Watanuki Eijirō) and chapter 2 (in Koreyasu Ryūkichi), plays a key role in this Osaka story, too. Tanizaki imagines the bonbon as an anachronistic masculinity that "curses" the Makioka family as it tries to move forward and adapt to "the current situation" of Japan's imperial project. Mapping images of tradition and modernity, nostalgia and futurity, expenditure and investment, and death and reproduction to the "merchant capital" and the imperial capital, Tanizaki addresses contemporary militarism and the role of Senba in the imperial imagination.

Sasameyuki

Tanizaki's novel follows the fortunes of four sisters, daughters of a once-prosperous, now declining Senba merchant house, from 1936 to 1941. The eldest sister, Tsuruko, moves with her growing family from the Uehonmachi main house to Tokyo after her husband is transferred there by the bank for which he works. They settle in Shibuya, at the time a suburb on the outskirts of Tokyo. The second sister, Sachiko, lives with her husband and daughter in Ashiya, at that time a recently developed suburb of Osaka, located in the cosmopolitan Hanshin-kan region. The third sister, Yukiko, shuttles between her two older sisters' homes as they try to arrange a suitable marriage for her, planning and attending several *miai*—formal meetings with prospective husbands. The youngest sister, Taeko—nicknamed "Koi-san"—stays at the Ashiya house and waits impatiently for Yukiko to marry, becoming involved with a series of men and gradually asserting her independence from the strictures of her bourgeois upbringing.[3]

The story moves with the sisters among these three households and locales: the family's old main house in downtown Osaka and the new homes in suburban Ashiya and Shibuya. The various sensibilities of these locales are embodied by the male characters associated with them. The old downtown is represented first of all by the sisters' father, who has already died when the story opens (as Senba has already declined) after damaging the family's financial situation through his extravagance. It is also represented by Taeko's first boyfriend, Okubata Keizaburō, or "Kei-bon." Ashiya is represented by Sachiko's husband, Teinosuke, and Shibuya by Tsuruko's husband, Tatsuo, who was adopted into the family as heir. The sisters link these spaces: Tsuruko, who reluctantly accompanies her husband to Tokyo, bringing mementos of the old Uehonmachi house with her to Shibuya; Sachiko, who travels from Ashiya to Shibuya to confer with her older sister but never feels comfortable in Tokyo; Yukiko, who reluctantly obeys the main house's directive to leave Ashiya and go to Shibuya; and Taeko, who resists a summons to the Shibuya house as long as she can, visiting Tokyo only to ask permission to study dressmaking in Paris and, at the end of the novel, to attend Yukiko's final *miai*.

The desultory narrative follows the diverging paths traveled by the two younger sisters, Yukiko and Taeko, plotted to their unrealized and realized connections with various other men. Yukiko's fortunes are falling throughout the story until, at the end, they seem to rise: she meets and rejects two suitors, and is herself rejected by a third and fourth, before accepting the fifth. The first suitor, Segoshi, is rejected when the family learns that his mother suffers from hereditary dementia. The second, Nomura, is thought to be too old and too attached to the memory of his deceased wife. The third, Sawazaki, is an attractive match from a prominent Nagoya family, but he turns down Yukiko; being the first rejection to come from the other party, this marks a low point in Yukiko's fortunes. The fourth suitor, Hashidera, is a widower with a good position in a pharmaceuticals company; though at first charmed by Yukiko, he grows frustrated with her shyness and rejects her. Finally, the family arranges a successful match with Mimaki, the illegitimate son of a noble family from Kyoto, who has trained as an architect.

In the meantime, Taeko takes a downward socioeconomic trajectory plotted to her three lovers. The first is Kei-bon, a revenant of outmoded Senba values. Taeko tries to elope with Kei-bon before the story's opening, but she is convinced by her family to wait until after her older sister marries. As she waits, Taeko tires of the frivolous Kei-bon and takes up with Itakura, a former servant in Kei-bon's family's firm in Senba. Itakura now works as a photographer, having learned the trade during a sojourn in the United States. The family demands that Taeko end this relationship, which they find socially unacceptable. Following Itakura's death and the loss of his baby in a miscarriage, Taeko takes up with an even less acceptable man, Miyoshi, who runs a bar in Kobe. At that point, the family cuts her off. As the story draws to a close, Taeko seems bound for a life of isolation and relative poverty, while Yukiko seems to have pulled out a social victory from the jaws of defeat. Although the story ends in 1941, the reader cannot help but speculate about how these two trajectories extend beyond the end of the war and into a postwar Japan for which the independent and practical Taeko and the bar owner Miyoshi would seem to be better prepared than the painfully reserved Yukiko and her pampered, dilettante husband.

Tanizaki began *Sasameyuki* during wartime, and Japan's militarization crops up in the narrative again and again: the navy ships in Kobe harbor, noticed by the sisters during the *miai* with Nomura; the sisters' conversation over dinner with their Russian neighbors about events in Europe; the naval parade taking place in Tokyo around the time of the final *miai*; the repeated references to the China incident and the current state of emergency. The effects of militarization and the global political situation are also evident in the many uncertainties that complicate the sisters' daily lives: Is it safe for Taeko to travel to Paris, or for the hairdresser, Mrs. Itani, to travel to America? What will become of their German neighbors, the Stoltzes?

The novel's apparently frivolous subject matter provoked government censors at the time of its release. They intervened to halt the serial publication of *Sasameyuki* in the popular literary journal *Chūō kōron* after the first few chapters had appeared in its pages in 1943, charging that the novel "goes on and on detailing the very things we are most supposed to be on our guard against during this period of wartime emergency: the soft, effeminate, and grossly individualistic lives of women."[4] Censors intervened again when Tanizaki published the first part of the novel in a small edition for friends. The author continued to work on *Sasameyuki* throughout the war and finally published the completed novel during the postwar occupation in 1948.

A Subversive Kansai?

Scholars have disagreed over whether and in what way Tanizaki's works of this period, *Sasameyuki* in particular, relate to the contemporary ideology of Japanese fascism. Some have seemed at pains to deny any such relationship, expressing surprise at the novel's censorship. Donald Keene, for example, states flatly, "It is completely unconcerned with any form of ideology," and goes on to suggest that "it was banned not because it preached subversive doctrines but because it described with evident nostalgia the Japan of the past when people were preoccupied not with the nation's sacred mission but with marriage arrangements, visits to sites famous for cherry blossoms, and the cultural differences between Osaka and Tokyo."[5] Similarly, Itō Sei asserts that "there is no direct social critique" in the novel, but continues, "The process of the collapse, amid the changes of the modern age, of the tradition produced by the unique merchant culture of Senba in Osaka is rendered more clearly than in so-called works of 'social critique,' since it arises here as an inevitable result of art."[6] Itō's reading of the novel concentrates less on economic history, however, than on the broader theme of Japanese beauty under threat from the West.

More recently, as Thomas LaMarre has observed, "Evaluations of Tanizaki tend to oscillate between . . . cultural nationalism or its subversion."[7] Those in the first category find complicity with the wartime state in Tanizaki's "turn to Japan" ("*Nihon kaiki*" or "*Nihon e no kaiki*"). This is the name given to the 1930s renunciation by Japanese cultural producers and intellectuals of progressive, Western modernity—its aesthetics, its themes and images, its technologies—in favor of traditional Japanese aesthetics, the subject of Japaneseness, and artistic modes that predated the influence of the West. Tanizaki made his particularly noteworthy "turn" after relocating to the Kansai region following the Great Kantō Earthquake of 1923. He manifested this turn in his novels, beginning with *Tade kū mushi* (Some prefer nettles, 1929); in his essays, most notably his statement of traditional Japanese aesthetics, *In'ei raisan* (In praise of shadows, 1933–34); as well as in his decision to translate the Heian-period classic *Genji monogatari* (The tale of Genji). Some scholars have supported their evaluation of Tanizaki's "turn" as complicit with cultural nationalism by noting that the author voiced his support of the war on several occasions. This support is detailed by Hosoe Hikaru and discussed by Brian Hurley in an essay linking Tanizaki and the linguist Yamada Yoshio. Hurley writes, "Like many of their contemporaries, Tanizaki and Yamada sought to resurrect what they thought of as auratic, authentic cultural forms in the early Showa years in order to counteract the fracture, hybridization, and homogenization that they thought accompanied Japanese modernization." Hurley explains their belief that "changes to the Japanese language following the Meiji Restoration . . . refracted the intrusions of an alien sensibility inimical to the Japanese national character (*kokuminsei*)."[8]

Other evaluations have, on the contrary, viewed Tanizaki's nostalgic idealization of prewar Kansai culture as a reproach to the ugly contemporary reality of Japan's militarism. Ken Ito, although rejecting the notion that *Sasameyuki* is "untouched by the dominant ideology," calls the novel "an elegy" to the blend of tradition and cosmopolitanism that flowered in the Hanshin-kan before the war, "a gentler culture that had been destroyed by the war and made irretrievable by defeat."[9] Anthony Hood Chambers goes further, arguing that Tanizaki offers in *Sasameyuki* "a subversive reminder of the non-military roots of Japanese culture, a lament for the decline of the Osaka merchant's way of life, and a sort of 'secret history' of Japan from 1936 to 1941."[10] Chambers elaborates on this reading in a later essay, writing that "to purge ultranationalism and militarism from the social landscape of *Sasameyuki* was to repudiate them and so to take a political position."[11]

Komori Yōichi, too, discovers a spirit of protest in Tanizaki's novel. In a dialogue with Hasumi Shigehiko published in *Kokubungaku*, he discusses reading *Sasameyuki* alongside contemporary newspapers, mentioning in particular the scene of the Great Hanshin Flood of 1938, a local event that received national coverage. Komori asserts that at a time of severe press censorship, "the insertion into that novel of news other than news of the war is itself an extraordinarily political choice." He goes on to suggest that *Sasameyuki* "effectively examines the question of what had become of the discourse of journalism overall in Japan," concluding, "I cannot help but feel it is a novel that, in some sense, directly confronts the reporting system of wartime imperialist journalism and the state of that centralized discourse, unfurling a flag of protest recognizable to those with eyes to see it."[12] Komori theorizes that as an "émigré" from Tokyo to the Kansai region, exposed to the difference of Kansai dialect, Tanizaki came to see his native tongue as a foreign language. "At a moment when the modern Japanese language was directly linked to nationalism and imperialism," Tanizaki "focused precisely on how *genbun'ichi*, as a modern Japanese language, occupied a position as only one among many Japanese languages." Likewise, Komori hypothesizes, Tanizaki found his understanding of Japanese history relativized to one among many Japanese histories.[13]

More recently, Greg Golley, in his study of *Tade kū mushi*, acknowledges that the "poeticization of an idealized past" in that novel (also set in Kansai) "supports the power structure by resonating with the dominant nativist idiom of state ideology." He argues, however, that this poeticized tradition asserts "a claim to an aesthetic exclusivity" that places it outside history and renders it inutile to the state. Repurposing the notion of "double profit" from Pierre Bourdieu (who used it rather to criticize Heidegger for camouflaging his support of fascism), Golley credits Tanizaki with accomplishing a double profit that yields "a brilliantly orchestrated message of subversion."[14]

Margherita Long proposes a way out of the question of the author's complicity or subversion "by shifting the terms of the debate from Tanizaki's ideas about nationalism to his ideas about the modern psyche."[15]

Examining three of the author's essays from this period, including *In'ei raisan*, Long argues that Tanizaki documented Japan's internalization of the West's racism and its response to "the West's contradictory injunctions, 'You must be like me, you may not be like me.' "[16] She concludes that Tanizaki "deserves to be counted with those rare culturalists who actually succeeded in using Japan's 'doubled' modernity to critique modernity itself."[17] Long offers a compelling account of the "moral masochism" involved in Tanizaki's exploration of Japanese fetishization of the West, and a convincing argument both that Tanizaki's culturalism cannot be reduced to a simple question of "complicity or subversion" and that it effects a critique of modernity. My own concern here is to examine the role of the local city in that critique.

The opposition of Kansai to Kantō that preoccupied Tanizaki throughout his later work is critical to his "turn" and its terms. He claimed to have rediscovered in western Japan traces of a Japanese culture that, he believed, had largely disappeared from Tokyo. In his essays and fiction from the late 1920s on, Tanizaki associated the Osaka-Kyoto region with a traditional Oriental culture, and associated the Tokyo-Yokohama region with a modern Western culture heavily influenced by the United States. That broad dynamic organizes *Sasameyuki*, too. However, other dynamics—spatial and narratological—complicate the dynamic. A closer examination of specific spaces within the Kansai and Kantō of the novel, and of their local and national associations, will help us both understand Tanizaki's response to contemporary militarism and ultranationalism and evaluate any complicity with or subversion of the ideology of cultural nativism. This examination will demonstrate that the Kansai Tanizaki constructs in *Sasameyuki* functions in the national imaginary in more complex ways than simple complicity or subversion. The first step is to map the relationship in the novel between Senba and the suburbs.

City and Suburb

At the outset, *Sasameyuki* establishes a contrast between the inner city and the suburb, as personified by the sisters' deceased father on the one hand, and by the two older sisters' husbands on the other. This contrast is cast in temporal and economic terms: the father, who is already dead when the story opens, belonged to a merchant culture whose time, like his, has passed. His sons-in-law, Tatsuo and Teinosuke, belong to a contemporary corporate world. The father helped bring the old order to an end, at least for the Makioka household: we learn in the second chapter that he was a lover of luxury who inherited a business with a long history and ran it into the ground through "the looseness of his lifestyle and management." The narrative then introduces the new generation of Makioka men. Tsuruko's husband, Tatsuo—the dispassionate son of a banker—is, the narrative notes, "quite the opposite of his ostentatious father-in-law . . . austere and retiring almost to the point of timidity."[18] The narration also makes a point of the fiscal discipline that distinguishes Tatsuo from his father-in-law. The two younger sisters criticize their brother-in-law for his cheapness, and Taeko blames him for the scandal that erupted when she and Kei-bon tried to elope and that might have been kept out of the newspapers were it not for the fact that Tatsuo "is always afraid to spend a little money."[19] Although adopted into the family as heir, an arrangement common among merchant families at the time, Tatsuo never took up the day-to-day management of the Makioka firm, continuing instead to work at his own family's bank. He purposely chose the work of a banker over that of a merchant. He confirmed this decision upon the death of the Makiokas' father by handing management of the business over to a family retainer rather than taking on the responsibility himself, an act for which Yukiko imagines her father reproaching Tatsuo from the grave.

The contrast with the father is drawn less sharply in the case of Sachiko's husband, Teinosuke, but he, too, is an office worker whose job suggests fiscal discipline and involves doing figures, not handling goods. Teinosuke graduated from a commercial school and works as an accountant in Osaka to supplement his wife's inheritance. Thus, in the generational shift from the father to his two sons-in-law, the novel personifies a shift in lifestyle from extravagance to discipline, as well as a shift in the model of masculinity that enacts it: from bonbon to manager of money. It locates the two sides of that shift in the city and the suburbs, so that the moves from Uehonmachi, in the center of Osaka, to the new suburbs of Ashiya, in Teinosuke's case, and to Shibuya, in Tatsuo's case, chart a historical development from a mercantile and urban model of modernity to a corporate national one.

As it introduces these characters, the narration emphasizes the difficulty with which the Makioka family is negotiating this historical shift. We read in the early chapters of a family friend's suggestion that the Makiokas are "living on the family's old glory." We learn that "they all remembered the luxury of their father's last years and the dignity of the Makioka name—in a word, they were thralls to the family name, to the fact that they were members of an old and once-important family"—and that "their prosperity lived now only in the mind of the Osakans who knew the old days well."[20] The arrangements for one of Yukiko's *miai* prompt these observations. Yukiko has attended several such meetings before the opening of the story and has rejected all suitors. As this first *miai* of the novel gets underway, Yukiko's older sister Sachiko sizes up the new prospect, Segoshi, who has been referred to as a "director" (*jōmu-san*) of his company. "Sachiko remembered that there had been just such a bald, clowning chief clerk [*bantō-san*] in the Makioka shop. Today, with the larger of the old shops for the most part reorganized as joint-stock companies, 'chief clerk' had become 'director.'"[21] Her observation alludes to the shift from merchant father to salaryman sons-in-law and to the broader economic change behind it: the recapitalization of the old economy.

In addition to a new economic model, the move from the central city to the suburbs also marks the debut of a new domestic space. At the turn of the century, two corporations, the Hanshin Electric Railway Company, founded in 1899, and the Hankyū Railway Corporation, founded in 1907, pioneered suburban development in the Hanshin-kan region, between Osaka and Kobe to the west.[22] These companies integrated their rail business with department stores and other attractions at terminal stations (including the hot springs resort that Hankyū established at Takarazuka) as well as new housing developments at intermediate stops, offering a complete commuter experience to a middle class eager to escape the crowding and the pollution of the city. Jordan Sand has described how Kobayashi Ichizō, the founder of the Hankyū Railway Corporation, changed the marketing of his company's new suburban developments early on, shifting away from associations with older modes of male pleasure and erotic play personified in the geisha or courtesan, and toward the "erotically charged yet safely domesticated commodity" of the bourgeois family, personified by the wife waiting at home.[23] Sand details how Kobayashi appropriated the emergent discourse of the family-centered household, or *katei*, to market the suburban home as a place in which the commuting businessman-homeowner could safely store away his investment in monogamy.

The Ashiya household exists within this new landscape: Teinosuke and Sachiko's house stands near Hankyū Ashiyagawa Station, which opened in 1920. The two younger sisters who stay at the Ashiya house, themselves representing significant investments on their family's part, inhabit this landscape in very different ways. While Yukiko remains largely tied to the house, Taeko strains against and eventually breaks free of the strictures of the suburban, bourgeois *katei*. She makes, exhibits, and sells fine dolls, and teaches doll making to other young women; as this business grows, she rents a studio in Shukugawa, one stop to the east, toward Osaka, on Hankyū's Kobe Line. Later, after she refuses to move to the new main house in Tokyo (where her movements would be more strictly circumscribed) and is kicked out of the Ashiya house on her eldest sister's orders, Taeko moves to an apartment in Motoyama, west of Ashiyagawa on the Kokudō bus line, going toward Kobe. Here she is able to entertain Kei-bon without her family's knowledge and generally exercise a freedom that contradicts the advertised image of the Hanshin-kan suburbs as a storehouse of carefully guarded female eroticism. Taeko even leaves the female preserve of the suburb on unchaperoned forays into the city. When the three younger sisters, along with Teinosuke, go for sushi to a small Kobe shop that Taeko has discovered, the narration notes that she often eats out at a variety of shops around the Motoyama and Sannomiya neighborhoods of downtown Kobe.[24] At the shop, the sisters fall into conversation with three local geisha also eating there. When Taeko later falls sick with what at first seems to be dysentery, she blames it on the mackerel she ate at a sushi shop in the Fukuhara licensed quarter, and her sisters note disapprovingly that "Koi-san is always eating out, and all kinds of things."[25] Together, these two scenes tie Taeko, through food, to suggestions of promiscuity and, through the geisha, to an older, urban idea of sexuality.

Taeko's gradual, inexorable slide into disgrace originates back in the city, in her affiliation with that archetype of Senba masculinity, the bonbon, whose malign influence follows her to the suburbs. Tatsuo may be the legal heir to the Makioka household, but the spiritual heir to the sisters' father is not to be found in the suburbs of Tokyo, nor is he to be found in Ashiya, with Teinosuke. Rather, he resides back in Senba, in the figure of Taeko's first boyfriend, Kei-bon. The son of an old Senba family that deals in jewelry and precious metals, Kei-bon possesses all the characteristics of the bonbon and is referred to as such again and again throughout the story. He is extravagant, racking up bills each month with "teahouses and tailors and haberdashers" that he afterward asks his mother to pay. He is morally undisciplined as well, continuing to spend time with both a geisha and a dancer while waiting for the Makioka family to accept him. Taeko herself makes the association between Kei-bon and her father, telling Sachiko that she had at first accepted Kei-bon's affairs because "his brothers and uncles were likewise rakes of the first order and the sisters' own father had been given to philandery."[26] Taeko twice tries to break from this bonbon and embrace a more modern, adaptive masculinity, but both attempts end in death.

Taeko first becomes involved with the photographer Itakura. Their association begins after Itakura risks his life to save Taeko during a flood that traps her on the roof of the studio where she makes her dolls. Kei-bon proves useless in this emergency, while Itakura rises to the occasion. A self-made man who has worked to distance himself from Senba, Itakura presents a sharp contrast to the bonbon. Born into a lower class, he once worked for Kei-bon's family. He has also lived and worked for a time in California. Since his return, he has opened a photography business, financed by Kei-bon's family. Taeko asks him to take promotional photos of the dolls she makes and sells, and a romantic attachment develops. When they learn of the relationship, Sachiko and Yukiko discuss Itakura's unsuitability, making direct comparisons between him and Kei-bon, repeatedly applying to Itakura the word "*teikyū*" (low class). Sachiko opines that although Kei-bon is not very impressive, his Senba roots mean that he is "something like the same race" as the Makioka family. A marriage to Itakura, on the other hand, "socially, would invite ridicule."[27] The sisters' judgment of Itakura reflects their loyalty to the values of Senba, but Teinosuke suggests that those values are outdated. He praises Itakura after witnessing his courage during the flood. And when Sachiko wonders why Taeko cannot see Itakura's vulgarity, Teinosuke explains, "Oh, Koi-san has thought about it carefully. Put it this way: even if he's a bit vulgar, it's all right as long as his body is strong, and he can deal with some hardship, and he seems reliable. She's being pragmatic, isn't she?"[28]

The divergence between their assessments of Itakura sums up the opposition between two masculinities and the values they represent: Sachiko defends Kei-bon and his anachronistic Senba values, according to which vulgarity is the only real fault; Teinosuke speaks for Itakura and the adaptive values of physical discipline and pragmatism. The narration encourages the reader to judge Itakura according to Teinosuke's ethics. Ultimately, however, Taeko's relationship with Itakura is doomed by his links to the old world of Senba. Kei-bon harries the couple, upbraiding

Itakura as the servant he once was. Soon after, Itakura falls ill and suffers a painful death.

After Itakura's death, Taeko takes up with another man, Miyoshi, who lives in a boarding house and works at a bar in Kobe. Miyoshi represents a complete break from the society of Senba; indeed, the family will eventually disown Taeko and require her to move out of the Ashiya house because of her relationship with Miyoshi. But the specter of Senba connections haunts this relationship, too. When Taeko discovers she is pregnant by Miyoshi, the Ashiya household resign themselves to letting Taeko marry him. After the baby dies at birth, Sachiko holds the infant body and wonders "if the child did not bear the curse of Okubata and Itakura."[29]

Kei-bon represents a merchant class that is being made anachronistic by Japan's imperial project. Teinosuke, Sachiko, and Taeko herself all comment on his inappropriateness to Japan's crisis. Discussing Kei-bon's recent excursions to the pleasure quarter of Sōemon-chō, Teinosuke says that such behavior is, "first of all, indecent *in the current state of emergency.*" Sachiko is compelled to agree that "*in light of the current incident*, one could not escape criticism for indecency."[30] And after Kei-bon objects to Taeko's move from doll making to the less genteel work of dressmaking, Sachiko, too, frames her reply in terms of the national situation, complaining that "Kei-*chan* was not sufficiently attentive *to current events*; this was not the time to be playfully making dolls and such."[31] Toward the end of the novel, Kei-bon seems at last to awaken to the national emergency, albeit in a manner peculiarly suited to a spoiled Senba bonbon: the sisters are incredulous when they hear that he may be headed to Manchukuō to take up a sinecure in the court of the puppet emperor: "'What?! To Manchuria?' Sachiko and Yukiko exclaimed together. 'That's ridiculous!'" Then, when Taeko adds that Kei-bon is hesitating to take up the post, one of the sisters replies, "That's hardly surprising. If even a Senba-born bonbon can end up in Manchuria . . ."[32] Their shock suggests that the bonbon does not belong on the international stage where the new imperial economy plays out its dramas. It is this figure, the bonbon—representative of Senba and branded as anachronistic—who frustrates Taeko's attempts to escape that society's outdated customs and mores.

The precise nature of Tanizaki's bonbon becomes clearer in comparison with Ryūkichi in Oda's *Meoto zenzai*—perhaps the most famous bonbon in literature. In *Sasameyuki*, the bonbon's connoisseurship is a shallow one to which the narrator's—and, by implication, the (national) reader's—is superior. As Sachiko helps Tsuruko pack up family heirlooms for the move to Tokyo, we are told that the father "really was a very bad judge of art, and, since he tended to think that the expensive must be good, he had occasionally made a foolish buy," after which the narrator invites us to sniff at one such purchase, a pair of flawed ink stones.[33] Likewise Kei-bon, though he enjoys hobnobbing with famous actors, has no patience to attend the theater.[34] Contrast this characterization with Oda's, of the bonbon as a devoted *jōruri* amateur and a *getemono* connoisseur who rejects expensive restaurants in favor of stalls and shops selling cheap snacks. The difference between Oda's bonbon and Tanizaki's is the difference between connoisseurship and pretension. Tanizaki caricatures the bonbon's connoisseurship: instead of searching out what is cheap and unknown but good, in *Sasameyuki* he overpays for worthless tchotchkes.

If Taeko's story begins with a bonbon, then Yukiko's ends with something like one. After rejecting several responsible businessmen, she settles on the son of a viscount with an estate in Kyoto. Mimaki is not a typical bonbon. He is from Kyoto, not Senba, and the sisters (together with the reader) first meet him in Tokyo; he belongs to the peerage, not the merchant middle class; and, having traveled the world, he is marked as international whereas the bonbon is parochial. He nevertheless manifests many of the characteristics of the bonbon. He is gregarious and likes to drink, growing wittier as he does. Though knowledgeable, he "had not been able to pursue one thing to the end; he was fond of entertaining people and otherwise doing favors, and good at spending money, but unfortunately he was not much of a hand at making money." Teinosuke judges him "a bonbon of the noble class" (*kazoku no bon-chan*).[35]

At the end of the novel, Mimaki has taken a job with an aircraft manufacturer in Osaka and is setting up a house in Kōshien, another new, upper-middle-class suburb on the Hanshin Line, not far from Sachiko and Teinosuke, while Taeko has moved with Miyoshi to Hyōgo, a working-class neighborhood of Kobe, heavily built up with factories.[36] Judged by the anachronistic values of Senba, Yukiko would clearly seem to be marrying up, while Taeko marries beneath her class. But does the reader feel that Yukiko's match will succeed? With her marriage, which ends the novel, is Yukiko permitted to recede into tradition and into the life of comfortable leisure that Mimaki's connections promise? The shadow of the worsening global political-economic situation hangs over the final *miai* in Tokyo. When Sachiko and Taeko arrive in Tokyo, a naval review is underway, as well as a festival at Yasukuni, the shrine commemorated to those who died in the service of the emperor. When the sisters stop by the main house in Shibuya before the *miai*, we learn in an aside that "the carefully guarded property of the main house had almost vanished with the collapse of the stock market."[37]

More than this, hanging over the entire novel is the reader's knowledge of what will follow: war with the United States; the bombing of Japan's cities, including the especially devastating firebombing of Kobe; then catastrophic destruction, defeat, and occupation. Which husband is better prepared to navigate all this: Miyoshi, with his plans to open a "not-too-vulgar bar for foreigners," or Mimaki, with his lukewarm interest in architecture and a new job in munitions, obtained through connections rather than through any demonstrated ability? Which will prove more appropriate to the times? And how will their wives, these two younger sisters, fare? A reader might well project, beyond the end of the novel and into the grim postwar, a reversal of fortunes. Taeko's painful efforts to break with the Senba world personified by the anachronistic bonbon and to embrace a more pragmatic masculinity may have prepared her in some small way for the trials of the occupation, while Yukiko's stubborn attachment to the extravagance and play characteristic of her father's lost world will likely make those trials harder to bear.

Kansai and Kantō

The spatial and temporal contrast between city and suburbs, between anachronistic play and a new pragmatism, is accompanied by another contrast: that between the two suburban households of Ashiya and Shibuya—or, more broadly, between the regions of Kansai and Kantō. One figures as a vestigial link to Senba, nostalgic in its expenditure; the other figures as a clean break, expectant in its economizing. The people in the Ashiya household practice the sort of cultural pursuits and live the sort of gracious life congruent with the family's Senba merchant past. They carefully select outfits for their annual outing to view the cherry blossoms at Kyoto's Heian Shrine; they write haiku together for the moon-viewing festival; they host a recital of traditional Osaka dance at their home. Although this household, headed by an accountant, does not indulge in the sort of extravagance that characterized the sisters' bonbon father, it spends money with relative freedom in pursuit of a fading tradition. The novel describes the Ashiya household's cultural practices as a vain persistence in the face of an inevitable passing of that tradition. The Osaka style of dance that Taeko practices is being overwhelmed by Tokyo's cultural hegemony, and its teacher is nearing the end of her life; the description of her death at the end of book 2, chapter 11, poignantly conveys a sense of impoverished local tradition. Again, contrast this to the *jōruri* in *Meoto zenzai*, which is a vital art, presented without reference to competition from any other city.

Meanwhile, the story follows the other household, headed by Tsuruko and Tatsuo, as they move to the Tokyo area and adapt to new economic and political realities. Tsuruko, especially, makes this break reluctantly; when she first learns of her husband's impending transfer, she is distressed: "Tsuruko tried to tell herself: she was not going off to a foreign country or even to some inaccessible spot in the provinces. She was going to the capital, she would be at the very feet of His Imperial Majesty. What was there to be sad about?"[38] As this passage associates Tokyo with Japanese nationalism and imperialism, it also marks, in Tsuruko's lack of enthusiasm, the distance between a national sensibility and a local sensibility. Tatsuo, on the other hand, welcomes the move. He had been asked by the bank to relocate once before but had begged off. The different outcome this time reflects the waning influence of one way of life and one model of family: "It had seemed afterwards that the bank would respect his status as head of an old family . . . but the bank had had a change in management and policy." The narrative then goes on to emphatically tie Tatsuo to a more disciplined, economically productive, and biologically reproductive regime, and to a rejection of the old model as insufficient to the times: "And then Tatsuo himself wanted to get ahead in the world, even if it meant leaving Osaka. . . . He had many children and while his expenses were growing, economic developments made it more difficult for him to rely on the property he had inherited from his foster father."[39]

After the move, Tsuruko quickly adapts to the new regime. She puts into practice various household economies: she does not wash Tatsuo's shirts as often as she did in Osaka, for example, and she writes to Sachiko requesting hand-me-down clothes. Such economies inspire gossip back in Ashiya; when Yukiko comes back from her first visit to the new Shibuya house, she tells Sachiko, Teinosuke, and Taeko that "Tatsuo's salary was higher now that he had become a branch manager . . . and yet he was far thriftier than he had been in Osaka."[40] The contrast between Ashiya's tendency to nostalgic expenditure and Shibuya's adaptive austerity also manifests in the plans for anniversary services commemorating the sisters' deceased parents. The Ashiya house wants to mark the anniversary in what they believe is a suitably grand manner, while the Shibuya house urges austerity in consideration of the political situation.

In general, the household that Tsuruko and Tatsuo establish in Shibuya, in contrast to the quiet and cultured Ashiya household, is associated with a frenetic energy, noise, and a lack of repose. The main reason for both this atmosphere and the need for economy in Shibuya is the size of the family that Tsuruko and Tatsuo are rearing. As Tanizaki describes it, with rambunctious children running up and down the stairs, quickly outgrowing their clothes, the Shibuya house is an emblem of the fecundity that the state encouraged under mobilization. Indeed, one scene of Tsuruko's son playing at soldier hints at the state's interest in reproduction.

Furthermore, the novel describes the Shibuya house itself as a material manifestation of the household's adaptability and of the contrast with Kansai. The slapdash quality of its construction, revealed to Sachiko when the house only barely withstands a typhoon, is utterly different from that of the sisters' old Uehonmachi house, as well as the Ashiya house, which serves as a reliable safe haven during the terrible flood. When Sachiko first visits her older sister in Shibuya, Tsuruko's new neighborhood reminds her of a frontier town in Hokkaido or Manchuria. With this explicit and ironic reference to imperial ambition, Sachiko's reaction reverses the order of nation and empire, locating the Tokyo suburb not close to the center of the nation but somewhere near the margin. Through the eyes of Tsuruko, the novel's purest personification of a Kansai sensibility, the narration disassociates the local from the Tokyo-centered modern nation.

Sasameyuki emphasizes the incongruity of the Shibuya household to the Senba main house in its description of several expensive *objet* bought by their father and brought by Tsuruko to Tokyo. In Sachiko's eyes, they seem out of place in the Shibuya house: "She could see the corner of the Osaka house where they had all been kept. No doubt Tsuruko had brought them out to help her remember the good days and to brighten up what was much too ugly to be called a guest room. But the treasures had a perverse effect: they only set off the shabbiness [*yasubushin*] of the room, and for Sachiko it was strange indeed to find relics of her father in a dreary section of Tokyo [*Tōkyō no basue*]. It seemed to show the depths to which Tsuruko had fallen."[41] The shabbiness or flimsiness that contributes to Sachiko's sense of incongruity is perhaps regrettable but is, in any case, a predictable effect of Tsuruko and Tatsuo's adaptation to a new regime of daily life—one that values economy in the service of reproductivity.

The generational, social class, and geographic shifts—from the merchant father in urban Osaka to the banker son-in-law in suburban Shibuya—that shape the contrast Tanizaki draws between Kansai and Kantō are driven by the modern economy with which Japan's imperial project is complicit. Sachiko's dismay upon visiting her older sister's home indicates her own failure to adapt to "the current situation" and her attachment to the anachronistic Senba lifestyle represented by her father's knick-knacks—a lifestyle she tries to preserve in cosmopolitan Ashiya. Despite the desperateness of life in Shibuya as witnessed through Sachiko's eyes, however, we cannot conclude that, in the novel's comparison between Kansai and Kantō, Kansai comes out on top. If the narrative describes Kansai as a repository of bourgeois culture, the valuation that it places on that culture is by no means unambiguously positive.

Kansai's Anti-futurity

Against a Shibuya household that is invested in the future—as indicated by its reproductive success, its economizing, and its attentiveness to the current state of emergency brought on by Japan's imperial adventures—the novel sets an Ashiya household that is not merely living in the past but marked as anti-future. This manifests, first of all, in the pervasive taint of illness, disease, and filthiness. There is the obsession with the spot over Yukiko's eye, purportedly a symptom of her unmarried and unreproductive state. There is Sachiko's jaundice and the "filthy" treatment for it that her guest Mrs. Niu suggests (keeping rice balls under the arms until the rice yellows). Sachiko also suffers a bout of bronchitis—a euphemism for tuberculosis at the time.[42] Sachiko's daughter, Etsuko, contracts scarlet fever. Itakura dies of gangrene after surgery to treat an ear infection. Above all, there is Taeko's bout of amoebic dysentery; visiting her sickbed, Sachiko observes in her "a certain sort of filthiness" (aru shu no fuketsu na kanji).[43] The sight prompts her to recall rumors that Kei-bon has contracted chronic gonorrhea. Minor details throughout the story underscore these associations, including the maid Oharu's habit of borrowing Sachiko's undergarments and the discovery of bed bugs at the hotel where the family stays during a trip to Nara.

Together with this pervasive presence of disease and filthiness, the novel characterizes the Ashiya household as having a concomitant obsession with medicine and hygiene. The famous opening scene has the sisters giving one another vitamin B shots to protect against beri-beri, perceived at the time as a "national disease" (*kokumin-byō*) that threatened the national body and its imperial mission.[44] The suitor at the fourth *miai*, Hashidera, works for a pharmaceuticals company; after Sachiko complains to him about the difficulty of procuring good foreign medicine under the control economy, he offers to get the family anything they need—an offer Teinosuke quickly accepts. Near the end of the novel, as Taeko struggles in childbirth, Sachiko brings from the house a cache of hoarded German medicine to trade to the doctor in exchange for drugs to induce the pregnancy. At another moment, seeing Etsuko play at giving her doll a shot, mimicking her mother and aunts, her father diagnoses the problem: "What a morbid little game, Teinosuke thought. That too was a result of a dangerous preoccupation with hygiene."[45] These associations culminate in a nervous attack suffered by Etsuko: seeing a dead rat in the street, the girl becomes convinced that she has touched it, although she has in fact given it a wide berth. Possessed by a paranoid fastidiousness, she is eventually sent by her parents to see a doctor in (where else?) Tokyo.[46]

These compounding associations underscore the Ashiya household's inability to respond appropriately to the national situation, which required healthy, disciplined bodies. It is certainly true that in *Sasameyuki*, "Tokyo's poverty, bleakness, and disorder serve to set off Ashiya's harmonious integration of tradition, modernity, and cosmopolitanism."[47] Tokyo's bleakness, however, is presented to us mostly through Sachiko's eyes. The narration, on the other hand, presents Ashiya's tradition as a dying one, and its modernity and cosmopolitanism as tainted by this filthiness and disease. Ken Ito has characterized the Ashiya of *Sasameyuki* as a place of "light and purity" and argues that "disease, defilement and moral lassitude" are presented as outside threats, introduced by the "class miscegenation" that Taeko commits in dating Itakura.[48] Building on this argument and borrowing from Judith Butler, we might consider that this act of miscegenation (with a man of a different "race," as Sachiko considers him) serves in *Sasameyuki* as an outside to the "racially pure reproduction" and bodily discipline required of the corporate state and demonstrated by the Shibuya household.[49] In that case, we could understand Tanizaki's novel to reinforce the productivist rhetoric of the contemporary state—though not in a way that state censors could be expected to recognize.

I would suggest, however, that "disease, defilement and moral lassitude" are essential characteristics of the Kansai locale as Tanizaki constructs it. They are manifestations of a certain morbidity—rooted in Senba and the merchant class—that has clung to Sachiko's family as it migrated to Ashiya and that Tsuruko's family has managed to shed only by moving to Kantō. It attaches to Itakura, who comes from Senba, but also to Taeko's other ill-fated liaison, Kei-bon. Furthermore, as previous examples indicate, associations of disease and pollution are not restricted to Taeko; indeed, they pervade the scenes at the Ashiya house. These associations stretch back into the past as well: William Johnson notes that Sachiko's bout with bronchitis calls to mind her mother's death from tuberculosis, then considered by most Japanese to be a hereditary disease, "a sign of 'tainted blood,'" and he goes on to identify this disease as "itself a cause of the Makiokas' decline."[50]

How do these images of disease, illness, and failed hygiene, and the issues they raise of heredity and infectivity, combine in this, the best-known novel of modern Osaka, to construct that city in the national imagination? In his analysis of disease as a trope in Shimazaki Tōson's *Hakai* (Broken commandment, 1906), Michael Bourdaghs contextualizes that novel's imbrication of disease (especially tuberculosis), socialism, and the socially marginalized status of the *hisabetsu burakumin* (descendants of pre-Meiji outcaste groups) within the contemporary development of germ theory and of hygiene as a medical discipline. Hygiene, Bourdaghs writes, developed "primarily as a form of military medicine designed to increase battle-readiness in the nation-state's wars of imperialist expansion" as germ theory placed human bodies and the national community "in a new relationship, wherein the purity/health of each was dependent upon that of the other."[51] Cultural production in modernity constructs certain bodies, and certain groups of bodies, as other to the national community; Bourdaghs quotes Tessa Morris-Suzuki's observation that modern national communities "encompass small groups that fail the tests of belonging because it is only through the visible failure of defined 'minorities' that the state can repeatedly reassure itself of the invisible homogeneity and loyalty of the 'majority.'"[52] He argues that the variety of diseases applied to the "othered" bodies of the *burakumin* characters in Tōson's novel amounts to an "*écriture* of discrimination" (borrowing a term from Watanabe Naomi) whereby the colonized are made to represent, indirectly and in negative, the identity of the dominant colonizer. The imaginary equivalence of those various diseases "becomes the grounding of the supposedly 'normal' Japanese."[53] Bourdaghs then demonstrates how those tropes, read in the context of competing medical practices of quarantine and vaccination, functioned in complex, sometimes contradictory ways to underwrite state policies of both isolationism and expansionism.

The application, in *Sasameyuki*, of tropes of disease and failed hygiene to bodies that are "othered" by their association with urban locality functions within the wartime and postwar national imagination in similarly complex ways. The Senba locality that makes them other is a cultural inheritance, of course, but *Sasameyuki* also figures it as a blood lineage: recall Sachiko's comment that the Makiokas and Kei-bon belong to the same "race." That inheritance is entwined with tuberculosis, which *Sasameyuki*—reflecting, like *Hakai*, a popular misconception—figures as perhaps hereditary. Sachiko's bout with bronchitis raises the specter of the tuberculosis that killed their mother, and Yukiko, the daughter who most resembles the mother, is said to look "as though she might come down with tuberculosis at almost any time."[54] Bourdaghs notes that the heredity of disease is linked to "broad ideologies of blood lineage that underlay the Meiji *ie* (family) system and the emperor system, as well as Western attitudes toward Japan and Japanese attitudes toward other Asians."[55] These ideologies were still in place when Tanizaki wrote *Sasameyuki*. The *ie* system figures in the disagreements between the main house in Shibuya and the house in Ashiya over issues big (Yukiko's suitors, Taeko's future) and small (arrangements for the parents' memorial service). The emperor system is referenced repeatedly. And the novel at least implies a link to Western attitudes toward Asians in the gaze of the Ashiya household's neighbors—the German Stoltzes and the White Russian Kyrilenko family. At other points, the novel figures Senba's taint as infectious—for example, when Sachiko involuntarily associates Taeko's dysentery (first misidentified by a doctor as anthrax) with Kei-bon's rumored gonorrhea. In this way, *Sasameyuki*, again like *Hakai*, confounds heredity and infectivity. Tanizaki's novel, then, imagines locality as a hereditary and infectious threat to the health of the national body and figures both a fear of contagion, in Taeko, and a fantasy of self-quarantine, in Yukiko.

Along with disease, the Ashiya household bears the stigma of a weak fertility. Sachiko has only one child, a daughter, and suffers a miscarriage during the narrative. Taeko, too, suffers a miscarriage—of Miyoshi's baby—while she is staying at the Ashiya house. Even before that, Sachiko has suggested to Taeko that it might be better not to bring the pregnancy to term. It is during the sisters' visit to Tokyo for the *miai* with Mimaki that Taeko first realizes that she is pregnant. When she informs Sachiko that the baby is Miyoshi's, Sachiko responds, "Do you plan to have it?" (Koi-san, umu ki ya non).[56] Later, Sachiko considers the possibility of obtaining an abortion, although that has become difficult under the military regime. All this happens amid repeated references to the "current situation" and concern over what is appropriate to it. Sachiko's response is one of the clearest indications of Kansai's betrayal of the reproductivist state, as the novel imagines it. In a satirical twist, the family cat, Suzu, is the only member of the Ashiya household to give birth successfully during the novel (at the end, just before Taeko's stillbirth), and even she requires Sachiko's assistance due to her age.[57] In this way, Tanizaki imagines Ashiya and the broader Kansai region in contradistinction not only to the Shibuya household and Tokyo as a locale, but also to a Tokyo-centered state government that directed sexuality toward nationalist goals through natalist policies as part of a campaign of positive eugenics that encouraged marriage and childbearing.[58]

A space of expenditure without return; of dirtiness, disease, and death; and of failed reproductivity, the Ashiya household in *Sasameyuki* registers as a denial of the future's promise. In his polemic on the subject of "reproductive futurity," *No Future*, Lee Edelman explains how the notion of futurity operates in both symbolic and social orders. In the symbolic order, the fantasy of the future encourages us to invest our desire in "the deferrals demanded by the signifying chain" in the hopes of undoing "the initiating fracture, the constitutive moment of the division by means of which the signifier is able to pronounce us into subjectivity"; in the social order, the fantasy of the future encourages us to invest in a state-sponsored ideology of reproduction in service to the state.[59] Edelman then argues for the potential of queerness, in the figure of the "sinthomosexual" as an incarnation of the death drive, to refuse meaning and to stand outside a politics that always takes the side of the future, of deferral, of "*promissory* identity."[60]

By imagining Ashiya as it does, *Sasameyuki* spatializes a similar refusal of national subjectivity and of a contemporary politics of sacrifice in the name of a promised empire. It does this in the symbolic order through its attention to local and national language. National subjectivity looms large among the various subjectivities into which moderns are pronounced, and the fracture that initiates Japanese national identity in each individual subject was aggravated by events of the late 1930s and early 1940s. Tanizaki's overwhelming concern with Kansai's difference after he relocated there from Tokyo betrays a sensitivity to that fracture, particularly the division between one's native tongue and the national standard—a division performed through state institutions, of course, but also through the institution of literature. Tanizaki's fascination with Kansai dialects together with his concern over what he perceived as *genbun'itchi*'s adulteration of ethnic-national sensibilities suggests a larger awareness of that division that pronounces us into national subjectivity.[61]

It is not only signification that is ordered by the future-oriented logic of deferral as investment in the hope of future compensation. At the historical moment of *Sasameyuki* (more precisely, the overlapping moments in which the story is set, during which the novel was written, and into which it was published, all spanned by the term "transwar"), the same logic ordered household, regional, and national economies, as families, communities, and the state deferred other needs and desires to invest financial, emotional, and human capital in Japan's imperial wager, tempted by the promise of unification and co-prosperity in a greater East Asian "sphere." *Sasameyuki* alludes to such deferrals in the dance recital at the Ashiya house, for example, and in the memorial service for the sisters' parents, both of which are held quietly and at minimal expense in deference to the political situation.

If one figure incarnates the death drive for this story in the place of Edelman's sinthomosexual it is the bonbon, in the characters of the sisters' dead father—avatar of the city's dying merchant culture—and of his spiritual heir, Kei-bon. The eldest sister flees the city and Kansai with her family, moving far enough away to evade that culture's baleful influence. The second sister remains within Senba's sphere of influence, and the two younger sisters with her. The result for them is death and disease. In the novel's last scenes, Taeko's baby by Miyoshi falls prey to what Sachiko imagines to be "the curse of Kei-bon and Itakura," and Yukiko, on her way to beginning a new life with one more bonbon, suffers from diarrhea, the novel's final image.

The Ashiya household's resistance to futurity is also figured in the delays and postponements that become a recurrent theme of the novel, which Watanabe Naomi has called a "tale of delay."[62] Yukiko postpones marriage and childbearing through countless small delaying tactics. Out of concern for her moods, the family delays its response to the marriage proposals that Itani and others bring them and repeatedly postpones the various *miai* even after they are arranged. Sachiko's miscarriage forces a postponement of the second *miai*, for example. Before the third, the train carrying the Makiokas stops suddenly on the way to Gifu, delaying their arrival. Itani, the almost annoyingly determined hairdresser—so committed to finding a match for Yukiko, so impatient to see her plans proceed, so quick to remind Sachiko not to rest on her family's past glory—is unrelentingly future oriented. This quality is confirmed at the end of the novel by her decision to travel to the United States, the source of the perceived threat to Japanese tradition. In this regard, Itani serves as an effective foil to the Ashiya household—one who, like Tsuruko, must try to leave Kansai behind. This theme of delay figures in subtler ways, too: Yukiko repeatedly postpones her return to the Shibuya household, preferring to stay in Ashiya. Postponement also characterizes many of Taeko's actions, even despite her intention to move forward. Yukiko's refusal of suitor after suitor forces Taeko to delay her own plans to marry Kei-bon, and the family's qualms about propriety force her to postpone her plan to travel to France to study sewing until the worsening geopolitical situation renders that impractical.

Yukiko's delaying tactics signify her attachment to the anachronistic lifestyle of the Ashiya household and her reluctance to invest herself in any reproductive future. This reluctance manifests as the worrisome, changeable dark spot on her face, sometimes fading until it is almost unnoticeable and then, at the most inconvenient moments, growing darker and strangely resistant to makeup. Her refusals will end only when she is presented with the ultimate anachronistic figure, the bonbon son of a Kyoto viscount. Yukiko's inaction in turn frustrates Taeko's investment in a future either with Kei-bon or without him. With each delay and refusal, the Makioka family sees the prospective return on their investment in these two younger sisters decline. The patterns of repetition and downward spiral give the lie to contemporary imperial politics' attempts to lend meaning to present deferral with the promise of future reward. Trapped within the repetition of *miai* as well as the seasonal cycle of events in which the Ashiya house (still) indulges—cherry-blossom viewings, moon viewings, and doll festivals—the family's profitless deferrals betray the state's attempts to impose meaning and encourage national identification through investment in the future.[63]

Yukiko, the instigator of these delays and postponements, demonstrates a "radical passivity" that resists such promissory identity. As part of an exploration of "the queer art of failure," Judith Halberstam identifies in a variety of texts the potential of "a feminism grounded in negation, refusal, passivity, absence, and silence." This is, Halberstam argues, an "antisocial, anti-Oedipal, antihumanist, and counterintuitive feminism . . . that thinks in terms of the negation of the subject rather than her formation, the disruption of lineage rather than its continuation, the undoing of self rather than its activation."[64] *Sasameyuki* models something akin to this in Yukiko's noncommittal responses and refusals. Two scenes in particular demonstrate Yukiko's startlingly (as the narrative presents it) antisocial behavior and how it repels two marriage prospects: in the first, Yukiko and Taeko run into her second suitor, Nomura, at a café in downtown Kobe. When he invites them to join him, Yukiko refuses to either accept or decline the invitation; instead, as Taeko explains later to Sachiko, "she stood there muttering and gurgling."[65] The family breaks off the marriage negotiations soon after. In the second scene, Yukiko's fourth suitor, Hashidera, after meeting the family twice, calls the Ashiya house to invite Yukiko to dinner in Osaka. Sachiko has stepped out to mail a letter, so the maid calls Yukiko herself to the phone, but Yukiko hesitates to take the call and sends the maid after Sachiko, who hurries back. When she gets to the house, she finds the receiver on the hook. She asks the maid whether her sister took the phone:

> "She waited and waited, and then finally . . ."
> "And did she talk long?"
> "No more than a minute or so."

Sachiko then speaks with Yukiko:

> "What did Mr. Hashidera want?"
> "He said he would be waiting at Osaka Station at four-thirty, and he wanted me to meet him."
> "I suppose he wanted to go for a walk with you."
> "He said he was thinking of walking through Shinsaibashi and having dinner somewhere, and he wondered if I would go with him."
> "And what did you say?"
> ". . . . ."
> "Are you going?"
> Yukiko muttered something that sounded very much like "No."
> "Why?"
> ". . . . ."[66]

Furious, Hashidera ends negotiations, telling the go-between that he hates "indecisive, missish young ladies."[67] These incidents are part of a broad pattern of passive-aggressive silence and diffidence that leaves the family constantly wondering what Yukiko is thinking about her suitors and afraid to press her too hard for an answer. In this way, Yukiko belongs in the company of women characters Halberstam identifies as "subjects who cannot speak, who refuse to speak."[68]

Like many of the English-language texts in which Halberstam grounds her argument, *Sasameyuki* "loses the mother." The sisters' mother, a "fragile, self-effacing Kyoto beauty," is long dead as the story begins, and we meet her only in Sachiko's recollections. The mother fell ill soon after the birth of her youngest child and was sent away from the family, first to the seaside, then to the mountains, in hopes the cleaner air would improve her condition. Sachiko, the second eldest, was allowed brief visits "once or twice a month," until the mother's death at the age of thirty-six, when Sachiko was just fourteen. Sachiko retains an idealized image of her mother, "joined to the lonely sound of the waves or the wind in the pines," but the two younger sisters must remember her but little. Halberstam argues that such a loss can signify a refusal of the knowledge passed down in a matrilineal line and "produce a theoretical and imaginative space that is 'not woman' or that can be occupied only by unbecoming women."[69] Sachiko remembers her mother as "the docile, long-suffering townsman's wife, managing the house with no hint of dissatisfaction" while her father pursued "an addiction to pleasure, verging on debauchery," that "only became more shameless with the mother's illness." Yukiko, the sister who most resembles the mother—and whom their father loved best because of that resemblance—recoils from the prospect of taking her place in such a tradition. The mysterious dark spot that marks her refusal to do so contrasts with the mother's face as Sachiko remembers it: "a cleaner white," even near death, that "took on no shadow."[70]

The youngest sister, Taeko, actively rebels against bourgeois convention: turning her genteel hobby into a paying job, dressing in less-restrictive Western clothes, renting a room of her own, and taking lovers. But such rebellion is itself a bourgeois convention. Furthermore, Tanizaki links this assertion of a liberal subjectivity to state interests: among the Ashiya household, it is Taeko who displays the greatest awareness of, and deference to, "the current situation"—that is, to Japan's imperial project. By contrast, Yukiko's resistance is closer to what Halberstam describes:

"a radical form of masochistic passivity that not only offers up a critique of the organizing logic of agency and subjectivity itself, but that also opts out of certain systems built around a dialectic between colonizer and colonized."[71] Yukiko's silences and refusals wreak havoc in the family: they divide the Shibuya and Ashiya households, lead to Taeko's downfall, and damage the Makioka name. Under a family-state ideology that analogized the imperial state to the patriarchal family, that havoc suggests resistance to the state's futurist aims. And, as he did in *Manji*, Tanizaki links that queer resistance to Osaka's locality. Yukiko deploys her radical passivity to postpone as long as possible her impressment into the reproductive futurity, but she is married off at last, to the "bonbon of the noble class," Mimaki. The novel ends with her on the train to the imperial capital, where the marriage will take place, and with a final symbolic evacuation: the diarrhea that plagues Yukiko as she rides toward married life.

Tanizaki's Ethnographic Irony

The narrative voice that describes Ashiya and the Kansai region in *Sasameyuki* has a distinctly ethnographic tenor. It asserts a position outside and above the city, the suburbs, and the region, observing the "ethnographic village" and exercising mastery over its culture and customs—a mastery that the narrator demonstrates by interrupting the story with pedantic asides addressed to an audience in the capital. For example, regarding Yukiko's marriage prospects, the narrator explains:

> She had been born in the year of the Ram. The year of the Fire-Horse is widely considered unlucky, but in Kantō there is no superstition against the year of the Ram, so Tokyoites will no doubt find it strange that in Kansai it is thought that women born in any year of the Ram bring bad luck and that merchants, especially, should avoid taking one as a wife. There is even a proverb, "Let not the woman of the year of the Ram darken your door." In Osaka, where there are so many merchants, it is a long-held superstition.[72]

Describing the sushi restaurant in Kobe where the sisters eat together, the narrator takes a moment to display his understanding of the region's cuisine, noting that the chef, though trained in Tokyo, was a Kobe native and "made his sushi from those things that appeal particularly to the Kamigata taste. For example, he used not Tokyo-style yellow vinegar but white.

For soy sauce, he used Kansai *tamari*, which no Tokyoite would ever use."[73] The narrator evinces a mastery of the region's architecture as well, in a description of the Makioka family's main house near Senba, built, he notes, in "the true Osaka style."[74] Above all, this narrator cannot resist drawing attention to his mastery of dialect. When the maid O-haru reports to Sachiko of having seen Kei-bon visiting Taeko, the author interrupts to explain parenthetically that "O-haru had used the world *mambō*, an old dialect word that survives only in the Osaka district. It describes a short tunnel, a sort of underpass, and it is believed to have come originally from the Dutch."[75] In all these fussy asides, the author presents the local phenomenon as a variation on a Tokyo standard, suggesting that his audience is national (that is to say, explicitly *not* local) and that his mastery is the sort that the national exercises over the local.

This quality in the narrative voice of *Sasameyuki* invites us to take the narrator for Tanizaki, the career author. It distinctly calls to mind essays Tanizaki published after moving to Kansai, sharing his impressions of the region with an audience back in Tokyo. Not long after his arrival, for example, he published an essay, "Hanshin kenbunroku" (Hanshin observations, 1925), that, as Ken Ito notes, "exudes from its opening sentence the Edokko's traditional hostility to Osaka."[76] That first line reads, "Osakans are a race of people who, as a matter of course, allow their children to urinate on the floor while riding a train. Tokyoites will be surprised to hear this, but I assure you I am not lying."[77] He then goes on to describe seeing a mother allow her child to do just that while riding on the Hankyū Line, as well as another mother allowing her child to defecate in the train car. The remainder of the essay details other examples of Osakans' lack of refinement, repeatedly applying to their behavior such words as *zūzūshii* (shameless) and *kebakebashii* (garish). Later, in passages that discuss the purportedly disappointing career of Koide Narashige, a well-known artist from Osaka, then recently deceased, and the lack of an Osaka novel to rival such novels of Tokyo as Ichiyō's *Takekurabe* (Comparing heights) and Kafū's *Sumidagawa* (The river Sumida), Tanizaki describes an Osaka inhospitable to art and literature, a city far less civilized than Tokyo.

Six years later, Tanizaki's opinion of Osaka has improved somewhat, as expressed in "Watakushi no mita Ōsaka oyobi Ōsakajin" (Osaka and Osakans as I see them), but his ethnographic impulse has, if anything, strengthened. For example, concerning people's faces, he writes, "Since coming to the Kansai region, as I take in the appearance of townspeople passing by, I am struck by the sort of faces that one never sees in Tokyo. . . . This is more the case in Kyoto than in Osaka, but if the residents of the former resemble *nō* masks in their quaintness, the latter are like *bunraku* puppets."[78] In such passages, Tanizaki presents Kansai as a storehouse of modern Japan's past, inhabited by a people who are distinguished from other Japanese not only by custom but by physiognomy.

Other passages describe Kansai people as unsuited to modern ways, even those living in Osaka. Tanizaki writes, for example, that "Osaka women dressed in Western style seldom seem stylish. These days, as I walk the neighborhoods of Shinsaibashi and Umeda, I sometimes see a terrific 'modern girl' dressed to the nines, but most of them are tourists visiting from Tokyo." He goes on to criticize the women of Kansai for their taste, which he finds more suited to the traditional than the modern, more inspired by nature than by urban life: "Certainly the color combinations of Japanese-style clothes in Kansai, which are much louder than those in Kantō, accord perfectly with the warm-climes scenery along the course of the Hanshin line—the deep blue skies, the bright green pines, the reflection of the white sands. However, when the flashy colors that are the taste in kimono there are applied as-is to a crepe-de-chine dress, well, it really is a bit much." He goes on to read the very bodies of Kansai women as incompatible with (a barbarous) modernity: "It is not just the color combinations they wear, but it certainly has to do with the women's anatomy and their movements, as well. From old, Kantō has had a barbarous character, and even the women there were encouraged to be lively. This conforms rather easily to the disposition of the modern-day flapper, and they have a great ability to adapt their gestures and facial expressions to the 'yankee' style, as well."[79]

Tanizaki regularly assesses Osaka and its people against a Tokyo standard and describes the difference as an essential matter, grounded in place. He writes, for example, of the local voice: "Above all, I sense the difference between the disposition of Tokyoites and Osakans in their speaking voice. More than words, it is the quality of the voice that clearly distinguishes east from west. As exchange between the regions grows more common, the gap between the dialect of the Kamigata region and that of Tokyo may disappear, but the difference in the sound of the voice produced from people's throats is unlikely to pass away so easily, since it is no doubt an effect of climate, topography, temperature, and so on."[80] Such pronouncements cast Kansai as a blood-and-soil ethnic nation rather than a metropolitan area shaped by centuries of migrant flows. As noted in earlier chapters, Osaka was at the time, as it remains today, a city of migrants, home to sizable communities of Ryukyuans, ethnic Koreans, migrants from Kyushu, and others. The inhabitants of Tanizaki's Osaka, however, are a distinct race rooted to the locale, their characteristics determined by geography and environment. This static, traditional Osaka is set against a modern Tokyo that is constantly changing and absorbing influences from all over. The dynamic is particularly remarkable in light of the fact that, at the same moment, such critics as Ōya Sōichi were warning readers of Osaka's dangerous ultramodernism and consumerism. In this way, Tanizaki recognizes in the locale of his destination the past that modernization had erased from his homeland.

In order to make such ethnographic observations, Tanizaki claimed a special status vis-à-vis the region. In "Watakushi no mita Ōsaka oyobi Ōsakajin," Tanizaki calls the Keihan region his "second homeland." However, he goes on to admit (or insist) that "I will probably never lose my natural disposition as a son of Tokyo, and so my observations will, after all, always be made through the eyes of an 'immigrant from Tokyo.' However, if I occasionally hurl a severe criticism at the faults of the people of Kyoto and Osaka, it is only out of concern for those who have put up with me for so long, and it is intended as an exhortation. I hope that you who read this, ladies and gentlemen of Kansai especially, will do so in that spirit."[81] Claiming this position of "immigrant," somewhere between "foreigner" and "native," allows the writer to maintain the ethnographic gaze. As Karatani Kojin writes, drawing a parallel with the "world of dreams": "We can say the same for the world of the primitive: the anthropologist can reside there and observe, but he can never *live* there. Even if he could, he would then cease to be an anthropologist."[82] Tanizaki's essays describe Kansai as modern Japan's—that is, Tokyo's—primitive past, uncannily manifesting in the present moment.

The migrant sensibility is carefully established between two anxieties: on the one hand, there is the anxiety that one will fail to attain the target identity, and on the other hand, the anxiety that one will lose one's original identity in the attempt. Tanizaki's essays betray the effort to maintain a position between these two anxieties. Tanizaki's insistence, at the beginning of "Watakushi no mita Ōsaka oyobi Ōsakajin," that he can never lose his essential character as a son of Tokyo is also an admission that he can never become a native Osakan. In "Hanshin kenbunroku," he repeatedly describes himself as an "Edokko," or "child of Edo," invoking a term used to describe those born in Tokyo, especially in the central neighborhoods of the merchant quarters of the "low city," rather than the "high city" of the former samurai estates. His use of the term comes to seem like an incantation against the threat of losing his original identity.

Similar observational migrant sensibilities structure earlier stories by Tanizaki. *Yoshino kuzu* (Arrowroot, 1931) and *Ashikari* (The reedcutter, 1932) both feature a primary narrator from Tokyo who is visiting the Kansai region with an interest in the premodern past and a secondary narrator from Osaka whom we might characterize as a native informant. In *Yoshino kuzu*, the narrator is researching the history of the Southern Court and accompanies his friend Tsumura to Yoshino. In *Ashikari*, a writer staying in Okamoto, in the Hanshin-kan, takes a short trip to the site of the detached palace of Emperor Go-Toba in Minase, outside the city, where he encounters a man visiting from Osaka, who tells him the story of a courtesan named Oyū. As Anthony Hood Chambers notes, both works shift from the Tokyo man's factual narration of the distant past to the Osaka man's romantic narration of the more recent past.[83] We have also seen in chapter 1 how a similar contest between the suspect, subjective narration of a Kansai local (this time a woman) and the confirming, objective narration of an author who writes in the national language structures the novel *Manji* (1928–29).

In *Sasameyuki*, this relationship is subtler. There is, however, something of the ethnographer–informant dynamic in the zero-focalization of the sometimes-intrusive authorial narrator, for whom the career author Tanizaki may reasonably be inferred, and the internal focalization of Sachiko, whose perspective and attitudes (especially toward Kansai and Kantō) the narration often takes. Social scientists speak of "ethnographic irony": a tone that colors the contrasts drawn between the practices, customs, and beliefs shared by the social scientist and the reader, on the one hand, and those of the other being studied.[84] We sense something of this sort in the contrasts that Tanizaki the national author draws for his national reader between the capital and the locale where he resides as an "immigrant."

The use of Sachiko as another focalization adds a dimension to this irony. The dynamic works rather like that visualized in the famous photograph by Robert Doisneau, "Un Regard Oblique" (1948), as analyzed by Mary Anne Doane.[85] In that photograph, the gaze of the woman, who is looking with interest at a picture in the window and seemingly commenting on it to the man beside her, is excluded by the gaze of the man, who is looking sidelong at another picture, of a female nude, in complicity with the (presumed male) viewer of the photograph. So, in *Sasameyuki*, Sachiko's focalization, and her estimation of Kansai culture, is if not excluded then ironized by that of Tanizaki in complicity with the (presumed national) reader. While the irony at work in *Sasameyuki* involves the same gender dynamic as that of Doisneau's photograph, it also involves the local–national dynamic. It is also the local that is being ironized through a complicity between the narrator writing in the national language and his national audience. In the same way that, as Doane argues, the female spectator must assume the position of transvestite to "get" the joke of Doisneau's photograph, so the local reader must assume a national sensibility to get the irony with which the play of narrative voices in *Sasameyuki* treats Kansai. Irony requires a victim, a butt of the joke, and here it is the local sensibility.

Sasameyuki produces, as another aspect of this irony, a sense of "historical irony" that, as Anthony Chambers notes, "lies thick on the last pages" of the novel, due to the reader's knowledge of the defeat and occupation to come.[86] This irony makes victims of Yukiko and Taeko and their husbands, as previously noted: how pointless seem all the strategies and the various *miai*, how pathetic seems the family's relief at finally marrying off Yukiko considering what the next few years will bring. The novel works this irony on its minor characters as well. Itani, the busybody hairdresser, arranges the match between Yukiko and Mimaki just as she is setting off to the United States for "six months to a year" in November 1940. The narrative notes: "Some of her friends pointed out that the international situation was most unstable, and that there might be trouble between the United States and Japan. Should she not wait a little longer?"[87] Before the final *miai* in Tokyo, the sisters and Mimaki meet in Itani's hotel room, where they tease her affectionately about the clothes she has packed for her trip. A few pages later, a letter from her daughter notes that Itani has sailed for America in high spirits. By the time of the novel's final publication, Tanizaki and his readers know, as the victim of his irony cannot, what lies ahead: Itani, so excited to be heading to America, so invested in her future, will see the international situation deteriorate quickly. In this way, the novel makes all the local characters the victims of its historical irony.

Tanizaki's irony works through this historical foreshadowing, through his ethnographic complicity with the reader, and through his use of the tropes of disease and death, to disfigure the traditional Japanese identity that his novel seems, at first, to celebrate. We might therefore identify a subversive quality in the novel that works not simply by elegizing an ideal Hanshin-kan culture destroyed by militarization but also by ironizing the essentialism represented in (Tanizaki's—or rather Sachiko's—idea of) that culture. The novel might then serve as another example of the strategy Greg Golley identifies in Tanizaki's earlier novel, *Tade kū mushi*, in which, he argues, the author uses irony to place his cultural essentialism "under erasure."[88] However, the politically and economically unequal relationship between local and national orders complicates such a subversion. *Sasameyuki* ironizes Japanese tradition. At the same time, it associates that tradition with a provincial Kansai characterized by an attachment to the past, and opposes this Kansai to an imperial Tokyo, "the lap of the emperor," characterized by an investment in the future. In doing so, it distances the national reader from the effects of that irony. The local becomes the negation of the national self. In order to "get" the irony, in order to recognize in it a potential subversion of the national project, we have to understand the local as the nation's past tradition, subsumed within and transcended by its present modernity. To do so is to reiterate the very operation at the heart of the national project: the subordination of one locale to another, disguised as transcendence.

A more effective subversion would require that the tables be turned. In his discussion of irony, Paul de Man suggests that in the opposition between the *eiron* and *alazon* of Hellenic comedy, "the smart guy and the dumb guy" (or, to put it into the terms of Osaka's *manzai* comedy tradition, the *tsukkomi* and the *boke*), "the smart guy, who is by necessity the speaker, always turns out to be the dumb guy."[89] Something like this threatens to happen in *Manji*, as Sonoko, the local female voice, manipulates her diagetic auditor, the writer Sensei, into copying down her tale and "arranging it like a novel." As Sonoko's story overwhelms the narrative frame, the sense grows that *Manji*'s "canny narratee" (to borrow Atsuko Sakaki's phrase) is playing "the smart guy," Sensei, for a fool. In *Sasameyuki*, on the other hand, the tropes of death and disease, the tone of ethnographic irony, and the overriding historical irony combine to keep the local in the role of victim to Tanizaki's national perspective.

Conclusion

Sasameyuki spatializes the relationship between tradition and modernity. It locates the former in Kansai, where one household clings to a dying tradition rooted in the culture of the Senba merchant quarter of Osaka, and it locates the latter in Kantō, where another household cuts ties with that tradition, adapts to present conditions, and invests in the future. Tanizaki's novel elegizes the anachronistic culture of Kansai, especially as viewed through the sensibility of the second sister, Sachiko. However, it overlays this elegy with heavy irony. The Kansai of the novel may be cultured, bourgeois, and cosmopolitan, a place of flower-viewing parties, dance recitals, French films, and colorful Russian neighbors, but it is also a place of disease and reproductive failure, empty expenditure, and investment without return. Tanizaki's novel comments on the processes of political and economic centralization and cultural homogenization that accompany the development of the modern capitalist nation-state, with wartime as a watershed. The Kansai of the novel, however fondly recalled, is nevertheless fatally associated with an outmoded economic model.

There are many reasons for the canonization of *Sasameyuki* as a classic not only of Japanese but of world literature, but certainly one is that Tanizaki so effectively reconciles Osaka's locality within the national form. For this reason, his novel has seemed more immediately germane and more interesting than, for example, Oda's *Meoto zenzai* to a discourse of national literature and, by extension, to the field of area studies, for which the unit of participation has long been the nation.

Chapter Five

The Afterlife of the Local Voice

Yamasaki Toyoko and Film Adaptation

The negotiation of Osaka's place in the national imaginary entered a new stage after the war, carried out in cinema. In 1951, the United States' occupation ended in much of Japan (although the occupation of Okinawa would continue until 1972) and with it most outright censorship of Japanese media. Freed from this restraint, film studios could participate more fully in the reexamination of recent history and the reevaluation of modern institutions to which the cataclysm of total war and defeat had prompted Japanese society. As part of this "golden age" of Japanese cinema, studios produced a string of notable films set in Osaka that reexamine the history of the city at a pivotal moment for the relationship between the local and the national. Sharing cast members, personnel, locations, and themes, these films form a distinct if loosely defined cluster with a significance greater than the sum of its parts. Together, they manifest a double consciousness of the city's status within the nation-state in the new circumstances of the postwar era.

By this time, Japan's conservative political establishment had begun to shift power back from local cities and prefectures to the state, reversing a process of decentralization initiated under the occupation by the Supreme Commander for the Allied Powers (SCAP). Convinced that the centralization of power in imperial Japan had encouraged militarization, SCAP had attempted to weaken state control and strengthen home rule for the prefectures. New legislation had provided for the local election of prefectural governors, previously appointed by the central government. Occupation reforms had also decentralized the police forces and education system and broken up the powerful Interior Ministry (Naimushō).

However, these efforts to effect lasting change in Japan's power structure were largely unsuccessful. Recentralization began even before the occupation's end, as Japanese bureaucrats endeavored to water down provisions introduced by SCAP. Popularly elected governors and other local officials were made dependent on the central bureaucracy. Once the occupation ended, conservatives in the Japanese government set about in earnest to dismantle the institutions of home rule, and this process only accelerated with the advent of high-speed economic growth. In 1954, a new Police Law subordinated prefectural police to a National Police Agency. Two years later, the Board of Education Law subordinated local boards of education to the central Ministry of Education. And in 1960, a new Ministry of Home Affairs (Jichichō) was instituted, reasserting many of the prerogatives of the prewar Naimushō. In their treatment of Osaka's locality, many of the films under consideration in this chapter responded to this contemporary process of recentralization.

The postwar golden age of cinema was, more specifically, a golden age of literary adaptation, or "*eiga-ka*," and this is evident from the Osaka films of the period.[1] Tanizaki Jun'ichirō's continuing popularity and Oda Sakunosuke's growing fame helped spur cinematic interest in the city. Two of Oda's novels were adapted in the 1950s: *Meoto zenzai* (Sweet beans for two), by one of the masters of literary adaptation, Toyoda Shirō, in 1955; and *Waga machi* (My town), by Kawashima Yūzō the following year. During the war, Kawashima had made his directorial debut film, *Kaette kita otoko* (The man who returned, 1944), from a script by Oda.[2] And in 1947, during the occupation, Takagi Kōichi had directed an adaptation of Oda's 1946 novel *Sore demo watashi wa yuku* (Even so, I'll go), set in Kyoto. As for Tanizaki, 1950 saw an adaptation of *Sasameyuki* (Fine snow, 1943–48, published in English translation as *The Makioka Sisters*), the first of several, by Abe Yutaka. An earlier novel, *Neko to Shōzō to futari no onna* (A cat, Shōzō, and two women, published in English translation as *A Cat, a Man, and Two Women*, 1936), set in the suburbs of Nishinomiya and Ashiya, west of Osaka, was adapted by Toyoda in 1956. Tanizaki's first Osaka novel, *Manji* (1928–29), would be adapted by Masumura Yasuzō in 1964.

The 1950s also saw noteworthy adaptations of works by other well-known prewar and wartime authors with less of a connection to Osaka. One of the most acclaimed was Naruse Mikio's *Meshi* (Repast, 1951), adapted from Hayashi Fumiko's unfinished novel—the beginning of that director's sustained engagement with Hayashi's works.[3] Although set in

Osaka, *Meshi* is not really an Osaka film. The story concerns a housewife (played by Hara Setsuko) who has moved from Tokyo to Osaka with her husband (Uehara Ken), and the crisis that besets their stale marriage when his cousin comes to visit. Hayashi is by no means an Osaka writer, nor are Hara and Uehara Osaka actors; rather, they are exemplary *national* stars. Their characters here are precisely not locals, and *Meshi* employs its setting primarily as background for the domestic drama at its center. When the film takes the husband and his cousin on a sightseeing bus through the city, it clearly positions the audience as visitors rather than natives. Other noteworthy Osaka film adaptations from this period include Gosho Heinosuke's *Ōsaka no yado* (An inn at Osaka, 1954), adapted from Minakami Takitarō's 1925 novel, and Kawashima's highly entertaining *Kashima ari* (Room for rent, 1959), which shifts the setting of Ibuse Masaji's 1948 novel from Tokyo to Osaka, turning the story into a raucous farce that Ibuse denounced as "vulgar and squalid."[4]

In addition to these established authors, a new talent who debuted in the postwar era proved an especially rich source for Osaka cinema. Yamasaki Toyoko saw three of her novels made into films during this period, each released in the year following the source novel's publication. *Noren* (The shop curtain, 1958) was adapted by Kawashima; *Hana noren* (The flowered curtain, 1959) by Toyoda; and *Bonchi* (1960) by Ichikawa Kon—a director recognized (like Toyoda) as a master of literary adaptation. (Ichikawa, who worked under Abe Yutaka, would go on to direct what is now the most familiar adaptation of *Sasameyuki*, released in 1983.) In this way, Yamasaki played a major role in the postwar literary construction of Osaka, both through her enormously popular stories of Osaka life and, crucially, through those stories' extended influence in film and television adaptation.

An examination of Osaka films of the 1950s will clarify the changing idea of the city within the national imaginary. An examination of film adaptations in particular, and the process of adaptation, will reveal how this idea was negotiated. *Noren*—Yamasaki's source novel as well as Kawashima's film adaptation—offers a particularly compelling object for such an examination, both because Yamasaki's works have generally demonstrated remarkable adaptability and because *Noren* addresses with unusual candor the fate of Osaka in the transition from the prewar to the postwar, memorializing and thematizing the adaptability of the Osaka merchant and his city. This chapter begins with an analysis of Yamasaki's novel. It then reviews several Osaka film adaptations produced in the

1950s and some of the characteristics common to them before moving to a detailed analysis of Kawashima's adaptation of *Noren*. Finally, it examines the role of actors in adaptation and their performance of locality, focusing on the star of *Noren*, Morishige Hisaya, who was a fixture of cinematic Osaka and one of the greatest male stars of the postwar era.

Noren, the Novel

Born in Osaka in 1924, Yamasaki Toyoko graduated from the Kyoto Women's University and joined the staff of the *Mainichi Shimbun* in 1944, where she worked under Inoue Yasushi (who would win the Akutagawa Prize in 1950 for his novel *Tōgyū* [The bullfight]).[5] She published her first novel, *Noren*, in 1957. A year later, she was awarded the prestigious Naoki Prize (awarded annually to a work of popular fiction) for her second novel, *Hana-noren* (1958). She went on to become one of Japan's most popular and prolific authors, active until her death in 2013. Despite this success, Yamasaki has attracted relatively little critical attention, in part because she wrote business novels and so-called social-question novels rather than "pure" fiction. Well-documented charges of plagiarism have also affected the critical reception of her work.[6] Nevertheless, her significance to Japanese literature and to the postwar literary production of Osaka cannot be ignored. Over her long career, Yamasaki took on a variety of topics, such as the experience of Japanese Americans during World War II in *Futatsu no sokoku* (Two homelands, 1980–83); Japan's colonial legacy in Manchuria in the four-volume series *Daichi no ko* (Children of the earth, 1988–89); and the 1985 crash of Japan Airlines Flight 123 in *Shizumanu taiyō* (The sun that never sets, 1999). For roughly the first twenty years, Yamasaki wrote mainly about Osaka and especially Senba. Those works, both in themselves and in adaptation for cinema and television, have played a major part in memorializing Osaka's merchant culture in the popular imagination.

Yamasaki's first novel, in particular, directly addresses the issue that has been the main concern of this study: the position of the city vis-à-vis the state and the nation. *Noren* does this with a concern for historical context that would become typical of Yamasaki's writing. Unlike Oda's *Meoto zenzai*, which for the most part writes out the broader context of Japan's militarization, or Tanizaki's *Sasameyuki*, which confines it to the margins of the story, Yamasaki's novel explicitly and continually locates

Osaka's merchant culture within the changing political-economic context of the transwar period. *Noren* opens in March 1896, just at the end of the Sino-Japanese War, and its second sentence refers to the postwar boom that Osaka, like other industrial centers, enjoyed. Throughout the story, the narration makes note of such milestone events as the start of World War I (p. 45), the Great Kantō Earthquake (52), the Nomonhan Incident of 1939 (78), the Shimoyama and Mitaka incidents of 1949 (145), and the Korean War (161), and takes care to explain the economic effects of Japan's imperialism on the economy and culture of Senba.[7]

The novel is divided into two books, the first running from the end of the first Sino-Japanese War to the end of World War II; the second set in the postwar period. The books follow the careers of two merchants, father and son, as they build and then revive the family business. In the first book, the father, Gohei, becomes an apprentice in a Senba merchant house, the Naniwa-ya; moves up the ladder; and eventually receives permission to open a branch shop. He guides this business through the vagaries of militarization and total war until it is all but destroyed in the firebombing of Osaka at the end of World War II. In the second book, Gohei's son Kōhei returns from the front to revive the business. It is a story of the ideal merchant as an embodiment of the culture of Senba and of the damage done to him by militarism and Tokyo's ascendancy. The name of the company whose fate *Noren* traces, the Naniwa-ya, suggests the importance of locality to the novel. Its line of business reiterates this: the firm deals in *konbu* (kelp), the seaweed that is the basis of Kansai-style stock and therefore one ingredient that fundamentally distinguishes Kansai cuisine from that of Kantō (where stock is traditionally based on dried bonito flakes). The story, then, follows the flavor of the local through the turbulent political economy of the modern era, with the war as watershed. In the process, it traces related shifts in the model of business and in the broader economy.

One important aspect of the business shift is a change in the model of succession, from affiliative to filial. In the prewar story, Gohei travels from the island of Awaji to Osaka at the age of fifteen. There he meets the master of the Naniwa-ya, also a native of Awaji, who takes the boy into the shop as an apprentice. The opening chapters establish the character of Gohei through a contrast with the young master, the biological son of the main house. While Gohei throws himself into even the most menial tasks and displays a native business sense, the young master devotes himself to the *jōruri* and neglects his responsibilities. The young master will eventually inherit the main shop, but that filial succession happens in the wings. The first book centers on Gohei, clearly identifying him as the spiritual heir to the Naniwa-ya by detailing the *noren-wake* (literally a division of the shop curtain) by which the old master grants him license to open his own shop under the main house's name. In contrast, the second book of *Noren* focuses on a filial succession from Gohei to his second-born son. Returning from the front, the lackadaisical Kōhei takes over despite reluctance on both sides, his more responsible elder brother having died in the war.

This shift from affiliative to filial is part of a broader adaptation in the organization of the business, from merchant house to corporation. When the story opens, the Naniwa-ya is conducting both processing and sales from its one location in Senba. After the *noren-wake*, Gohei begins marketing his products through independent retailers—first a gourmet shop run by the well-known restaurant Nadaman and then department stores, starting with the Mitsukoshi in Kōraibashi. The narrative notes that when Gohei began selling in the department store, "his eyes were opened to the modern institution [of business]."[8] By 1930, the Naniwa-ya's *konbu* is known throughout the nation. In 1937, Gohei opens a boutique in the new Hankyū Department Store in Umeda, gateway to the recently developed western suburbs of the Hanshin-kan. To meet increased demand, he builds a processing plant and makes a fundamental change in the organization of the business, employing workers for the plant as wage laborers rather than apprentices.

The Naniwa-ya also adapts to developing consumer tastes and buying habits. When Kōhei is preparing to move into the Tokyo market, he schools his father, Gohei, on the difference between Osaka and Tokyo, saying that while Osakans value what is good and cheap, the people of the capital believe something is good only if it is expensive. Kōhei's dialogue suggests that another shift is taking place. The first book has Gohei traveling to Hokkaido to meet with suppliers in 1924; he builds the business on his relationship with them and his ability to judge the quality of the *konbu* itself. In the postwar, Kōhei travels to Tokyo and revives the business through his understanding of consumer desire and a sensitivity to packaging and convenience as much as taste. The shift from merchant house to corporation thus accompanies a shift from connoisseurship to consumerism.

These shifts in the business model respond to a broader economic shift, from a networked regional economy with Osaka as one node to a national economy centered in Tokyo. The opening scene of the novel, in which the young Gohei arrives in Osaka and meets up with the master, who made the same migration in his youth, establishes the geography of this shift: in the prewar, Osaka is a regional metropolis to which provincials flock. Later in the first book, the description of Gohei's trip to Hokkaido emphasizes Osaka's place in a far-flung mercantile network—one to which Tokyo is not central. To underscore this, Yamasaki, like Oda in *Meoto zenzai*, makes reference to the Great Kantō Earthquake. Gohei is returning with an assistant to Osaka from Hokkaido and has stopped in Tokyo on the way when the earthquake hits. His shipment of *konbu* is destroyed in the fires that follow. In response, Gohei sends the assistant home to Osaka and heads back to Hokkaido to replace the lost shipment. Tokyo here is little more than a way station, and the signal event in its modern history (which is to say national history) is reduced to an interruption in Osaka's supply chain. By the second book, however, Tokyo has become the metropolis, and Osaka has been provincialized in turn. Visiting the capital after the war, Kōhei is stunned to see the scale of the retail districts there.

The control economy imposed during the war represents a fundamental threat to the Naniwa-ya and to the very role of the merchant. In the penultimate chapter of the first book, the narrative records that "the new wartime economic system was announced, and suddenly it became more difficult to do business." When the new controls are explained to Gohei, he cries, "That can't be! Are you saying I can't do business freely?" The narrative then goes on to explain the effect on Osaka's merchant economy: "Until now, *konbu* from Hokkaido and Karafuto had passed right through Tokyo and Nagoya and on to Osaka, due to the particular fondness for *konbu* and the skill of processors there. But although the executive plan attempted to ration *konbu* uniformly according to population, surpluses developed in those provincial cities where there was no particular taste for it."[9] Distribution was rationalized in a way that treated the population as a national whole, ignoring local tastes. Before the control economy, Osaka consumed as much as 120,000 *kan*, the narration notes; but under the new controls, all Osaka processors together are allotted just 20,000 *kan*—the amount that Gohei's shop alone had previously handled.[10] As a result, Osaka companies are forced to choose between selling *konbu* and processing it.

Unable to abandon the Naniwa-ya's merchant roots, Gohei decides to focus on selling and gives up the factory, which he rents to a munitions manufacturer. His resentment surfaces when he turns the plant over to the manufacturer and says, in his strong Osaka dialect, "Take care of what's in that plant, at least. I didn't get it by riding the wave of the munitions-manufacturing nouveau riche, like you. I built it through grain upon grain of suffering."[11] The munitions manufacturer, significantly, speaks standard Japanese, though one detail, the use of the suffix "*-han*" instead of "*-san*," betrays his Kansai roots—roots he betrays in another sense by speaking to a fellow Osakan in the national, rather than the local, language. The symbolism of the plant's repurposing—from the processing of *konbu*, the essence of local everyday life, to the manufacturing of munitions—is hardly subtle, but Yamasaki's narrative of Osaka's fate in the wartime economy is admirably clear.

Kōhei's recognition of the economic injustice visited upon Osaka motivates him to revive the company in the postwar. The novel ends with a remarkable combination of political-economic analysis and emotional appeal, as Kōhei recognizes what has been done to Osaka and resolves to undo it:

> Beginning with the wartime economy, the center of the Japanese economy had shifted to Tokyo. Then, with the loss of China and Manchuria, Osaka's business activity, centering as it did on trade, had been snuffed out like a flame, and with it Osaka's small- and medium-sized companies. . . .
>
> * * *
>
> His father, Gohei, had called Osaka Japan's navel. That Osaka was losing its economic strength—the Osaka that had nurtured capitalism through its infancy in Meiji and Taishō, the Osaka that had done business under the same *noren* for hundreds of years. "I won't accept defeat like this," Kōhei thought. "With the help of each and every merchant, I'll return Osaka to its former economic strength. If we persevere ten more years, just ten more, we'll show you the old Osaka!"—Kōhei whispered it in his heart.[12]

Such sentiments of patently futile defiance are easily recuperated into the sort of nostalgia that confirms, rather than challenges, Osaka's subordinate status. Kōhei's assertion, at the end of the story, that "We'll show you the old Osaka!" draws its affective power precisely from the reader's suspicion (by 1958, the year of the novel's publication) that the city's preeminence is irretrievable. Such futile defiance has since become a sentimental cliché of Osaka. It echoes, for example, in the 1986 hit song *Tonbori ninjō* (Dōtonbori kindness), sung by native daughter Tendō Yoshimi in the voice of a woman who returns to the supportive Osaka neighborhood of Dōtonbori after being dumped by her boyfriend in Tokyo, which rises to a chorus expressed in dialect: "maketara akan, maketara akan de, Tōkyō ni" (I mustn't be defeated, I mustn't be defeated by Tokyo). Coming at the end of Yamasaki's novel, however, with its clear-eyed accounting of Osaka's subordination, Kōhei's whisper communicates more than just nostalgia. *Noren* emphasizes that the city's economy, represented by the Naniwa-ya, was already modern under Gohei's ownership, before the war. The military state subordinates that economy through the application of wartime controls. After Japan's defeat, Kōhei vividly imagines a regeneration—of the family's fortunes, of the Naniwa-ya, and of Osaka. The structure of the novel underscores this idea of regeneration. The father's death initiates the Naniwa-ya's rebirth under the management of his son, who carries the code of the merchant—a modern sense of innovation and adaptability—into a new economic cycle.

Yamasaki's Adaptability

Yamasaki's stories have, since the start of her career, manifested another sort of adaptability: a remarkable propensity to regenerate in the afterlife of intermedial translation. The adaptation of her first three novels established a pattern that would continue throughout her career. Yamasaki's 1965 novel *Shiroi kyotō* (Ivory tower) became perhaps the most remarkable example of this adaptability; set at a fictional Osaka hospital, the story of two doctors—one kindhearted, the other ruthlessly careerist—became a phenomenal success across several media. It was originally serialized in the *Sunday Mainichi* newspaper beginning in 1963, published as a novel in 1965, and made into an award-winning film the following year.[13] A sequel was serialized in print from 1967 to 1968. The story was then adapted for Japanese television four times (in 1967, 1978, 1990, and 2003), and for Korean television in 2007. Another Yamasaki novel, *Nyokei kazoku* (A matrilineal house, 1966), about a venerable Senba cotton-merchant house ruled by the women of the family, has been adapted for television a remarkable eight times. *Karei naru ichizoku* (A splendid clan, 1973), a best seller about a Kobe banking and steel dynasty, was another multimedia success, adapted for film in 1974 and for television in 1974 and 2007. One tally lists forty-eight TV and film adaptations of Yamasaki's works between 1958 and 2009.[14]

What makes Yamasaki's stories so extremely adaptable is the author's brand of realism, which transfers easily to mass film and television and suits the special claim of those media to authenticity. Yamasaki's style is dry and straightforward, often journalistic. Her writing does not offer the humor and pathos of Oda, nor the perverse wit of Tanizaki, nor either writer's elegance of expression; rather, the appeal of her work lies in how it indexes social relations and urban (and, later in her career, national) history to carefully observed details of everyday life. In *Noren*, for example, she painstakingly describes the apprenticeship system in Senba under which young men enter as *detchi* and, if they show promise, move up to *tedai* and then to *bantō*. Yamasaki devotes several extended passages to the workings and the incidental details of this system, down to the appropriate costume on New Year's Day for each class of worker. In particular, her Osaka novels (like the writings of such earlier Osaka realists as Saikaku and Oda) reproduce a rich local language, including terms specific to the Senba merchant class. The 1959 story "Senba-gurui" (Crazy for Senba), in fact, describes one character's childhood awareness of Senba's borders and the special language used within.[15]

The elaboration of realistic detail in Yamasaki's Kansai works amount to a self-ethnography of the local as a response to the relentless homogenization and centralization pursued in modernity. Rethinking ethnography through Laura Mulvey's notion of "to-be-looked-at-ness," Rey Chow has argued that "the state of being looked at not only is built into the way non-Western cultures are viewed by Western ones; more significantly it is part of the *active* manner in which such cultures represent—ethnographize—themselves."[16] The non-West's act of subjective self-ethnography through looking, Chow argues, is informed by the memory of its objectification by the West, its "to-be-looked-at-ness"; this self-ethnography therefore "destroys the operational premises . . . of classical anthropology," of a world divided between viewing subject and viewed object.[17] Yamasaki's ethnography of the local similarly decenters the relationship between local and national. Informed by a recognition of its own objectification within the national imagination, this ethnography claims the subject position for the local and challenges the assertion of transcendence by which the nation attempts to objectify and subordinate the local. If we think of film adaptation, like literary translation, as a product of a work's "afterlife" or "after-ripening," then this self-ethnography is the genetic code that is carried forward as Yamasaki's novels regenerate in film and television. Next, I consider what becomes of this code in the new medium of film. After a general discussion of the value of fidelity in adaptation, I briefly review common strategies of adaptation in several notable Osaka film adaptations, before moving on to a discussion of Kawashima's film version of *Noren*.

Osaka in Adaptation

What, if any, significance should we attach to an adaptation's fidelity to its source material? The process of adaptation inevitably involves changes. As Robert Stam notes, "The source text forms a dense informational network, a series of verbal cues which the adapting film text can then selectively take up, amplify, ignore, subvert, or transform."[18] Those changes can reveal new significances that emerge in the process of carrying information across the gaps—temporal, medial, and more—that separate the source novel, or hypotext, from the film, or hypertext. That information may include plot points, dialogue, descriptions, characters—what one theorist has termed the story's "genetic material."[19] The model of inter- or hypertextual analysis that Stam, among others, has argued for is often contrasted with the use of fidelity as a value by which to judge an adaptation—a model that, its critics suggest, is based on a discredited concept of the originary text. Indeed, as the field of adaptation studies has grown over the past dozen or so years, seemingly every new attempt at a general theory has begun by tilting at a simplistic notion of fidelity. Yet even as one recently reissued guide declares the "fidelity debates" over, what Frederic Jameson has called "the scarecrow of 'fidelity'" still overshadows the field.[20] Jameson describes the service that the "scarecrow" performs in this way: it "stages a well-nigh Derridean vigilance to the multiple forms difference takes in the object of [adaptation] studies and insists on fidelity to that difference rather than to this or that ideology of the original."[21]

Eric Cazdyn has discovered another use for fidelity in the context of Japanese cinema. In *The Flash of Capital*, Cazdyn examines how an adaptation's fidelity to the "dominant canonical reading" of its source text manifests the character of popular regard for national origins at the historical moment of the adaptation's production. Cazdyn argues that in the 1930s, for example, literary adaptations characterized by fidelity to the source novel helped validate colonialism, establishing the origins of the Japanese people in a cultural canon. In the 1990s, Cazdyn argues, a new, "transformative" mode of literary adaptation that "seeks to delink and deterritorialize the adaptation from the original" parallels a challenge to the centrality of nation presented by the rise of transnational corporatism.[22] Similarly, we can examine the selective exercise of fidelity—the film's regard for certain aspects of the source text and its disregard of others—in postwar adaptations of Osaka literature to discover not only the hypotext's usefulness to the film but, more broadly, Osaka's usefulness to the postwar national imaginary. The following analyses of source novels and film adaptations, then, are undertaken not in an effort to evaluate the success or failure of an adaptation but to consider and compare differences in the representation of Osaka and thus better understand the deployment of the local in postwar cinema.

WAGA MACHI

Many postwar adaptations take liberties with the time setting of their source novel's prewar or wartime story. Often this has the effect of distancing the story from commercially impractical aspects of Japan's recent history. In Oda's 1942 novel *Waga machi* (discussed in chapter 3), for example, the story begins in the Philippines around 1901 and ends in 1941, with the news that Japanese forces have invaded those islands. Kawashima's adaptation shifts most of the action to the postwar. The early episodes in the Philippines are still set at the turn of the century, but they are dispatched hastily in voiceover, as the pages of a history book turn to show animated illustrations depicting events there. This awkward device relegates to memory the activities of Japanese immigrants in the Philippines and the Japanese state's imperial ambitions there, removing them from the film's reality. It also severs the link between local Osaka and the South Seas, which grounds the novel's exploration of the discourse of imperial transcendence; in the film adaptation, those two locales exist in different visual realms. The war itself Kawashima dispatches with an intertitle, after which comes an image of doves circling Osaka Castle on a bright new day as Takichi, in the foreground, pulls a GI in his rickshaw. The film thus repurposes a scene from the novel that held very different significance there. In the novel, Takichi returns from the Philippines to Japan in the early years of the twentieth century, entering through Kobe. He immediately takes a job there as a rickshaw driver, planning to work for a year and save some money before returning to his family in Osaka. That plan ends abruptly after just three months, when, for no apparent reason, he overturns his rickshaw, dumping his passenger, an American, to the ground in front of a hotel. The scene suggests a festering resentment of the U.S. presence in Asia, born of Takichi's experiences in the Philippines. In the film, on the other hand, as the American (now a GI in occupation-era Osaka) urges him to move faster, Takichi merely grumbles, then bears down. In one sense, the transposition of the scene highlights the continuity from prewar to postwar of a U.S. presence perceived as overbearing. The change in Takichi's response, however—from prewar swagger to postwar subservience—suggests a reluctance to confront this aspect of recent history.[23]

ŌSAKA NO YADO

Changes to the time setting may, on the other hand, enable a director to address the effects of the war. This is the case with Gosho's adaptation of *Ōsaka no yado.* The source novel, written by Minakami Takitarō and published in 1925, deals with the struggles of the contemporary urban lower classes in the interwar era as witnessed by an office worker in an insurance firm who takes a room in a cheap inn after being transferred from Tokyo to the Osaka office. For the film, Gosho, who worked throughout his career to dramatize the social conditions of the lower classes, moves the story forward to the present day, when the war's aftermath has compounded their struggles.[24] The characters in the film make candid reference to Japan's defeat. In a key scene—one of the few relatively happy moments in a film filled with sorrow—the main character, Mita, takes two maids from the inn on a picnic in the precincts of Osaka Castle. As the women discuss their lives, one remarks with offhanded bitterness that she sometimes thinks it would have been better if all the men had died in the war. In another scene, Mita talks with a male colleague who refers to Mita and himself as "*santō jūyaku*," or third-rate executives. This term, popularized by the Osaka author Genji Keita, became a buzzword in postwar Japan, used to describe those salarymen who had been promoted beyond their true abilities after General Headquarters forced a purge of corporate executives thought to have acted in complicity with the military state.[25] Taken up by the mass media and by Gosho here, "*santō jūyaku*" came to define a generation of corporate managers and their sense of insufficiency. In such asides, *Ōsaka no yado* links urban dissatisfaction to the war and suggests a transwar continuity with the earlier conditions that Minakami's novel detailed.[26]

MEOTO ZENZAI

Another film that meddles with the time setting of its source text, and in a seemingly gratuitous way, is Toyoda Shirō's 1955 adaptation of Oda Sakunosuke's *Meoto zenzai* (Sweet beans for two), and this film invites a more extended consideration for several reasons.[27] First of all, Oda's novel, discussed in chapter 2, has primary significance for the subject of Osaka in the Japanese imagination. Second, the film was a great critical and popular success. Its director, Toyoda Shirō, was a leading exponent of Osaka film and of postwar *eiga-ka* in general. As previously noted, in addition to *Meoto zenzai* (and a 1962 sequel), Toyoda adapted Tanizaki's *Neko to Shōzō to futari no onna* and Yamasaki's *Hana noren*. His non-Osaka films include adaptations of important works by Mori Ōgai, Arishima Takeo, Murō Saisei, and Shiga Naoya.[28] *Meoto zenzai* also boasts a superlative cast of actors closely associated with Osaka. These include Morishige Hisaya and Awashima Chikage, who star as Ryūkichi and Chōko, the couple at the center of the story, and Naniwa Chieko as O-Kin, who runs the contract-geisha service for which Chōko works. The film garnered three Blue Ribbon awards—for best director, best actor, and best actress—and Mainichi Concours awards for best actor and best screenplay. It ranked second on *Kinema junpō*'s annual top-ten list for 1955, and thirty-first on that journal's 1999 list of the best 100 Japanese films of all time. Finally, the differences between novel and film versions of *Meoto zenzai* raise issues that will inform the discussion of *Noren* that follows.

Toyoda's film suggests from the very start that it is reimagining Oda's local story through national eyes. The opening titles run over a series of illustrations of representative Osaka sights. The first depicts the statue of the plump, jolly folk character Otafuku that stands outside the titular snack shop in Dōtonbori, near the shrine at Hōzen-ji. The shop and statue are mentioned in the final scene of Oda's novel, and they also figure prominently in a well-known earlier short story, Kamizukasa Shōken's "Hamo no kawa" (The skin of the pike conger eel, 1914). The use of the illustration in the film's opening would therefore have indicated to some portion of the audience not only the film's setting but also its literary antecedents. The use of illustration rather than photography underscores this literariness; this is a frankly represented, storybook Osaka. The next illustrations show buildings beside a canal, presumably the Dōtonbori, crossed by bridges; whitewashed warehouses; tenements; and then the front of the restaurant Izumoya—a local landmark that Oda mentions in his story. All of these would suggest to a local audience the southern part of the city. The final illustration addresses a wider national audience, offering a panoramic view of city rooftops and, looming above them in the distance, Osaka Castle, a nationally recognized landmark. A superimposed title then indicates the year: "Showa nana-nen no koro" ("Around Shōwa 7," or 1932).

This approach to Osaka differs markedly from that of Oda's novel, in which we enter at street level, *in media res*. "There were always bill collectors hanging about," the first sentence reads, before shifting to a description of Chōko's father, Tanekichi, standing at the entrance to an alley, frying tempura. The first line of dialogue, spoken in unmistakable Osaka dialect, establishes the setting: "Ossan, hayo gonbo ageten kai na" (Mister, hurry up and fry some burdock!).[29] The film, by contrast, enters Osaka with more ceremony, from above, swooping down and in from the panoramic illustration of Osaka Castle to an illustration of the Koreyasu shop front, which fades into a camera shot of the shop itself. The film returns to that superior perspective several times, in overhead establishing shots of Hōzen-ji Yokochō and other downtown neighborhoods.

Many postwar film adaptations establish their setting through the use of these devices: the montage of local sites, the panoramic shot of the city, and the supertitle. Abe's 1950 adaptation of Tanizaki's *Sasameyuki*, for example, begins with an aerial panning shot of Nakanoshima, an island in the Yodogawa that flows through central Osaka, showing the architecturally distinctive public library and the city hall (locations that do not figure in the story at all). The next shot shows the river in the foreground, barges passing under the Suishōbashi bridge, as a superimposed title appears: "Ōsaka Shōwa 12-nen [1937]." The film then cuts to an exterior shot of an old house in the Japanese style and another title identifying the neighborhood as "Uehonmachi 9-chōme [Ninth Ward]." Again, it is a far less subtle approach than that of the novel, which, like Oda's, establishes the setting indirectly through dialogue; the first word of *Sasameyuki*, "Koi-san," is a term peculiar to Senba households, where it was used to address the youngest daughter.

Similarly, Ichikawa's adaptation of Yamasaki's *Bonchi* begins with a quick-cut montage of city images, including a detail of Osaka Castle; a shot of the Glico "Running Man," the massive neon sign that hangs along the Dōtonbori advertising the Osaka-based confectionary company; and then a low-angle shot of Osaka's landmark tower, Tsūtenkaku. Again, this differs from Yamasaki's novel, which, like Oda's and Tanizaki's, establishes the setting through the use of dialect. Just a few sentences into the story, the *bonchi* of the title asks a servant, "Dō yanen, mise no hō wa?" (How are things going in the shop?), and we know immediately that we are in Osaka.[30] Clichés of the period drama and the travelogue, the opening montage and panoramic shot, together with the supertitle identifying the setting, betray an impatience to locate the story immediately and precisely, rather than allowing the audience to figure it out. These devices also highlight the otherness of the setting. In these films, they suggest that Osaka has become strange or distant to a postwar audience, and in *Meoto zenzai* in particular, these devices utterly divorce the visual narrative's point of view from its object in a way quite contrary to the source novel's descriptive passages. The use of a supertitle to indicate the reign year of the story (as in *Meoto zenzai* and *Sasameyuki*) also betrays an eagerness to fix the story in time in a way that contains it within national history.

The superimposed title at the beginning of *Meoto zenzai* indicating the time setting as 1932 introduces another fundamental difference with the novel. There, although the Osaka setting is clear from the first line, the exact time setting is ambiguous throughout the first chapter. The chapter is studded with the names of actual shops and restaurants, but most are businesses of long standing, whose presence would not indicate a precise year or even decade. This ambiguity lends the town and the protagonists who inhabit it a timelessness very different from the specificity of the film's opening title. More to the point, the time setting that the film establishes so immediately and so specifically is different from the one eventually established in the novel. There, as Ryūkichi and Chōko are stopping at the hot springs resort of Atami on their way home after a jaunt in Tokyo, they suddenly feel the earth tremble: it is an earthquake. Train service is disrupted. Eventually, the couple catch a special train transporting victims and make their way back to Osaka, where newspaper extras are reporting a catastrophic earthquake in the Kantō region. This episode unmistakably refers to the Great Kantō Earthquake and allows us to date the opening of the novel to 1923—nine years earlier than the date given at the start of the film and a very different historical moment.

The novel appeared in 1941, looking back on a period that begins in 1923 and ends around 1936. The film appeared in 1955, looking back on a seemingly shorter period that begins in 1932. In terms of national history, then, the two versions of the story are set on either side of an acute shift in national politics, from liberalization to militarization. The early 1920s, when the novel begins, represents the height of "Taishō democracy," a period that witnessed the brief ascendancy of political party rule, the expansion of suffrage, and the legalization of unions. The 1930s, when the film begins, saw the reversal of these liberalizing tendencies, the rise of violent ultranationalism, the expansion of state control, and the escalation of imperial adventurism. In particular, the year blazoned across the screen at the start of the film marks the beginning of a national state of exception (*hijōji*) that, as Alan Tansman writes, "transformed Japan into a place of eternal crisis."[31]

Just as the novel and film look back at two very different moments in national history, so, too, do they look back at distinct moments in Japan's urban history and in the relationship between its two largest cities. The novel is set at precisely the moment when Osaka's gradual subordination to Tokyo briefly reverses. The Great Kantō Earthquake decimated the capital, prompting an exodus of people, capital, and industry. In that same year, Osaka gained a visionary and capable leader in its new mayor, Seki Hajime. A year and a half later, in 1925, Seki expanded the city's borders to make Osaka the largest city in the nation and the sixth largest in the world, ushering in the era of "Great Osaka." The film, on the other hand, is set at the end of Osaka's brief ascendency. The year 1932 marks Tokyo's substantial recovery from the effects of the earthquake, as the capital expanded its own borders to reclaim the title of Japan's largest city. As noted in chapter 2, Oda's story largely ignores—even denies—the geographical as well as historical contexts of state and nation; the story unfolds within an oddly self-contained and timeless urban chronotope, sealed against events beyond its boundaries. The brief mention of the Great Kantō Earthquake near the beginning only highlights this quality, relativizing Tokyo to an Osaka that is central to the novel's world, as if to say that, whatever cataclysm may have occurred off in the political capital, life went on in the merchant capital. By retaining the scene of the earthquake but changing the year, the film muddles the historical reference and eliminates the association with Osaka's ascendency. At the same time, by bannering the year 1932—a year with strong associations of centralized state power, particularly for an audience in the immediate postwar era—the film relativizes Oda's story to national history, wrapping the city within a larger narrative of militarization and war.

The other key difference introduced by Toyoda's film adaptation is subtler and more pervasive: several changes combine to deemphasize the economics of Oda's novel and turn the film into a more conventional romance, with Chōko alone at its center. First, the film deemphasizes the couple's business activities and Ryūkichi's frustration of Chōko's financial ambitions. In the novel, Ryūkichi sabotages three of the couple's business ventures (and loses another job due to laziness). In the film, however, we see only one business failure, the *Kanto-daki* shop, along with their final success, the café. Though a few scenes mention money, the running account of debits and credits that keeps Oda's story focused on the economies of Chōko and Ryūkichi's relationship finds no equivalent in the adaptation. Moreover, in the novel, the *Kanto-daki* shop fails because Ryūkichi cannot control himself around alcohol, but in the film, its failure is due more to his worsening health than to indolence or intemperance.

The film makes Ryūkichi a more conventionally attractive romantic object, who does not seem mentally weak in the way that the Ryūkichi of Oda's novel does. Morishige has suggested that this was intentional: the actor writes in his memoirs that he was concerned about making his character more appealing, and chose to play him with an endearing, childlike charm. At the same time, the film introduces another side to Ryūkichi. As the Osaka author Fujii Shigeo notes in a contemporary review, several scenes set in and around the Senba house show us a rougher, more aggressive character who is nowhere to be found in the novel: a "hooligan" who extorts his young daughter, curses out his father and then demands a glass of water, storms out of his father's funeral service, and snarls at his uncle.[32] This forceful Ryūkichi is utterly unlike the yielding and submissive bonbon of Oda's novel.

The most salient feature of Ryūkichi's recharacterization is the elimination of his stutter. The novel carefully inscribes this speech impediment; when Ryūkichi takes Chōko out to one of his favorite cheap food stalls, for example, he says to her, "Do-, do-, doya, umai yaro ga, ko-, ko-, konna umai mon doko i itta ka te taberarehen ze," or, roughly, "Wha-, wha-, what do you think of that? Delicious, right? You won't find anything this g-, g-, good anywhere else!"[33] His stutter is presented in this way throughout the novel. This impediment suggests Ryūkichi's unsuitability to the work of a merchant, for whom loquacity and verbal acuity—cajoling, badgering, and bargaining—are considered to be both characteristic and necessary. It also suggests a fundamental incompatibility with Chōko's economic aspirations. Morishige, however, delivers his lines fluently, smoothing over that incompatibility.

The film underscores its adaptation of Ryūkichi into a more romantic character by expanding the role of his brother-in-law as a foil. The novel mentions this character only briefly, explaining that he is adopted into the family to take over the business in place of Ryūkichi. In the film, he becomes a more fully developed character. Frugal and fastidious, impatient but self-controlled, he manifests all the self-discipline that Ryūkichi lacks but in a way that makes him suspect and unlikable. When Ryūkichi's sister confides to Chōko that her husband "likes everything to be clean—almost obsessively so. And so I'm cleaning from morning to night" (a line original to the film), Chōko pities the browbeaten girl, as we are meant to do. Set beside this ill-tempered brother-in-law, the Ryūkichi of the film seems far more sympathetic.

With these changes, the film deemphasizes Ryūkichi's practice of unproductive expenditure and dulls the edge of Chōko's affection for him—an affection that the novel presents as irrational within the productivist economy of the militarist state. Though the film, like Oda's novel, depicts Ryūkichi as lazy, it does not show him repeatedly draining Chōko's savings and frustrating her ambitions. Compared to her desire for the Ryūkichi of the novel, Chōko's desire for the more conventionally masculine and sympathetic Ryūkichi of the film seems less perverse, less a self-sabotage of her state-sanctioned impulses to economic productivity and bourgeois propriety. By adapting Ryūkichi into a more ordinary male lead, the film dilutes the distinctively local masculinity of the bonbon, whose weakness and inutility Oda's novel described at a moment of convulsive nationalism.

NOREN, THE FILM

We find similar strategies at work in the film adaptation of *Noren*, directed by Kawashima Yūzō.[34] Although his name may not arise immediately in discussions of *eiga-ka*, Kawashima directed several excellent adaptations, including a 1962 adaptation of Mizukami Tsutomu's Naoki Prize–winning novel *Gan no tera* (Temple of the wild geese, 1961). For *Noren*, Kawashima gathered an impressive cast of Osaka actors, headed by Morishige, Yamada Isuzu, and Otowa Nobuko. Although the resulting film was not the unqualified hit that Toyoda's *Meoto zenzai* was, it ranked twenty-fifth on *Kinema junpō*'s list of best movies in a year crowded with good and great films. Like Toyoda's film, Kawashima's

Noren places an emphasis on romance and alters the chronology of the source novel's story.

First, Kawashima's film fundamentally restructures the first half of Yamasaki's story as a romantic triangle involving Gohei; his childhood sweetheart, O-Matsu, whom he meets when he comes to the Naniwa-ya as an apprentice; and O-Chiyo, the master's niece, whom Gohei is destined to marry in a financially advantageous match arranged by the master. A film poster plays up this triangle, showing Morishige as Gohei flanked by Otowa as O-Matsu and Yamada as O-Chiyo. The frustrated love between Gohei and O-Matsu resurfaces in the second half and in the next generation, when O-Matsu's daughter charms Gohei's son, Kōhei. This restructured storyline necessitates a vast expansion of O-Matsu's role. She appears only briefly at the beginning of Yamasaki's novel and is incidental to its story; there is no suggestion that Gohei harbors any special feelings for her and no mention of a daughter. In the film, early scenes show a friendship developing between Gohei and O-Matsu as children. Later, O-Matsu goes to work for Gohei in the shop he opens, and a scene there establishes the grown-up O-Matsu's charming but problematic character. Returning to the shop to find two unsupervised apprentices trimming *konbu*, scraps littering the floor, O-Matsu picks up a broom and blithely sweeps the scraps into the street. When Gohei arrives, the sight of the precious *konbu* lying in the dirt outrages him. The scene sets up a clear contrast between love and business: the winsome O-Matsu is a questionable marriage prospect from a business standpoint; O-Chiyo is the opposite: aloof but business minded, and a savvy alliance.

The climax to this romance comes at the annual Tōka Ebisu festival, where Osakans honor the god of commerce and pray for prosperity in the new year. On festival day, the old master summons Gohei to the main house and expresses his wish that Gohei marry O-Chiyo. Gohei tries to explain that he loves someone else, but the master and his wife quickly put a stop to such talk. Coming out of the meeting, Gohei heads to the festival and finds O-Matsu there. As festival music plays and the pressing crowds in the temple precinct chant "Shōbai hanjō de sasa motte koi" (So that business will thrive, fetch the bamboo), O-Matsu smiles bravely and congratulates Gohei. He protests and tries to explain his feelings, but she runs away. As he chases after her, they are separated by a procession of men carrying a festival palanquin—the two lovers driven apart by Ebisu, the god of merchant ambition. After this scene, Gohei marries the master's niece, O-Chiyo. Their wedding night gets off to a rocky start, but they quickly find a common interest in entrepreneurial plans for expanding the business.

The film contrasts this prewar story of romance sacrificed to pragmatism with a postwar story of romance fulfilled. In the second half of the film, Gohei and O-Chiyo try to encourage a romance between their son Kōhei and O-Matsu's daughter, but Kōhei ignores them and chooses his own bride. That contrast, too, is new: in Yamasaki's novel, both generations, Gohei and his son Kōhei, agree without any difficulty to marriages arranged on the basis of the advantageous connections they bring. The film thus rehearses the conflict between responsibility and desire, but this time with a different ending. In this way, Kawashima's *Noren* relegates the practice of arranged marriage to the prewar world of the Osaka merchant and links the modern love match, with its associations of individual subjectivity and personal choice, to the Tokyo-centric postwar world. The film thus introduces to the story a sharp contrast between local traditionalism and national modernity, with the war as the dividing line.

Second, to support this contrast, Kawashima's *Noren* distorts the chronology of economic change. As noted earlier, the novel has the Naniwa-ya begin selling its products through department stores before the war. After opening its first counter in the Mitsukoshi at Kōraibashi, the Naniwa-ya opens a second in the new Hankyū Department Store in Umeda, in north Osaka—like the Mitsukoshi, an actual store, one that opened in 1929. In the film, however, this development must wait until the postwar. Kōhei (not Gohei) opens the Naniwa-ya's first postwar shop, in a new department store being built in Umeda. Immediately preceding a scene of father and son arguing over the location, we see a shot of a street with what looks like a U.S. military jeep passing by; "For Sale" is written on its side, suggesting that the year is around 1952, the end of U.S. occupation on the main island. After their argument, the scene cuts to an overhead shot of postwar Umeda with the Hanshin Department Store on the right side of the frame, its sign clearly legible. This store in fact opened in 1951.

Whereas in the novel the father identifies and pursues this new market as one in a string of innovations, in the film it is the son who pursues it against the father's protests. By altering the chronology, the film associates the growth of consumer culture exclusively with the postwar generation and the postwar economy, contrasting that period with the prewar era. At the same time, the film deemphasizes the war itself, moving abruptly from pre- to postwar and largely ignoring the wartime control economy. The film thus minimizes the central economic lesson of

Yamasaki's novel: that Osaka's subordination was dictated by central planners in Tokyo. The shift in economic power from Osaka to Tokyo remains, but the cause is elided, naturalizing the process of national centralization.

The most significant change, however, is that the film reframes *Noren* as one man's life story by keeping the father alive until the end. In the novel, Gohei dies early in the second book; most of the Naniwa-ya's postwar success is realized by Kōhei on his own. In the film, the father lives to witness (and meddle in) his son's innovations and the shop's revival. While the novel, by tracing the career of one master, his death, and then another master's career, narrates Osaka's modern history as a tale of death and regeneration, the movie reframes the narrative, containing the son's story of revival within the framing narrative of the father's decline.

In short, the film's introduction of a love triangle shifts the story's focus from economics to romance and from a social class to individuals, and its reordering of history and heightening of generational contrasts relegate Osaka as local space to tradition, reserving modernity to Tokyo as the space of nation. As the representative of the earlier generation, the father—an innovator in Yamasaki's novel—becomes an embodiment of tradition. By keeping him alive, the film emphasizes his increasing anachronism. His lingering presence seems to contradict a narrative of Osaka's regeneration: How can the son mature into the Naniwa-ya's master while the old master lives? How can the new corporate economy occupy the same time and space as the outmoded merchant economy? Unable to regenerate, the Naniwa-ya must instead graduate to a new economic order centered in Tokyo. The cumulative effect of these changes is to turn Yamasaki's story into a narrative of national progress.

In this way, cinema reclaims the subject position for the nation. Writing of the challenges facing a minor cinema, Gilles Deleuze notes that "the cinematic author finds himself before a people which, from the point of view of culture, is doubly colonized: colonized by stories that have come from elsewhere, but also by their own myths become impersonal entities at the service of the colonizer."[35] While recognizing the great differences between the colonial condition and the condition of the local city in a highly centralized state economy, we can at the same time apprehend a similar process at work where a national cinema takes up local stories, such as Oda's and Yamasaki's, and adapts them for an audience (imagined to be) centered in the capital. Decisions to deemphasize the story of business development and social relations in favor of romance, and to smooth out the contradictions that local history introduces to national history, effectively draft the source novel into the service of recentralization.

The Star's Authenticity

Chapter 1 examined the competing values of mastery and authenticity: the mastery of the local that Tanizaki demonstrated through his ethnographic approach to describing Osakans' language, customs, sensibilities, and character, combined with his frank acknowledgment of outsider status, both as narrator in his novels and as author in his public life; and, on the other hand, the authenticity that Osaka writers asserted to support their criticism of Tanizaki. Writers such as Oda and Yamasaki assert authenticity in their fiction, too, through their self-ethnographic description—especially their rendering of local speech, presented without the narrative distancing that we find in Tanizaki's work. Does that authenticity survive the process of adaptation? I have argued here that differences introduced in the process of adaptation from novel to film draft stories into a national narrative. How might a star's performance of authentic locality undermine this nationalization of plot?

A novel's signifiers of authenticity transfer to film in various ways. The audience's foreknowledge of the source text and the public image of its author, including his or her personal history and oeuvre, play a part. For instance, Oda's status as a favorite son of Osaka, strengthened by his untimely death, likely influenced the reception of Toyoda's adaptation of *Meoto zenzai*. This transference, though, depends on how faithful the adaptation is perceived to be. The director's public image, too, may lend authenticity to a film adaptation—the audience's awareness, for example, that a director has already adapted other novels by the same author, or directed other films set in the same milieu. A film also gains authenticity for its representation of local space by shooting on location when that fact is recognized by audiences. The use of local amateurs, again readily identified or promoted as such, can likewise lend authenticity, as in Kinoshita Keisuke's casting of local children in *Nijūshi no hitomi* (Twenty-four eyes, 1954). (Of course, the contrast with such locals can also expose the artifice of the professional actors who share the screen with them.) From such intertexts, a film that purports to represent a particular place accrues power to claim that its representation of that place is not only realistic but authentic.

Perhaps the most important element for establishing the authenticity of a local film, however, is the star. Biography and filmography may influence an audience's willingness to accept a star in a particular role and enhance the pleasure they take in his or her performance. Certainly we see this at work in Osaka films of the 1950s and early 1960s, in which a certain group of stars and supporting actors born or trained in and around Osaka turn up again and again, functioning almost as an informal repertory company. Yamada Isuzu (1917–2012), one of the greatest stars of Japanese cinema, was born in Osaka and appeared in many films set in Kansai, including Mizoguchi Kenji's prewar classics *Naniwa erejī* (Osaka elegy, 1936) and *Gion no shimai* (Sisters of the Gion, 1937), the latter set in Kyoto. In the postwar era, she appears in *Neko to Shōzō to futari no onna*, *Noren*, and *Bonchi*, among others. Otowa Nobuko (1924–94), born in Tottori Prefecture and raised in Osaka, stars in *Noren*, *Hana noren*, and *Kashima ari*. Awashima Chikage (1924–2012), who stars as Chōko in *Meoto zenzai* and appears in *Hana noren* and *Kashima ari*, was not born or raised in Osaka but was trained at the Takarazuka Music School, in a suburb of Osaka, from the age of fifteen and later joined the Takarazuka Revue. Then there is Morishige (1913–2009), who became perhaps the most familiar fixture of Osaka films, starring in *Neko to Shōzō to futari no onna*, *Meoto zenzai*, *Noren*, and *Hana noren*, as well as Ozu Yasujirō's Kansai film (from an original screenplay), *Kohayagawa-ke no aki* (The autumn of the Kohayagawa family, 1961; released in the United States as *The End of Summer*).

In addition to these stars, talented character actors brought to supporting roles their native fluency with Osaka speech and, in some cases, an authenticity legible in their very names. The inimitable Naniwa Chieko (1907–73) appears in *Noren* as the mistress of the Naniwa-ya in the earlier generation; she also appears in *Neko to Shōzō to futari no onna*, *Meoto zenzai*, *Kashima ari*, and *Kohayagawa-ke no aki*, owning the category of the no-nonsense middle-aged Osaka woman (a type that remains closely associated with the city). Naniwa also played many non-Osaka roles over a long, distinguished career. She has a brief turn in Mizoguchi Kenji's masterpiece *Sanshō dayū* (Sansho the bailiff, 1954), for example, and she plays the leader of a group of comfort women in Kawashima's *Gurama-tō no yūwaku* (Temptation on Glamor Island, 1959). Nevertheless, her renown was tied to the locale specified in her stage name, Naniwa, and to the local voice that she could never completely suppress. Nakamura Ganjirō II (1902–83), who appears in *Noren* as Naniwa's husband, the prewar master of the Naniwa-ya, as well as in *Bonchi* and *Kohayagawa-ke no aki*, also carried a name that signaled Osaka to audiences. Ganjirō II was part of a dynasty of kabuki actors in the Kamigata style associated with the Kyoto-Osaka region. As such, his name was a potent symbol of resistance to Tokyo's cultural hegemony: the demise of the more restrained Kamigata style of kabuki known as *wagoto* is often dated to the death of his father, Nakamura Ganjirō I, and its revival is credited to Ganjirō II's son. Another fixture of these films is the Osaka native Sazanka Kyū (1914–71), who appears in *Meoto zenzai*, *Neko to Shōzō to futari no onna*, *Noren*, *Hana noren*, *Kashima ari*, and *Kohayagawa-ke no aki*. Sazanka's stage name also subtly links him to the city. Although written with different characters, it is a close homonym for a line from the multiplication tables—"sazan ga kyū" (three threes are nine)—suggesting Osaka's merchant history and the fascination with figures that Saikaku and Oda identified as characteristic of the city. It also suggests the sort of roles the actor often played: Sazanka is the fastidious brother-in-law who takes over the family business in *Meoto zenzai*, the young master in *Noren*, and a clerk in *Kohayagawa-ke no aki*.

Richard Dyer, in his seminal study *Stars*, examined how film stars' images influence our understanding of identity, arguing that the star image helps resolve ideological tensions of the age. In *Heavenly Bodies*, he elaborates this argument, writing, "We're fascinated by stars because they enact ways of making sense of the experience of being a person in a particular kind of social production (capitalism) with its particular organization of life into public and private spheres."[36] In Japanese modernity, increasingly in the transwar period and particularly at the time of Japanese film's postwar golden age, one critical aspect of that division between public and private was the division between national and local selves. Thus, in addition to Dyer's considerations of gender, class, and race, we can examine locality in order to understand how the stars of that golden age influenced audiences' perceptions of themselves and broader society.

Authenticity was a key factor in this function of the star image. The authenticity that accrued to these stars and that they brought to the films in which they appeared results from a combination of performance and public image. These actors' native (or, in Awashima's case, native-like) facility with the distinctive Osaka dialect and their familiarity with other cultural specificities beyond grammar, vocabulary, and intonation—including tone of voice, pitch, volume, and pace of speech; posture, gesture, and speed of movement; facial expression; and so on—identify them as authentic. More generally, the audience's foreknowledge of actors' Osaka connections lends a sense of authenticity to the performance. Fans' foreknowledge that Yamada and Morishige were natives of Osaka who lived through the war, for instance, likely intensifies their appreciation of a key scene in *Noren* in which the two actors, playing an elderly married couple, walk through the ruins of the firebombed city—their city. The fact that the two played another Osaka couple three years earlier in Makino Masahiro's *Jinsei tonbogaeri* (Life is like a somersault) also contributes to that appreciation. To what degree are we watching the characters' pain and their tenderness toward each other, and to what degree the stars'?

Examining the function of authenticity in the production of the star image, Dyer has argued that "authenticity is both a quality necessary to the star phenomenon to make it work, and also the quality that guarantees the authenticity of the other particular values a star embodies (such as girl-next-door-ness, etc.). It is this effect of authenticating authenticity that gives the star charisma."[37] As an example of this process, Dyer details how Judy Garland's performance in *A Star Is Born* authenticates the "charisma" or "star power" that Garland's character, Vicki Lester, must be seen to possess. Analyzing the pivotal scene in which Judy/Vicki sings "The Man That Got Away," Dyer argues that Garland's bravura delivery of the song does not, in and of itself, suffice to authenticate her "talent" for the purposes of the star image, and that the film "has to marshal markers of authenticity" indicating that the performance is uncontrolled, unpremeditated, and private, thus asserting the authenticity necessary to secure the fundamentally unstable star image.[38] The artifice of Judy/Vicki's deployment—what Dyer calls a "rhetoric of authenticity"—paradoxically authenticates her talent as "born," not made.

What Morishige, Otowa, Awashima, and other stars embody for Osaka films is, first of all, "Osaka-ness," and then, more abstractly, that urban locality, characteristic of Osaka, that resists (or at least resents) subsumption within a national identity. Their performance of that quality must be secured against not only the inherent instability of the star image but also the increasing instability of local identity in the postwar era. The prominence that Osaka enjoyed in the 1910s and late 1920s ends with militarization, the shift to heavy industry, and the institution of a control economy. The occupation offers a brief reprieve, as SCAP pursues decentralization, but as previously noted, the end of the occupation brings an emphatic recentralization. By the mid-1950s, the political, economic, and cultural forces of national subjectification have cast into doubt the authenticity of local identity in most of its manifestations: by the postwar, is "Osaka-ness" anything more than a nostalgic performance in which necessarily national subjects indulge? In response, the locality of the star itself (like Garland's charisma) became a powerful signifier, but one that required continual rhetorical authentication. The performed authenticity of local stars buttressed Osaka identity.

Performing Locality

No one more successfully performed this function than Morishige Hisaya (1913–2009), who was the consummate Osaka film actor and at the same time indisputably one of Japan's great *national* stars. Born in the city of Hirakata in Osaka Prefecture, Morishige moved to Tokyo to attend Waseda University but dropped out to act. He became an announcer with NHK (Nippon Hōsō Kyōkai, the Japanese Broadcasting Corporation) in 1939 and was posted to Manchuria. NHK was and is a bastion of standard Japanese language, much as the BBC used to be for British English, and by becoming an announcer there, Morishige demonstrated his overcoming of the local voice. He continued with NHK after the war and, in 1950, became cohost of a regular music program, *Yukai na nakama* (Delightful companions). In the meantime, Morishige had moved into film, making his screen debut in 1947 in *Joyū* (Actress). His big break in film came with *Santō jūyaku* (Third-rate executives, 1952), adapted from Genji Keita's best-selling novel, and its three sequels (1952–53). Then, in 1955, Morishige vaulted to a new level of stardom, appearing in eighteen films in one year and winning the Mainichi Concours award for best actor for four of them—*Meoto zenzai*, *Jinsei tonbogaeri*, *Keisatsu nikki* (A policeman's diary), and *Wataridori itsu kaeru* (When will the migratory bird return?)—as well as the Blue Ribbon best-actor award for *Meoto zenzai*. He went on to star in two of the definitive film series of the postwar era, both long-running comedy series produced by Tōhō: the *Shachō* (Company president) series, which, together with four new *Santō jūyaku* films (1959–60), ran to forty films between 1956 and 1971; and the *Ekimae* (In front of the station) series of twenty-four films between 1958 and 1969.[39] Altogether, over his long and prolific career, Morishige appeared in more than 250 films.[40] At the same time, he built a highly successful career on the stage, where his signature roles included the title role in *Sadojima Takichi no shōgai* (The Life of Sadojima Takichi), an adaptation of Oda Sakunosuke's *Waga machi* (Tatsumi Ryūtarō starred in the film version), and Tevye in *Fiddler on the Roof* (Yane no ue no baiorin-hiki). He also published many popular collections of essays and memoirs and performed in radio and television dramas.

During his early career, Morishige came to personify the *dame-otoko* (no-good guy), which was representative of Osaka in postwar cinema. His body pale and soft; his posture slack; his expression by turns ingratiating, petulant, and sheepish; his voice now whiny, now wheedling, the *dame-otoko* expresses an undisciplined masculinity with literary antecedents in the bonbon discussed in earlier chapters. Unrepresentable in the heavily censored media of wartime (though the notion circulated even then of the unfit Osaka soldier; see chapter 2), he resurfaces in postwar cinema. We do not find the *dame-otoko* among the small number of major "social types" that Dyer addressed in his original analysis of the star image—the "good Joe," the rebel, the independent woman, the pin-up, and so on. But Andrew Spicer, looking outside Hollywood to British cinema, has proposed adding several types to Dyer's list, including two alternative masculinities, "Fools and Rogues," that help us recognize the potential in Morishige's performances. Spicer writes,

> Both Fools and Rogues occupy a liminal, licensed space on the margins of society for "unacceptable" masculine traits, which can include deviousness and incompetence. Their ideological function varies, but they can be empowering for subordinated groups as their resourcefulness, ingenuity and resilience often expose the arbitrariness of social systems.[41]

The language of liminality and marginality may confuse the issue when applied to Osaka; the *dame-otoko* is central to urban society and a full participant in cultural negotiations over ideas of masculinity. Spicer's point about "the arbitrariness of social systems," on the other hand, applies fully to this Osaka character.

As perhaps the best known of all *dame-otoko*—Ryūkichi in *Meoto zenzai*—Morishige authenticates the Osaka-ness of both his character and his star image with a performance of local language as native language. Morishige was not unaware of the language politics that informed his performance. He had campaigned energetically for the role of Ryūkichi, going so far as to perform an impromptu read-through of Oda's novel for the director Toyoda over drinks one night. In a memoir, the actor recalls his excitement at winning the role and his determination to demonstrate through his performance the potential of the local language. "I was eager to emancipate *Ōsaka-ben*," he writes, "which had for quite some time been held in contempt by the people of Edo, from a 'dialect complex' (*hōgen konpurekkusu*) and insert it into the language of Japan (*nihon no kotoba ni irete yaru*)."[42] Note Morishige's allusion to the historical roots of Osaka's present condition in his use of "Edo" rather than "Tokyo." Morishige manifests this determination in his performance, which signals the authenticity of his local identity through a combination of markers like those Dyer identifies in Garland's authentication of "talent": uncontrolled, unpremeditated, and private.

From the very start, Morishige's delivery of his lines is characterized by his distracted manner. The first time we see Ryūkichi, in the film's second scene, he bustles into the room of the inn at Atami in a burst of dialect, grumbling about the resort town in a bit of business original to the film. Talking half to himself, he continues his grumbling as he settles into a seat on the balcony and then moves to a low table and begins to squirm as Chōko combs his hair. In a pivotal later scene, in which Ryūkichi returns to Chōko after a long absence spent at the Umeda Shinmichi, he grumbles as he wriggles out of his rain-soaked kimono and lets Chōko dry him off and dress him, then collapses on the floor and begins crooning softly. As the two of them begin scheming to open a restaurant, excitement overcomes him, but as the scene ends, he is whining again, this time that he is hungry. When illness confines him to a hospital bed, he grows petulant. On a visit to the main house, he throws a tantrum. This lack of emotional control is consonant with the undisciplined character of the bonbon, but Morishige's annoyed, distracted delivery also marks the flow of local speech as private, spontaneous, and authentic.

The film also frames Morishige's performance within situations that show Ryūkichi behaving like a child. He interrupts some children in the street who are playing at having tea and asks to join their game. After they leave, Chōko finds him there. As Ryūkichi picks up the toy teapot and plays at pouring tea, she scolds, "You're just like a child, aren't you!" Again, at the restaurant Jiyūken, when Chōko offers Ryūkichi her handkerchief to wipe his mouth and he offers his face for her to wipe, she teases, "Oh! You're like a baby!" This childishness lends an unpremeditated quality to the actor's verbal performance of a language not yet trained to national identity.

These qualities of distraction, annoyance, and childishness constitute a rhetoric of authenticity that supports Morishige's Osaka-ness. This rhetoric would have accorded with the knowledge of the actor's Osaka roots that much of the audience brought to the film. In addition, Morishige's reputation for ad-libbing, earned early in his career, supported this impression of naturalness. In an article that ran in *Kinema junpō* in February 1957 (two years after the release of *Meoto zenzai*), Morishige acknowledges the reputation and defends the practice: "If I go off-script, it is because I have determined that it is necessary to the naturalness of the character in that situation."[43] This reputation further supported the impression of "unpremeditated" local speech as a mark of the star's local authenticity. That quality contradicts the scripted, "deliberate and calculated" nature of filmmaking, and reiterates the sense of Osaka language as speech rather than writing.

Ōya Sōichi, the noted transwar critic of modernity and mass culture, responded to this rhetoric of authenticity when he reviewed the film adaptation of *Meoto zenzai* upon its release:

> The *manzai*-like flavor in which the film is completely soaked comes not simply from the accent or idiom of Morishige's words; it radiates from the Kansai-ness that suffuses his whole person. This is not something you can gain simply by studying. And the same could be said for the wonderful success of [the film] *Meoto zenzai*. Since the Edo period, the popular life of Tokyo and that of Osaka have diverged. The expression of a Tokyo sensibility is rectilinear, like a triangle, a square, or a rectangle, while in the case of Kansai people it is curvilinear, like a circle or an oval. Morishige is a curvilinear artist. His words and his character take on a rounded flavor.[44]

Ōya suggests that only a native Osakan could give a performance such as Morishige's. According to this assessment, Osaka-ness is in fact more than a performance; it is an essential quality, and one defined against that of Tokyo. In this way, the review participates in the performance's reinforcement of an increasingly unstable local identity. It is worth noting that Ōya's judgment, like Morishige's performance, is authenticated by the author's Osaka origins: Ōya was born in Mishima-gun in Osaka Prefecture and went to school in Osaka before moving to Tokyo for college. As a prominent critic of Japan's modernity from the 1920s on, he often wrote for a national audience about Osaka and its cultural influence.

Morishige's performance elicited a very different response from another contemporary Osakan. In the same review criticizing the hooligan-like roughness of Morishige's Ryūkichi, the novelist Fujii Shigeo also faults the actor's use of language, finding his Osaka dialect too crude for the character. Fujii notes that such language would have been inappropriate enough to the character in the novel but is made even less appropriate by a change to the story that relocates Ryūkichi's family's shop from the Umeda Shinmichi, a "new road" constructed in 1908 linking Osaka Station in Umeda and Yodoyabashi, to the more historic and exclusive precincts of Senba. As Fujii points out, families with a shop in Senba at that time would have been well-to-do, and so the rough speech that the film scenario gives Ryūkichi suits the new setting even less than the old.

Here again, the changes introduced in adaptation point to how Osaka is made to signify in the postwar. "Senba," a place-name familiar from history books, would have registered with a popular national film audience, whereas "Umeda Shinmichi" would likely not have. At the same time, Morishige's rougher speech may have sounded like "Osaka" to that audience, who had by the postwar begun to associate the city with a contemporary urban underclass rather than the glories of its merchant past. As a locale becomes more and more thoroughly subordinated within a homogenized national popular culture, and as it is reimagined and performed for a national audience, the diversity and nuance of local spaces and practices is simplified to a relatively few, easily recognized signs. It is the same process that Oda and other Osaka literati identified in the "standardized" Osaka dialect of Tanizaki's *Manji.* The reinforcement of genuine Osaka-ness in the context of postwar deterritorialization requires a *rhetoric* of authenticity rather than the documentary record Fujii seems to have wanted. Though Morishige's crude language and the Senba setting were dissonant for him, they harmoniously signified an authentic Osaka-ness for a postwar national film audience—and even for an Osaka native like Ōya, who understood that mass audience as well as cinema's mass appeal.

We hear the authentic local voice in the performances of the supporting cast, too. Naniwa Chieko steals her first scene as O-Kin, in which Chōko visits seeking work, and she steals it in large part through her quicksilver vocal performance of dialect (Fujii, in his largely negative review of the film, praises Naniwa's Osaka dialect, calling it, "as one would expect, orthodox and pleasing to the ear").[45] The fluid, shifting intonations of Naniwa's line readings pull the focus from the star, Awashima (whose own performance of dialect Fujii also praised). We hear that quality, as well, in the performance of Yorozuyo Mineko (1919–), another Osaka-born actress, who plays Kinpachi, Chōko's friend from their time working together as geisha. And we hear it in the hammy performance of the stage actor Tamura Rakuta, who, as Chōko's father, lays on the dialect with a knife, slurring his words and rolling his "r"s.

At the same time that the star's performance authenticates Osaka-ness in the face of the city's deterritorialization, however, it also acknowledges the loss associated with that process—particularly the gradual fading of the local voice, which haunts both Oda's novel and Toyoda's adaptation. Throughout the novel, numerous references to *jōruri* point to the containment of a primarily oral mode by a textual one, just as Toyoda's film adaptation highlights the subsequent containment of that textual mode by a cinematic one. Chōko and Ryūkichi's enjoyment of the *jōruri*—competing in amateur recitation contests, practicing from published scripts, crooning famous passages to each other—reminds us that it is an artistic form with strong local roots, an ephemeral art of the live voice, and a heavily participatory practice, all in contrast to the two signal modern cultural forms: the novel (as it develops in the twentieth century) and the classical narrative film. *Meoto zenzai* both thematizes and models the reduction of oral performance to an artistic tradition serving newer forms that are national and purport to record or fix the voice.

Mladen Dolar distinguishes voice from speech as "what does not contribute to making sense" and argues that the voice in film possesses the potential to undermine the domination of visual discourse.[46] He writes, "The visible world presents relative stability, permanence, distinctiveness, and a location at a distance; the audible presents fluidity, passing, a certain inchoate, amorphous character, and a lack of distance. The voice is elusive, always changing, becoming, elapsing, with unclear contours, as opposed to the relative permanence, solidity, durability of the seen."[47] Dolar ignores dialect and touches only briefly on the related topic of accent. He acknowledges that accent "appears as a distraction, or even an obstacle, to the smooth flow of signifiers and to the hermeneutics of understanding," but goes on to dispute its disruptive potential, arguing that "the regional accent can easily be dealt with, it can be described and codified. After all, it is a norm which differs from the ruling norm," and adding that "the ruling norm is but an accent which has been declared a non-accent."[48] However Dolar dismisses the potential of the local voice too easily. Oda, in his theorization of "Osaka's potential," defined it precisely as the potential to elude codification and disrupt repetition. Understood in this way, some aspect of the Osaka dialect resists becoming a norm. As Toyoda's *Meoto zenzai* authenticates local identity for a postwar audience for whom it has come to seem increasingly unstable, it also allows the excess of the local voice to haunt the image, a phantom threat to its stability. The film adaptation of *Noren* makes this operation overt.

Morishige in *Noren*

Three years after his career-making performance in *Meoto zenzai*, Morishige starred in Kawashima's adaptation of *Noren*, this time playing not one but two archetypes of Osaka masculinity. As previously noted, Yamasaki's novel is constructed as a repetition: it tells a story of building a company in the prewar and rebuilding it in the postwar. The film visualizes this repetition by casting Morishige as both Gohei and his son Kōhei, prewar and postwar generations of the Osaka merchant. In the first half, as he builds the business, Morishige/Gohei demonstrates the qualities of the ideal merchant: humility, diligence, economy. In the second half, Morishige/Kōhei rebuilds it employing qualities more adaptive to the immediate postwar. As a boy (played by a juvenile actor), Kōhei is a typical spoiled second son of the merchant class, more interested in rugby than trade. Even when he returns home from the war, Kōhei (now played by Morishige) retains the undisciplined demeanor of the *dame-otoko*, flopping on the floor and crooning to himself (a posture familiar to the actor's fans from Toyoda's *Meoto zenzai*). Now, however, he also demonstrates a merchant's instincts, quoting the price of *konbu* on black markets in Kobe and Osaka. As he involves himself in the business, Kōhei displays other traits useful in the chaos of the occupation: he takes risks, breaks rules, and even brawls to protect his territory. Spicer, in his study of male types in British film, pairs the Fool with another model of "alternative" masculinity, the Rogue. Kōhei, as a new sort of merchant, demonstrates some of the features of this type, who "is best placed to adjust to rapidly changing social conditions and 'get away with it' against various regulations, restrictions and authoritarian institutions."[49]

In Yamasaki's novel, repetition serves her theme of Osaka's regeneration. However, Morishige's appearance throughout the second half of the film as both father and son alters that theme. The film calls attention to the double role with several winking comments. When a clerk at the warehouse meets Kōhei for the first time, for example, she immediately guesses who he is: "You must be the young master of the Naniwa-ya. You're the image of your father!" Later, someone at the buyers' market comments on the resemblance. The film uses a split screen in several scenes to allow Morishige to appear in both roles, side by side. This gimmick culminates with a scene in which Morishige/Kōhei, on the right-hand side of the screen, works to develop products to sell in the Naniwa-ya's new Tokyo location, carefully measuring out ingredients with scales and test tubes and fussing over pots, while Morishige/Gohei watches doubtfully from the left-hand side. As the more intuitively inclined Gohei begins to criticize his son's methods, Kōhei insists he is working in "a spirit of rationality" (*gōriteki seishin*). The exchange grows heated, and the camera cuts to a close-up of the two, arguing nose to nose, like a mirror image. Finally, Gohei storms out of the room and up the stairs, where he complains to his wife about their son's attempts to turn *konbu* into a "luxury item" (*zeitaku-mon*). "We aren't a luxury item!" he insists.

By showing the two occupying the same space, the film crystallizes a pivotal postwar moment of graduation from a local to a national economy (in the film's version of economic history), presenting us with the merchant past and present coexisting and confronting each other: one traditional and intuitive, the other modern and scientific; one understanding his product as a basic commodity, the other recognizing its potential as a retail luxury. While they coexist, the film suspends the graduation to a national order, which this version presents as inevitable. The trickery involved in having Morishige play both roles underscores the unreality of that extended moment of suspension, inviting us to indulge in nostalgic reverie. That moment ends with the father's death at the end of the film, a climax that permits the film's linear history to move forward, beyond the end of the story, toward a modern, Tokyo-centric, corporate, and consumerist future.

The fading Osaka voice, however, protests against the triumphalism of this new narrative. Kawashima cast several stars whom audiences would have recognized as native speakers with special claims to an authentic voice. In particular, the scenes with Nakamura Ganjirō and Naniwa Chieko as the old master of the Naniwa-ya and his wife record a vanishing local sphere of which not only the distinctive Senba idiom but the rhythm of speech, the intonation, and the quality of the voice is a vital part. Ganjirō and Naniwa bring Senba archetypes to life in an early scene, in which Gohei learns that he is to marry O-Chiyo and haltingly expresses reluctance. The scene is set in the private rooms of the Naniwa-ya main house. Ganjirō is seated on the floor at a desk, going over accounts. Naniwa kneels in an adjoining room, praying at an impressive *butsudan* (home altar). The generous size of the rooms, the quality of the architecture, the discreet luxury of the finishes, as well as the careful dress, well-maintained look, and earnest occupation of the master and mistress of the Naniwa-ya, all communicate an ideal image of the prewar Osaka merchant: disciplined, prosperous, and restrained. Festival music bleeds in from the street. Morishige/Gohei bustles in, and the old master moves to a large ceramic hibachi in the middle of the room and lights a pipe. As Naniwa turns from the altar to join their conversation, the old master comes quickly to the point:

利兵衛： お千代をもろうてくれへんか 。お千代早うから両親を失(うしの)うて、家を取り仕切ってきたよってに、ちいと年くうてるけど、しっかりしたもんやで。

五平： へっ、そら、ま、しっかりしすぎてはるぐらいのお人でござりますけれども。

利兵衛： それに、弟の娘というもんの、まるでわしの娘みたいように、気性も考えもようにとる。

きの： お前も親旦さんの身内からいただいたら、心丈夫でええやろがな。

五平： あの、それにつきまして—。

利兵衛： 何や。

五平： あぁ、私はちょっと実はその、心当てござりまして。

利兵衛： それは困る。いや、いや、それは困るで。嫁はわしのいう通りにしてもらわな。

きの： その心づもりで、親旦さんも、暖簾分けてあげなはったんやで。

* * *

Master: O-Chiyo o morōte kurehen ka. O-Chiyo wa hayō kara ryōshin ushinōte, ie o torishikitte kita yotte. Chii to toshi kūteru kedo, shikkari shita mon ya de.

Gohei: He-, sora, ma, shikkari shisugiteharu gurai no o-hito de gozarimasu keredomo . . .

Master: Sore ni, ototo no musume to iu mon no, maru de washi no musume mitai yō ni, kishō mo kangae mo yō nitoru.

Mistress: Omae mo, Oyadan-san no miuchi kara itadaitara, kokorojōbu de ee yaro ga na.

Gohei: Ano, sore ni tsukimashite . . .

Master: Nan'ya?

Gohei: Aa, watashi, chotto, jitsu wa, sono . . . kokoro-ate gozarimashite.

Ganjirō: Sore wa komaru. Iya, iya, sore wa komaru de. Yome wa washi no iu-tori ni shite morawana.

Mistress: Sono kokoro-zumori de Oyadan-san mo noren-wakete agenahattan ya de.

Master: Would you take O-Chiyo as your wife? O-Chiyo lost her parents at a young age, so she's learned how to manage a household. She's a little old, but she's steady.
Gohei: Yes, as to that, well, she's a bit too steady . . .
Master: What's more, she's my brother's daughter, and just like a daughter to me. Our values and way of thinking are quite similar.
Mistress: And if you're received into your master's family, you'll be good and secure, won't you.
Gohei: Um, about that . . .
Master: What?
Gohei: Well, that is, actually, I have someone in mind . . .
Master: What?! That's no good. That is no good! You should take the bride I tell you to take.
Mistress: That's what your master had in mind when he gave you your own shop.

Many of the usual markers of Kansai dialect—and of Osaka dialect in particular—crop up in this short excerpt from the dialogue, including the "*-hen*" negative in "*kurehen*," the sentence-ending emphatic "*de*" and "*ga na*," the imperative "*morawana* [*akan*]" ("*morawanakereba ikanai*" in standard Japanese), "*ee*" for "*ii*" meaning "good," the copula forms "*ya*" for "*da*" and "*yaro*" for "*daro*," the "be" verb "*oru*" for "*iru*" (in the contracted form "*nitoru*" for "*nite oru*"), the polite suffix "*-haru*" in "*shisugiteharu*" and "*agenahattan*" ("*agenasatta*"), and the conjugation of verbs such as "*morau*" and "*ushinau*" as "*morōte*" and "*ushinōte*" rather than "*moratte*" and "*ushinatte*." Of course, the pronunciation (for instance, the short "o" sounds of "*ototo*" and "*iu-tori*") and intonation of these two Osaka-native actors weave these individual elements into a seamless fabric of local speech. Although this scene and the tension that motivates it (Morishige's desire to choose his own bride) are original to the movie, the mode of expression effectively does the same work as Yamasaki's self-ethnography: it indexes a pivotal moment in the city's history to the carefully observed, thickly described details of everyday life and language.

The interactions between Morishige and Isuzu record another facet of this vanishing world. The scene of their wedding night with its awkward repartee provides a record of two great stars deploying their native idiom. After Naniwa, as the old master's wife, leaves them at their new house, bidding them good night with meaningful looks and a teasing remark to Gohei about "being gentle," the newlyweds begin awkwardly to undress, and O-Chiyo sets some ground rules for this arranged marriage:

お千代：五平どん。
五平：へぇ。
お千代：「へぇ」はやめておくれやす。
五平：そんなら何とゆうたらええ。
お千代：「何や」と言わはったらよろしいねん。
五平：ほな、何や。
お千代：私、な、あんさんにちょっとお聞きしたいことござりまんねんけど。ほんまにあてを気に入って迎えておくれやしたんでっか。
五平：そんなこと—。
お千代：しょうことなしに一緒になりはったんでっしゃろ。
五平：そんなことあれしまへんが、ありがたいこっちゃ思うて。
お千代：あてはな、一旦ここに来た以上、帰れ言わはったかて、帰れしまへんよってな。

***

O-Chiyo: Gohei-don?
Gohei: He-?
O-Chiyo: "He-" wa yamete okure yasu.
Gohei: Sonnara nan to yutara ee?
O-Chiyo: "Nan'ya" to iwahattara yoroshii nen.
Gohei: Hona, nan'ya?
O-Chiyo: Watashi, na, an-san ni chotto o-kiki shitai koto gozariman nen kedo. An-san, honma ni ate o ki ni itte mukaete okure yashitan dekka?
Gohei: Sonna koto . . .
O-Chiyo: Shō koto nashi ni issho ni narihattan desharō.
Gohei: Sonna koto arishimahen ga. Arigatai kotcha omōte . . .
O-Chiyo: Ate wa, na, ittan koko yome ni kita ijō, kaere iwahatta ka te kaere shimahen yotte na. Yoroshu gozaimasu na.

O-Chiyo: Gohei?
Gohei: Yes?
O-Chiyo: Please stop saying "Yes."
Gohei: Then what should I say?
O-Chiyo: Say, "What?"
Gohei: OK, What?
O-Chiyo: I have something I want to ask you. Did you really marry me because you liked me?
Gohei: That's—
O-Chiyo: We're together because you had no choice, isn't that right?
Gohei: That's not true. I was grateful for the opportunity.
O-Chiyo: Look: now that I've come here to be your wife, even if you tell me to leave, I won't leave. You understand me?

This exchange offers another deep description of dialect, with the use of "*-haru*" in the past tense ("*iwahattara*," "*narihattan*"), the emphatic "*nen*" ("*yoroshii nen,*" "*gozariman nen*"), and the polite command form "*okure yasu,*" to point out just a few elements in what is really *Kansai-ben* from start to finish. In the slightly hammy or camped-up quality of the dialogue, we hear these two stars authenticating their locality. It is interesting to compare Isuzu's vocal performance here with that in Mizoguchi's classic *Naniwa ereji* (Osaka elegy, 1936), in which the dialect seems unself-conscious, its locality less emphatically authenticated. In that prewar film, we hear the voice of a city that has not yet recognized its own subordination and does yet feel the need to insist on its difference.

Noren's nostalgic investment in the local voice becomes clear in a pair of scenes near the end of the film. The first is set at a wholesale auction of *konbu* in Osaka, where the father, Gohei, faces off against a buyer from Tokyo. It is midsummer and the day is hot; the Osaka buyers are sweaty and unkempt, frantically fanning themselves, but the Tokyo buyer, in a crisp white suit, looks cool as a cucumber. As the auction proceeds, he buys every last lot of *konbu*, one after the other, in what seems like the ultimate defeat for Gohei and for Osaka. But a few days later, at the opening of the Naniwaya's new main shop, the Tokyo buyer seeks out Gohei; he has been unable to unload all the *konbu* he bought at auction and is forced to sell to Gohei at a loss. The negotiation between the two men becomes a linguistic negotiation between standard Japanese and *Osaka-ben*, a contest Gohei wins. The scene suggests the same sort of proudly stubborn local identification that Mike Featherstone recognizes in the images of Gracie Fields and George Formby, British "working-class film star heroes" of the 1930s. Those stars, Featherstone writes, evinced "a strong sense of community and loyalty to place, and the retention of a local accent showed their unwillingness to lose their roots and reinforced their apparent 'naturalness.'"[50] As Gracie and George got the better of London toffs, so Gohei, with his local knowledge, bests the Tokyo businessman. Afterward, Gohei goes out to the warehouse. He is helping an apprentice move bales of *konbu* when he suddenly collapses. Kōhei, O-Chiyo, and O-Matsu rush out to find him dead, his clenched fists gritty with salt from the *konbu*. Whereas the novel ends with the son's defiant oath, the film ends with the father's death—a merchant's death in the storehouse—signifying the passing of a social and economic class. Gohei's final victory is that class's last hurrah: a victory of business savvy, temperament, and language, won against Tokyo.

Senescence and the City

In this way, the persistence of the fading local voice haunts the narrative of *Noren*, as the lingering presence of the father can be taken for a ghost. Morishige's persistence in the role of the father after his entrance, halfway through the film, in the role of the son does have the uncanny effect of an apparition. Giving the actor both roles produces a temporal confusion that troubles the progressive history the film tries to tell. And, since that history proceeds from a past that is local to a present that is national, Morishige's ghostly doubling troubles the spatial order, too. Meanwhile, the local voice infiltrates the narrative into which such films as *Noren* attempt to draft the imagined city and reminds us of its dependence on the specter of the local.

Like ghosts, this aural haunting is perceptible only to certain people—those used to hearing it and those, like ghost hunters, actively listening for it. In this sense, Morishige's performance, and those of the other local stars, make a dual address. While Dyer argues that stars synthesize contradictions, Daisuke Miyao, in the introduction to his study of the international silent-film star Hayakawa Sessue, asserts that "stardom is not a stable form of synthesis but an ongoing process of negotiation," and that "this process of cross-cultural negotiation sometimes synthetically reconciles contradictions of images, but in many cases... enhances the contradiction." Miyao is writing specifically of a transnational negotiation between the two film industries in which the star image of Hayakawa circulated, Hollywood and Japan, and of contradictions between two national audiences. Miyao insists, "Hayakawa's stardom has different meanings and modes of reception in different geographical and historical sites. It did not necessarily own a synthetic power over various contradictions but kept maintaining ambivalences."[51] Considered in the context of Osaka films, Miyao's observation suggests a way to think about stars who played to a different pair of audiences, "local" and "national" (or, more correctly, Kansai and Kantō, western and eastern Japan), and negotiated their sometimes conflicting expectations without necessarily synthesizing the contradictions between those two orders.

In fact, Dyer himself alludes to different audiences and dual address. He writes that the extraordinary appeal Judy Garland held for gay men after 1950 arose in part out of "the sense of Garland performing herself," which signaled "a recognition of the theatricality of experience that gay sensibility is attuned to." Her performances appealed to a gay sensibility that "holds together qualities that are elsewhere felt as antithetical:

theatricality and authenticity" and, equally, "intensity and irony."[52] As the homogenization of Japanese culture regained momentum after the occupation, local identity became, in its own way, a combination of theatricality and authenticity, and Osaka, privileged by its historical significance, its continued cultural relevance, and its carefully tended otherness, became a primary locus for the cinematic exploration of local identity. Just as queer audiences could recognize in Garland the embrace of artifice, so, too, could locals watching Morishige play an Osaka character recognize (as most nonlocals likely could not) the artifice of locality; appreciate the bravura performance of it that only a local star could give; and delight in seeing and, especially, hearing that performance infiltrate the national cinema. Such a performance must have given particular satisfaction when produced by a code-switching star like Morishige, who enjoyed equal success playing unmarked characters. So, while his performance authenticated Osaka-ness to an outside audience, to insiders it acknowledged the loss. As a sign of what Marilyn Ivy calls "the relationship between the historical erasures effected by industrial capitalism since the late nineteenth century in Japan and the ongoing reinscriptions of those lost differences as identities," Morishige's performance can only be "phantasmatic."[53]

Conclusion

The spate of films set in Osaka that appeared throughout the 1950s attest to the changing image of the city in the postwar national imaginary and to the increasing instability of local identity. Many of these films drew source material from popular novels of Osaka life written by wartime and postwar local authors, including Oda Sakunosuke and Yamasaki Toyoko—works that recorded and responded to the cultural economic subordination of Osaka to the state. An analysis of the differences between novel and film indicates which aspects of these imagined Osakas filmmakers found useful or potentially profitable and which they did not, and the tactics by which they emphasized the former and deemphasized the latter. In *Noren*, Yamasaki commemorates Osaka as the site of Japan's early economic modernity, a modernity hijacked by militarism and a control economy administered from Tokyo. Kawashima's adaptation of *Noren* alters time setting and chronology and minimizes concerns of economics and class in favor of the personal and the romantic. As such, the adaptation dulled the critique offered by its source novel. It refit Yamasaki's local story into a national history of the smooth progress of the centralizing state. Amid a postwar process of recentralization, this and other Osaka films served the purpose of reassuring audiences faced with the loss of local identity. At the same time, the performance of locality in each film offers a reminder of that loss. Such stars as Yamada Isuzu, Otowa Nobuko, Awashima Chikage, Naniwa Chieko, Nakamura Ganjirō, and especially Morishige Hisaya gave performances that simultaneously authenticated an increasingly unstable local identity and acknowledged its loss. In particular, their performance of local voices haunts the national history these films tell.

As a postscript, we may note that more recent adaptations of Yamasaki's work have registered the continuing loss of the Osaka voice in a different way. Consider, for example, Fuji Television's 2003 adaptation of *Shiroi kyotō*, starring Karasawa Toshiaki as the power-hungry Doctor Zaizen and Eguchi Yōsuke as the ethical Doctor Satomi. It is in many ways a satisfying adaptation, but if we compare it with the 1966 film adaptation starring Tamiya Jirō as Zaizen and Tamura Takahiro as Satomi, we immediately notice the remarkable degree to which local forms of speech have dropped out. The stars of the 1966 adaptation were completely comfortable in Kansai dialect—Tamiya was born in Osaka and Tamura in Kyoto—whereas the pop idols who star in the more recent adaptation, Karasawa and Eguchi, were both born in Tokyo and demonstrate no special mastery of Osaka dialect in their performances. Karasawa's Zaizen speaks standard Japanese even with his mother (who also speaks standard). The only main character left to speak dialect consistently in the later adaptation is Zaizen's father, a loud, crass man (played by Nishida Toshiyuki). Perhaps producers and directors no longer expect stars to have a facility with local languages and no longer consider idiom and voice to be a key aspect of Yamasaki's stories, or else they have decided that such educated characters would no longer speak in dialect in a contemporary setting. The resulting performances eloquently attest to the instability of the local identity that Yamasaki's novels memorialize.

Conclusion

National Drag

In the summer of 2011, television and newspaper advertisements, billboards, video screens, and shop-window displays across Japan revealed the existence of an independent "Osaka Nation," established at the beginning of the Meiji period and maintained in secrecy until the present day. This campaign supported the release of Tōhō Studios' live-action film *Purinsesu Toyotomi* (Princess Toyotomi), an alternate history in the manner of *The Da Vinci Code*. The film, starring established actors Tsutsumi Shin'ichi and Nakai Kiichi, as well as rising star Okada Masaki, scored the second-highest box office numbers for its opening weekend, but its overall take was unspectacular, ranking thirtieth for the year. Regardless of this lackluster performance, the novel from which the film was adapted can accurately be called a sensation. Written by Makime Manabu, *Purinsesu Toyotomi* was originally serialized in the journal *Bungei shunjū* in 2009. It was promptly adapted for a ten-episode radio drama broadcast by NHK. The novel was released in paperback in 2011, just before the debut of the film. It was nominated for the Naoki Prize, a prestigious award for popular fiction; it ranked second for the year on Kinokuniya's fiction best-sellers list; and it was the most downloaded novel of 2011—a record of success that demonstrates both the persistent resonance and the shifting relevance of Osaka as "treason."

Both novel and film restage two watershed events in the history of Osaka and Japan: the Siege of Osaka Castle and the Meiji Restoration. The central figure in the first event is Toyotomi Hideyoshi, who completed the task of unifying Japan's domains and built Osaka Castle as his seat, making Osaka the political and economic center of Japan. After Hideyoshi's death, as every Japanese schoolchild knows, Tokugawa Ieyasu betrayed his former lord, defeating Hideyoshi's son Hideyori at the Battle of Sekigahara in 1600 and stamping out the remnants of Toyotomi-loyalist resistance in 1615, in the Summer Campaign, or *Natsu no jin*. Osaka Castle burned, Hideyori committed suicide, and Tokugawa forces beheaded his son, Kunimatsu, bringing an end to the Toyotomi line. (Or *did* they?!). The center of political power shifted irreversibly from West to East, from Osaka to Edo. The Meiji Restoration of 1868 confirmed this shift by bringing the emperor to the city of Edo, making it the new imperial capital, Tokyo.

Purinsesu Toyotomi's alternate history develops from two premises. First, it posits that Hideyoshi's grandson Kunimatsu escaped the Tokugawa forces and that the Toyotomi line has survived, concealed by loyal Osakans, down to the present day. Second, it posits that Meiji leaders borrowed money from Osaka merchants at the time of the Restoration in 1868 to pay for modernizing reforms and, in return, officially recognized an independent Osaka nation, which has since then maintained a secret government beneath Osaka Castle, in an interior identical to that of the National Diet building (in a nice detail, it turns out that the Osaka version is the original; the national Diet Building in Tokyo is the copy). The Japanese government pays Osaka an annual fee to cover administration of the secret nation and to protect Hideyoshi's descendants.

The novel and film relate the discovery of this secret history and its impact on several lives. Three investigators from the federal Board of Audit come to Osaka to review several grants. The chief investigator is Matsudaira Hajime, who bears the name of the clan from which the Tokugawa descended. His assistants are Torii, an awkward chatterbox with strong intuition; and Gainsbourg, a tall, half-French, half-Japanese beauty who is all business. One of the grants they investigate is paid annually to an association called "O.J.O." (a near homonym for "*o-jō*," or "princess," in Japanese), which is a front for the government of Osaka Nation. This is no random audit. Gainsbourg is in fact a cryptocitizen of Osaka Nation and opposes the policy of keeping its existence a secret. Gainsbourg longs to see Osaka stand up and declare its independence and has added O.J.O. to the list of audits in the hope that the punctilious Matsudaira will cancel the long-standing annual payments and precipitate a war. In the course of their investigation, Matsudaira, Gainsbourg, and Torii become involved in the lives of two schoolchildren: Hashiba Chako and Sanada Daisuke. Chako is the princess of the title, a direct descendant of Hideyoshi. Daisuke is her best friend. His family name, Sanada, references Sanada Yukimura, a hero of the Siege of Osaka Castle. Daisuke's father, Kōichi, runs a shop serving *okonomiyaki*, the savory pancake that is one of Osaka's representative foods, but he is also the current prime minister of Osaka Nation. As a citizen, Daisuke shares a responsibility to protect the princess, but in fact he is protected by her—from the bullies who have harassed him since he started wearing girl's clothes to school.

The desire to restage the Meiji period is hardly surprising in a city with the highest percentage of welfare recipients in Japan and the highest rate of homelessness, a prefecture that ranked dead last in a recent study measuring residents' "happiness."[1] Osaka's economic powerlessness has fueled resentment of the concentration of power in Tokyo. The film version of *Purinsesu Toyotomi* arrived at a critical moment in the local politics of resentment. In the elections of April 2011, just a month before the film's release, the Osaka Restoration Party (Ōsaka ishin no kai), founded by Hashimoto Tōru, won a majority in Osaka's prefectural assembly. Hashimoto, a lawyer who had made a name for himself as a television personality, was elected governor of Osaka Prefecture in January 2008. A key element of his campaign was a plan to streamline local government and reduce costs by merging the operations of Osaka city (Ōsaka-shi) and Osaka urban-prefecture (Ōsaka-fu) into a metropolitan prefecture. This new entity would be designated "Ōsaka-to," claiming the suffix (written with the same character as "*miyako*," also the second character in "*teito*") that has always been reserved for the capital, Tokyo ("Tōkyō-to"). Hashimoto founded the Osaka Restoration Party in 2010. Following the group's success in the April 2011 elections, he resigned the office of governor to run for mayor of Osaka city while his hand-picked successor, Matsui Ichirō, ran to replace Hashimoto as governor. Both were elected in November 2011.

After this success, Hashimoto expanded his scope, forming a new national political party, the Japan Restoration Party (Nippon ishin no kai), in 2012. He then joined forces with the Sunshine Party, led by outspoken right-wing politician Ishihara Shintarō, former governor of Tokyo Prefecture, who replaced Hashimoto as the head of the new national party. Hashimoto has often framed his positions in the language of decentralization of power. This includes not only the plan to reorganize Osaka as a metropolitan prefecture but, for example, a proposal that would allow the prefectural government to have more say over education policies, which have long been dictated by the state Ministry of Education.[2] When the central government announced plans to restart nuclear power plants that had been shut down after the multiple meltdowns at the Fukushima Daiichi power plant, Hashimoto again asserted local authority, opposing (at least at first) the restarting of the plant at Fukui, near Osaka, run by Kansai Electric, in which Osaka city is a shareholder. On the other hand, he has embraced issues dear to nationalists, requiring, for example, that public school teachers stand and sing the national anthem at official school events. The alliance with Ishihara was seen by the media as confusing his original message. At the same time, certain statements and actions led critics to brand Hashimoto's politics "Hashizumu" ("Hash-ism," playing on the word "Fascism"). These include his statement that "the most important thing for current politics in Japan is dictatorship—a strength such that it could be called dictatorship," as well as his order, in February 2012, that city employees complete questionnaires with detailed questions about their labor-union activity and their support for political parties.[3] The Restoration Party's fortunes turned in the 2013 elections. It lost its majority in the Osaka assembly, and candidates with ties to the group were defeated in mayoral elections in Sakai city—which would have been subsumed within the planned new metropolitan prefecture—as well as in Kishiwada city. Hashimoto and Ishihara disagreed over the latter's support for revision of Japan's "peace constitution" and dissolved their alliance in May 2014.

Like Hashimoto's calls for decentralization and greater local autonomy, the alternate history imagined by *Purinsesu Toyotomi* appeals to Osakans' lingering resentment over the city's subordination to a central authority located in Edo/Tokyo. It does this by playing on several of the tropes that I have identified in the preceding chapters. The result, however, suggests the increased difficulty of tapping the city's potential.

In its production of Osaka's essential difference, the story picks up on the same characterization of Osaka as "*yayakoshii*" that local authors promoted in the 1930s (a process detailed in chapter 1). *Purinsesu Toyotomi* introduces manifold signs of incongruity and contradiction: the city that is really a state, the *okonomiyaki* cook who is really the prime minister. Gainsbourg, although identified as French, insists to everyone that she is Japanese. Matsudaira's name associates him with the Tokugawa, and he leads a team from Tokyo, but we learn that he, like Gainsbourg, is an Osaka native. Above all, *Purinsesu Toyotomi* deploys the notion of *yayakoshii* in its treatment of gender. There is, of course, Chako, the girl who fights like a boy. More important to the story, however, is Chako's best friend, Daisuke, who looks like a boy but dresses like a girl. Both book and film carefully trace his decision to wear a girl's uniform and the effects of that decision. (The film adds a layer to this complication, reversing the genders of Torii and Gainsbourg from the novel.)

Sex and gender, and their complications, also play an important role in transmitting and preserving the secret of Osaka Nation. This secret is passed down from all Osaka-born fathers to their sons—and only their sons. The initiation takes place in the secret government's inner sanctum, which is reached after a long walk down a tunnel, during which the father explains the true history of Osaka, and the son vows to defend the nation. When the nation is threatened, the castle will glow red, a signal for all sons of Osaka to gather there while the women retreat to their homes.

This preoccupation with gender suggests one way to understand the dynamics of urban and national identity explored in *Purinsesu Toyotomi*: as a type of passing. Matsudaira passes as Tokyo/national when he is in fact Osaka/local. After his parents separated and he moved with his mother to Tokyo, Matsudaira disowned his father and concealed his roots as he climbed the ladder of the state bureaucracy. This personal history of national passing surely resonates with readers and viewers born in the "provinces," who recognize Matsudaira's trajectory from margin to metropolis (a trajectory familiar from colonial discourses) and the pressures of cultural homogenization. Language is a key aspect of Matsudaira's disavowal: his speech betrays no sign of the local language in which he was raised. A flashback to a conversation between the adult Matsudaira and his father contrasts the father's deep *Ōsaka-ben* with the son's impersonal *hyōjungo*.

Passing requires association with the chosen group, of course; but as Judith Butler points out, it also compels association with the disavowed group in order to satisfy the desire to constitute and display one's purity. At the same time, association with the disavowed risks the betrayal of one's true identity. Butler writes that in Nella Larsen's 1929 novel *Passing*, "race itself is figured as a contagion transmissible through proximity."[4] In this way, passing sets filial and affiliative associations in opposition. Matsudaira's trip to Osaka provides just such an opportunity for renewed association with the disavowed local, an opportunity to display the cool, business-like detachment—birthright of the Tokyo/national subject—that distinguishes him from the garrulous and colorful locals he meets on his audits. His trip also provokes the return of repressed childhood memories and regrets, prompting a crisis of identity. This crisis culminates in an extremely public self-outing, when he acknowledges his local Osaka identity over a public address system, to an enormous crowd in front of Osaka Castle. The agent of Matsudaira's outing is Gainsbourg, another Osakan who is passing as national. Gainsbourg's own local identity is betrayed by language in unguarded moments throughout the film, when he obviously understands and even speaks Osaka's distinctive dialect.

Daisuke seems at first to serve as Matsudaira's foil. His boy's buzz cut in stark contrast to his girl's uniform, Daisuke is an emblem of not passing. He is the *yayakoshii* heart of the film, frankly contradictory. His relationship with his accepting father seems to be all that Matsudaira's relationship with his own father was not. A pivotal scene in both book and film involves Daisuke's initiation, after his father recognizes the threat posed by the Tokyo bureau's investigation. Daisuke is allowed to make his walk down the long tunnel in his girl's sailor suit. This initiation, however, confirms a condition of the nation-state's belonging. His father allows Daisuke to dress as a girl but requires him to fulfill his destiny as a son and a man of Osaka. Daisuke must suppress his gender identification in order to belong to Osaka Nation. As he takes the walk that all local boys take, he subordinates his difference to the patriarchal bond that secures the Osaka Nation, just as Matsudaira has suppressed his locality to belong to the nation of Japan. His character therefore demonstrates how "national" identity takes precedence over gender identity.

The climax of *Purinsesu Toyotomi* offers a vivid image of national belonging. Once O.J.O. recognizes the threat posed by the audit, it gives the signal for the men of Osaka to gather and defend the city. After a shot of the castle glowing red, the film cuts to scenes of Osaka's streets. They are eerily still, entirely depopulated. These scenes make clear the terms of *Purinsesu Toyotomi*'s alternate history: reimagining Osaka as a nation empties it of all those who were not born there, whose fathers were not born there, the very migrant populations that make Osaka a city, that produce its heterogeneity and any potential it bears. *Purinsesu Toyotomi* thus trades the potential of the city for that of the nation. By imagining an Osaka defined by filial bonds, *Purinsesu Toyotomi* transforms the city into a caricature of ethnic nationalism—a city in national drag.

Because both the survival of the Toyotomi line and the establishment of Osaka Nation have been kept secrets throughout Japan's modernity, the main dramatic tension of the novel concerns what will happen if those secrets are revealed. But Matsudaira is convinced to keep them. This, then, is the denouement: things stay the same. We might well ask whether the story amounts to an alternate history at all. Rather, it explores the frustration of an alternate history. *Purinsesu Toyotomi* is about keeping secrets, eschewing independence, suppressing the promise or the threat of another history. It suggests one strategy available to the local in contemporary Japan, if suppressing difference can be called a strategy rather than a capitulation.

The reticence of *Purinsesu Toyotomi* is a far cry from the strategies explored in cultural production of the transwar period. The preceding chapters have shown how popular literature and cinema from the 1920s through the 1950s negotiated the shifting status of Osaka in Japanese imaginaries. Processes of political and economic centralization and cultural homogenization that accompany the development of the modern state were subordinating urban forms to national forms. As these processes continued across militarization, total war, and occupation, writers and directors imagined Osaka as a treasonous city that, in the insistent locality of its language, its daily life, its flows, and its spaces, betrayed its subordination as the result of hegemony, rather than an ideal transcendence of the partial and fragmentary by the unified whole.

The strategies employed by these authors changed as the irreversibility of Osaka's containment became clearer with the passing years. When Tanizaki Jun'ichirō relocated from Tokyo to the Kansai region, Osaka still constituted a legitimate rival to Tokyo in the spheres of industry and popular culture. In *Manji*, Tanizaki imagined a personal history, confessed in a local voice, that called attention to the negotiation of local and national authority. In the "dark valley" of the 1930s and early 1940s, Oda Sakunosuke could still recall the era of Great Osaka during which he had grown up. Under the heaviest censorship, Oda imagined in *Meoto zenzai* an alternative local practice of expenditure that willfully ignored a state ideology of rational consumption. Then, in *Waga machi*, he produced an alternate history of cosmopolitanism from below, rooted in the local city. Writing through the war, Tanizaki identified in Osaka the source of a "secret history" of militarism as a paroxysm of national transcendence, told ironically through a local sensibility in *Sasameyuki*. By the postwar era, when Yamasaki Toyoko began to write about Osaka, the idea that a local urban sensibility could trump a national sensibility, or that local forms could challenge national forms, had begun to recede into nostalgia. Even so, Yamasaki produced an alternate history of economic centralization as seen from the old merchant capital, indulging her audience's wish, however futile, for the local economy's rebirth.

The difference between these transwar deployments of the local and that in *Purinsesu Toyotomi* particularly reveals itself in speech as the vehicle of local and national sensibilities. Oda made idiom one measuring stick of Osaka's literary potential in his criticism, and his characters speak the local language heedless of any so-called standard. Tanizaki turned his own prose over to local "dialect consultants" and forced Sensei, his fictional stand-in in *Manji*, to transcribe Sonoko's local speech. Sachiko in *Sasameyuki*, on a trip to Tokyo, worries about dialect giving her away in "enemy territory." And in *Noren*, Yamasaki stages a linguistic duel between dialect and standard language as spoken by her protagonist, on the one hand, and a pretentious shaper from the capital, on the other. The Osaka characters in these stories speak the national standard reluctantly if at all; contrast them with the characters Matsudaira and Gainsbourg in *Purinsesu Toyotomi*, whose linguistic passing underpins the elaborate plot.

Other recent popular novels and films have, in contrast, made a point of revealing rather than suppressing local histories, especially of the migrant communities absent from *Purinsesu Toyotomi* (and largely absent from the popular literature of the transwar era, too)—the communities that help make Osaka a city. Principal among these have been the stories of Osaka's *zainichi* Korean community, notably the 1998 novel *Chi to hone* (Blood and bones) by Yang Sogiru (Yang Seok-il) and the award-winning 2004 film adaptation by Sai Yōichi, which explore the violent history of that community and trace its subnational links to the island of Jeju.[5] Another is Yang Yong-hi's *Dia Pyonyan* (Dear Pyongyang, 2005), a documentary about the director's family and her father's decision to repatriate her brothers to North Korea. It tells a new chapter of Osaka's eccentric cosmopolitanism and its migrant flows, most vividly manifested in the father's exuberant idiom, which mixes the languages of Korean and Osaka. (It is interesting to note, however, that when Yang treated similar themes in a dramatic film, *Kazoku no kuni* [Our homeland, 2012], she chose to make Tokyo the setting, a decision that abstracts and nationalizes the story and flattens out the idiom.) Such works suggest that Osaka remains a privileged site for interrogating the relations between locality and nation, city and state.

Notes

Introduction

1. Taylor, *Modern Social Imaginaries*, 23–31. See also Anderson, *Imagined Communities*, which Taylor identifies as a key influence on his own conception of the social imaginary.

2. Berry, "If China Can Say No," 142. See also Walsh, "National Cinema," to which Berry's essay is, in large part, a response.

3. Appadurai, *Modernity at Large*, 31.

4. McClain and Wakita, *Osaka: The Merchants' Capital*, xvii. The authors note that the *Nihon shoki* dates the event at 313 CE.

5. Ibid., 26.

6. McClain and Wakita cite a 1499 reference to a community of seven thousand households around Shitennōji (6).

7. On this history, see Hauser, "Osaka Castle and Tokugawa Authority," 153–72.

8. See Murata Michihito, "Osaka as a Center of Regional Governance," in McClain and Wakita, *Osaka: The Merchants' Capital*, 243–60.

9. Steiner, *Local Government in Japan*, 50–54.

10. In 1930, Osaka had total industrial production worth 996 million yen to Tokyo's 818 million yen, and Hyogo Prefecture, which includes the city of Kobe, had total production worth 629 million yen. For the three contiguous prefectures of Osaka, Hyogo, and Kyoto combined, the figure is 1.8 billion yen, compared to 1.1 billion yen for Tokyo and fifth-ranked Kanagawa combined. Nakamura, *Economic Growth in Prewar Japan*, 186.

11. On the early Osaka jazz scene, see Atkins, *Blue Nippon*. On Osaka's cinema history, see Sasagawa, *Meiji Taishō Ōsaka eiga bunka no tanjō*.

12. On suburban development, see Sand, *House and Home in Modern Japan*, particularly chapter 3.

13. Elise K. Tipton explains how, after the Kantō earthquake, Osaka capital flowed into Tokyo, establishing big cafés in the Ginza that introduced innovations in

design, in advertising, and in the *ero* (erotic) service waitresses offered; see "The Café: Contested Space of Modernity in Interwar Japan," in Tipton and Clark, *Being Modern in Japan*.

14. The five larger cities were New York, London, Paris, Berlin, and Chicago. On Seki and Great Osaka, see Hanes, *The City as Subject*.

15. On the transwar, see Yamanouchi, Koschmann, and Narita, *Total War and "Modernization,"* and Gordon, "Consumption, Leisure and the Middle Class."

16. Steiner, *Local Government in Japan*, 60–61.

17. Williams, "Region and Class in the Novel," 230.

18. On locality in Japanese literature, see especially H. Long, *On Uneven Ground*. Long's study focuses on the peripheral locale of Miyazawa Kenji's Iwate, but discusses locality and regionalism generally.

19. Smith, "Tokyo as an Idea," 46.

20. The first film in the series, *Akumyō*, was based on Kon's 1960 novel of the same name; see Kon, *Akumyō*. The film adaptation was directed by Tanaka Tokuzō and stars Katsu Shintarō. The series eventually ran to sixteen films, the last released in 1969.

21. See, for example, Miike's *Naniwa yūkyōden* (released in the United States as *Osaka Tough Guys*, 1995), *Ōsaka saikyō densetsu: Kenka no hanamichi* (*The Way to Fight*, 1996), and *Kishiwada shōnen gurentai: Chikemuri junjō-hen* (*Young Thugs: Innocent Blood*, 1997).

22. The phrase resonated with later scholars. In a collection of essays on Oda and his work, edited by Kawahara Yoshio and published in 1971, four essays employ the word "*hangyaku*" in their title. See *Oda Sakunosuke kenkyū*.

23. See Fowler, *The Rhetoric of Confession*.

24. Deleuze and Guattari, *Kafka: Toward a Minor Literature*, 16–23.

Chapter 1

1. For a detailed description of the Osaka dialect in literature, see Murakami-Smith, *Dialects and Place*.

2. On the transition from *Kyōto-go* to *Edo-go* as a common and then a standard language, see Twine, "The Genbun'itchi Movement."

3. On these reform movements, see Twine, *Language and the Modern State*. On script reform in particular, see Seeley, *History of Writing*. In Japanese, see Komori, *Nihongo no kindai*; Yasuda, *"Kokugo" to "hōgen" no aida*; Lee, *"Kokugo" to iu shisō*; and Sanada, *Hyōjungo wa ika ni seiritsu shita ka*.

4. Mozume, "Genbun'itchi."

5. Tatsumi, "Baku-genbun'itchi-ron."

6. Contemporary reformers in the United States likewise saw spelling reform as a means of at once "democratizing" language and standardizing it. In *Strange Talk*, Gavin Jones quotes the philologist Thomas Lounsbury: "Exact pronunciation would be imposed upon the word by its very form" (26).

7. On the critique of this top-down narrative, see Torrance, review of *Language and the Modern State*.

8. "A common unitary language is a system of linguistic norms. But these norms do not constitute an abstract imperative; they are rather the generative forces of linguistic life, forces that struggle to overcome the heteroglossia of language, forces that unite and centralize verbal-ideological thought, creating within a heteroglot national language the firm, stable, linguistic nucleus of an officially recognized literary language, or else defending an already formed language from the pressure of growing heteroglossia." Bakhtin, "Discourse in the Novel," in *The Dialogic Imagination*, 270–71.

9. Okakura, *Nihongogaku ippan*, quoted in Sanada, *Hyōjungo wa ika ni seiritsu shita ka*, 91.

10. For example, Yamada Bimyō; see Lee, *"Kokugo" to iu shisō*, 45–46.

11. Lee, *"Kokugo" to iu shisō*, v.

12. In literature produced before the institutionalization of standard Japanese, we find rustic language spoken by bumpkins (*inakamono*), who are treated as figures of fun on this account. The urban-rural dynamic at work, however, is different from the local-national dynamic that informs the use of standard language.

13. Originally published in the journal *Jinruigaku* in 1927.

14. Yasuda, *"Kokugo" to "hōgen" no aida*, 163.

15. Ibid., 149.

16. "General Language" in the group's name was changed to "Standard Language" (*hyōjungo*) in 1937.

17. Tanizaki moved first to Kyoto, then lived in several different locations in Kobe, to the west of Osaka.

18. Tanizaki, "Gendai kōgobun no ketten ni tsuite" (November 1929), in *Tanizaki Jun'ichirō zenshū*, vol. 20, 183.

19. From the introduction to the book version of *Manji*; "Manji shogen," *Tanizaki Jun'ichirō zenshū*, vol. 23, 137. Tanizaki's was not the first such novel. Uno Kōji's story "Nagai koinaka," originally published in the journal *Yūben*, October 1919, is framed as the oral narration of an Osaka man. See Uno, "Nagai koinaka," 282–309.

20. Tanizaki, "Kansai no onna o kataru" (July 1929), in *Tanizaki Jun'ichirō zenshū*, vol. 22, 242.

21. The Hanshin Electric Railway Company commenced its real-estate business in 1909 in Nishinomiya. On the development of these suburbs, see "Landscapes of Domesticity" in Jordan Sand, *House and Home in Modern Japan*. On private rail in Kansai, see Hara, *"Minto" Ōsaka tai "teito" Tōkyō*.

22. For a discussion of narration as performance in *Manji*, see Sakaki, *Recontextualizing Texts*. My reading here benefits from Sakaki's discussion of what she calls the "polarity" of orality and literacy in the novel, the first associated with Sonoko as woman and the other associated with Sensei as (presumed) man. Sakaki's reading explores both the power to narrate and how Sonoko becomes a "canny narratee." It does not address the relation between local and national that is my interest here. Furthermore, Sakaki's concern with polarity differs from my concern with citation and containment.

23. Tanizaki, *Manji*, in *Tanizaki Jun'ichirō zenshū*, vol. 11, 395. Translations (and underscores) are mine. I have consulted Howard Hibbett's translation, published as *Quicksand*.

24. Kōno, *Tanizaki bungaku to kōtei no yokubō*, 22.
25. Yoda, "First-Person Narration and Citizen-Subject."
26. Tanizaki, *Manji*, 403.
27. Ibid., 404.
28. Ibid.
29. Ibid.
30. Ibid., 424.
31. Inoue, *Vicarious Language*, 53.
32. Shibata, "'Monogatari'-enai katarite."
33. Ivy, *Discourses of the Vanishing*, 81.
34. Ibid., 89.
35. Bakhtin, *Problems of Dostoevsky's Poetics*, 202.
36. Tanizaki, *Quicksand*, 26.
37. Tanizaki, *Manji*, 481.
38. Ibid., 502–6.
39. Noguchi, *Tanizaki Jun'ichirō-ron*, 150.
40. Irigaray, *Sexes and Genealogies*, 14, quoted in Margherita Long's study of Tanizaki, *This Perversion Called Love*, 76–77.
41. Gangloff, "Tanizaki's Use of Traditional Literature."
42. On the development and marketing of the suburbs as such a space, see Sand, *House and Home in Modern Japan*.
43. One historically significant instance of Kannon's shape-shifting with relevance to the painting of Mitsuko in *Manji* is recorded in accounts of the life of Shinran. According to legend, the bodhisattva appeared to Shinran at the Rokkakudō and promised to take the form of a beautiful woman and allow the monk to violate her, thus satisfying his carnal desire while following the doctrine of Pure Land Buddhism.
44. One of these consultants discusses her work for Tanizaki in a memoir, *Tanizaki-ke no omoide*, published under the name Takagi Harue.
45. Kōno, *Tanizaki bungaku to kōtei no yokubō*, 17–18.
46. Oda, "Ōsaka no kanōsei," in *Oda Sakunosuke zenshū*, vol. 8, 268–69. Here Oda anticipates the observation by Sumner Ives, in his seminal work on literary dialect, that "when an author uses dialect as a literary medium . . . it is [a] typical set of usages—[a] sort of koinē—that he employs. . . . From the total linguistic material available, he selects those features that seem to be typical . . . of the sort of person he is portraying. These features he generalizes so that the literary dialect is likely to be more regular in its variants than the actual speech it represents." Ives, "A Theory of Literary Dialect," 144.
47. Oda, "Ōsaka no kanōsei."
48. Koide, *Koide Narashige zuihitsu-shū*, 100.
49. Ibid., 101.
50. Tanizaki, "Watakushi no mita Ōsaka oyobi Ōsakajin," in *Tanizaki Jun'ichirō zenshū*, vol. 20, 373.
51. Kubota Mantarō (1889–1963), an author, playwright, and haiku poet, was born in Asakusa and wrote stories of prewar Tokyo.
52. Nabei, "Ōsaka damashii," 45.

53. Uno, "Samazama no Ōsaka katagi," 12:136.
54. Oda, *Meoto zenzai: Kanzenban*, 64.
55. Ibid., 66.
56. Ivy, *Discourses of the Vanishing*, 89.
57. Benjamin, "Task of the Translator," 82.
58. Derrida, *Monolingualism of the Other*, 62.
59. Benjamin, "On Language as Such and on the Language of Man," 28.
60. Here I use Carol Jacobs's retranslation of this passage from *In the Language of Walter Benjamin*, 81. The corresponding passage is found in Benjamin, "The Task of the Translator," 78.
61. Derrida, "Des Tours de Babel," 175.
62. Derrida, *Monolingualism of the Other; or, The Prosthesis of Origin*, 66–68.
63. Ibid., 8.
64. Ibid., 40.
65. Ibid., 62.
66. Ibid., 63.
67. Ibid., 42–43.

Chapter 2

1. Burton Watson's English translation of this novella is included in *Stories of Osaka Life*. Quotations here are from Watson unless otherwise noted. The title of the story can be understood in two ways, as indicated by his translation, which I adopt here.
2. Shah, *Contagious Divides*, 77–79. Shah writes that "the space and social relations of queer domesticity countered or transgressed . . . normative expectations. It included emotional relations between men and women that upset normative heterosexual marriage, as well as homosocial and homoerotic relations" (78).
3. On the Burai-ha, see Dorsey and Slaymaker, *Literary Mischief*. In Japanese, see especially Okuno, *Burai to itan*. Watson gives "hooligan school" in his introduction to Oda, *Stories of Osaka Life* (xii); William Tyler gives "libertines" in his collection of translated stories by Ishikawa Jun, *Legend of Gold* (203); see Joel Cohn, *Studies in the Comic Spirit*, for "outlaw school" (132); Marvin Marcus in Mostow, ed., *Columbia Companion to Modern East Asian Literature*, for "wastrel faction" (57); and Ikuho Amano, *Decadent Literature in Twentieth-Century Japan*, for "Group of Ruffians" (25).
4. Miyoshi, *Off Center*, 19.
5. Oda, "Waga bungaku shūgyō," in *Oda Sakunosuke zenshū*, 8:162–4.
6. Oda, "The State of the Times," in *Stories of Osaka Life*, 147.
7. Maeda, "Oda Sakunosuke, *Meoto zenzai*," 224.
8. Watson's collection is currently out of print. Murakami-Smith deals extensively with Oda's work, particularly through a linguistic approach. Matthew Fargo deals with humor in the work of Makino Shinichi, Ango, and Oda. In Japanese, see Nakaishi, *Oda Sakunosuke*; Maeda, "Oda Sakunosuke, *Meoto zenzai*"; and Kawahara, *Oda Sakunosuke kenkyū*. For considerations of Oda's life and work, see

Taguchi, *Oda Sakunosuke no sekai*, Ōtani, *Iki aishi kaita*, and novelist Aoyama Kōji's recollections of his long friendship with Oda, *Seishun no kake*. Oda's complete works have been published by Kōdansha (1970) and Bunsendō Shoten (1976, 1995).

9. *1946–1996 "Kinema junpō" besuto-ten zenshi*. See chapter 5 for a discussion of this film.

10. The opera, also entitled *Meoto zenzai*, was composed by Ōguri Hiroshi (1918–82). Two performances were given in Osaka, and one each in Kyoto and Kobe. For a panel discussion of the opera, see Ueno Akira et al., "Opera 'Meoto zenzai' o megutte."

11. Miyako Chōchō recalls her life and career in *Onna hitori*.

12. *Asahi hōsō 50-nen ippon shi*, 61.

13. Ibid., 96–97. The concept was revived in 1987 with new hosts for a program called *Shin meoto zenzai* (New sweet beans for two).

14. Makimura, *Ōsaka kotoba jiten*, 654.

15. Yamasaki, Afterword to *Bonchi*, 643.

16. Kobayashi, *Ōsaka to kindai bunka*, 50.

17. Yamasaki, *Noren*, 25.

18. Oda, *Meoto zenzai*, in *Oda Sakunosuke zenshū*, 1:78, my translation; cf. Oda, *Stories of Osaka Life*, 19.

19. Iwano, "Bonchi," 107–29.

20. From the afterword to the paperback edition, quoted in Uranishi, *Ōsaka kindai bungaku sakuhin jiten*, 82.

21. Ishimaru, *Senba no bonchi*.

22. See chapter 4 for a discussion of *Sasameyuki*.

23. Garon, "Fashioning a Culture of Diligence and Thrift," 319.

24. Frühstück, *Colonizing Sex*, chap. 1. See also Ueno, *Nationalism and Gender*.

25. Mosse, *Nationalism and Sexuality*, 5.

26. Bataille, *Accursed Share*, 9.

27. Ibid., 23–25.

28. Ibid., 37.

29. Bataille, *Accursed Share*, 198.

30. Bataille, "Notion of Expenditure," 118.

31. Noys, "Georges Bataille's Base Materialism," 501.

32. Ibid., 508–9.

33. Bataille, "Notion of Expenditure," 129.

34. See Amano, *Decadent Literature in Twentieth-Century Japan*, in particular chapter 6, which discusses Mishima Yukio's debt to Bataille. Amano's study does not deal with Oda Sakunosuke but does include a chapter on Oda's friend and colleague Ango.

35. Oda, *Meoto zenzai*, 74; Oda, *Stories of Osaka Life*, 12.

36. Oda, *Meoto zenzai*, 81; Oda, *Stories of Osaka Life*, 26.

37. Oda, *Meoto zenzai*, 92; Oda, *Stories of Osaka Life*, 50.

38. Oda, *Meoto zenzai*, 78; Oda, *Stories of Osaka Life*, 21.

39. Oda, *Meoto zenzai*, 82; Oda, *Stories of Osaka Life*, 29.

40. Oda, *Meoto zenzai*, 90; Oda, *Stories of Osaka Life*, 45.

41. My translation. "Androgynous" is "*chūsei no*," and "the fag" is "*okama*"; Oda, *Meoto zenzai*, 86–87; cf. Oda, *Stories of Osaka Life*, 39.

42. On the reform movement, see Garon, *Molding Japanese Minds*.

43. On the Osaka style of café, see Tipton, "The Café."

44. Oda, *Meoto zenzai*, 83; Oda, *Stories of Osaka Life*, 30–31.

45. Oda, *Meoto zenzai*, 83; Oda, *Stories of Osaka Life*, 32.

46. Bataille, *Accursed Share*, 199.

47. On food and eating in the Japanese novel, see Shindō, *Shokutsū shōsetsu no kigōgaku*. In English, see Aoyama, *Reading Food in Modern Japanese Literature*.

48. Oda, *Meoto zenzai*, 73–74; Oda, *Stories of Osaka Life*, 9–10.

49. An adage dating back to the Tokugawa period, "*Kyō no kidaore, Ōsaka no kuidaore*," expresses the perception that in Kyoto, people bankrupt themselves over clothes, while in Osaka, they bankrupt themselves over food. A longer version adds, "*Kōbe no hakidaore*": in Kobe, they bankrupt themselves over shoes. On *kuidaore* and the history of Osaka's food culture generally, see Sasai, *Ōsaka shoku-bunka taizen*, and Watanabe Tadashi, *Kinsei "kuidaore" kō*.

50. For a discussion of *getemono ryōri* in Oda's novel and in Kamizukasa Shōken's "Hamo no kawa" (The skin of the pike conger eel, 1914), a novel that prefigures Oda's in some ways, see "Getemono to umaimon" in Shindō, *Shokutsū shōsetsu no kigōgaku*. Shōken's story has recently appeared in an English translation by Andrew Murakami-Smith.

51. Oda, *Meoto zenzai*, 73; Oda, *Stories of Osaka Life*, 9.

52. Oda, *Meoto zenzai*, 77, my translation; cf. Oda, *Stories of Osaka Life*, 18.

53. Oda, *Meoto zenzai*, 82.

54. Bataille, *Accursed Share*, 77.

55. Oda, *Meoto zenzai*, 74, my translation; cf. Oda, *Stories of Osaka Life*, 10.

56. Oda, *Meoto zenzai*, 77; Oda, *Stories of Osaka Life*, 19.

57. Bataille, *Accursed Share*, 55.

58. Ibid., 58–59. Italics in the original.

59. Shindō, *Shokutsū shōsetsu*, 80–81.

60. Heine, "Tragedy and Salvation," 369.

61. Ibid., 371.

62. Oda, "Saikaku shinron," in *Oda Sakunosuke zenshū*, 8:11–12.

63. Chikamatsu, *Major Plays of Chikamatsu*, 170. For the Japanese, see *Meido no hikyaku* in Chikamatsu, *Chikamatsu zenshū*, 7:293–94.

64. Chikamatsu, *Major Plays of Chikamatsu*, 180; Chikamatsu, *Chikamatsu zenshū*, 7:311.

65. Chikamatsu, *Major Plays of Chikamatsu*, 405; cf. Chikamatsu, *Chikamatsu zenshū*, 11:724.

66. Chikamatsu, *Major Plays of Chikamatsu*, 415; cf. Chikamatsu, *Chikamatsu zenshū*, 11:742.

67. Najita, *Visions of Virtue*, 227.

68. Ibid., 227–37. Najita's account of the intellectual environment among *chōnin* in the early Tokugawa period provides insight into the importance of money as a subject of ethical inquiry at the time.

69. Sheldon, *The Rise of the Merchant Class*, 105.

70. Noys, "Georges Bataille's Base Materialism," 500–501.

71. Chikamatsu, *Chikamatsu zenshū*, 4:10–11, my translation; cf. Chikamatsu, *Major Plays of Chikamatsu*, 40. Note that the original audience would have been sitting in a theater in Dōtonbori as they heard Tokubei's injunction to avoid the area.

72. Chikamatsu, *Chikamatsu zenshū*, 11:721–22.

73. Chikamatsu, *Major Plays of Chikamatsu*, 40; Chikamatsu, *Chikamatsu zenshū*, 4:11.

74. Chikamatsu, *Major Plays of Chikamatsu*, 47; Chikamatsu, *Chikamatsu zenshū*, 4:22–23.

75. Shively, *The Love Suicide at Amijima*, 64; Chikamatsu, *Chikamatsu zenshū*, 11:701.

76. Chikamatsu, *Major Plays of Chikamatsu*, 173–74; Chikamatsu, *Chikamatsu zenshū*, 7:297–98.

77. Chikamatsu, *Major Plays of Chikamatsu*, 53; Chikamatsu, *Chikamatsu zenshū*, 4:34.

78. The shrine is Tsuyutenjinja, now known popularly as Ohatsu Tenjin.

79. Borgen, *Sugiwara no Michizane*, 320.

80. Shively, *Love Suicide at Amijima*, 126n219.

81. Oda, *Meoto zenzai: Kanzenban*, 63. Ryūkichi's shrine is identified as Ōsaka Tenman-gū, an alternative name for Tenma Tenjin.

82. Oda, *Meoto zenzai*, 98, my translation; cf. Oda, *Stories of Osaka Life*, 64.

83. On *nichijō seikatsu*, see Harootunian, *History's Disquiet*, and Silverberg, *Erotic Grotesque Nonsense*. On the everyday-life reform movement and the related discourse of *bunka seikatsu* (culture life), see "Middle-Classness and the Reform of Everyday Life" in Sand, *House and Home*, 162–202.

84. Oda, *Meoto zenzai*, 95, my translation; cf. Oda, *Stories of Osaka Life*, 59.

85. Hanes, "Osaka versus Tokyo," 241.

86. Ōya, "Ōsaka bunka no Nippon seifuku," quoted in Hanes, "Osaka versus Tokyo," 244.

87. Gonda, "Minshū goraku," 72–82.

88. Gonda, "Gin-bura to Dō-bura: Santo jōshu," 68–71.

89. Hanes, "Media Culture in Taishō Osaka," 278.

90. Gonda, "Minshū goraku," 77. Hashizume Setsuya's delightful *Modan Shinsaibashi korekushon* provides plentiful pictorial evidence of south Osaka's modernity in the 1920s and includes a chapter on Shinsaibashi flanerie.

91. Bataille, *Accursed Share*, 23.

92. Silverberg, "Constructing the Japanese Ethnography of Modernity," 31.

93. The rediscovered manuscript has been published together with the original novel in Oda, *Meoto zenzai: Kanzenban*.

94. Hidaka quotes the letter, dated August 24, Shōwa 15 (1940), in his afterword to Oda, *Meoto zenzai: Kanzenban*, 202.

95. Oda, *Meoto zenzai: Kanzenban*, 85. Elements of local speech in this line include "*i*" for "*e*" as the postposition after "*Senchi*"; the polite suffix "*-haru*" embedded in "*ikihattara*" and "*soriharahen*"; the negative suffix "*-hen*" instead of "*-nai*"; "*yaro*" for "*darō*"; and the final verb formation, which in standard Japanese might be rendered "*omoidashite kudasai*."

96. Oda, *Meoto zenzai: Kanzenban*, 85.

97. See Nakano, *Ōsaka to hachirentai*. Nakano traces the dissemination of this stereotype and thoroughly refutes it.

Chapter 3

1. Kawamura, "Ōsaka to iu shokuminchi," 159.

2. Aoyama, "Sakuhin kaidai," in *Oda Sakunosuke zenshū*, 3:353. Aoyama cofounded the coterie journal *Kaifū* with Oda.

3. Kawamura, "Ōsaka to iu shokuminchi," 163; emphasis in original.

4. Oda, *Waga machi*, 3:336.

5. For an analysis of the use of the term "*waga machi*" in Oda's novella, see Miyagawa, "Oda Sakunosuke no 'Waga machi' ni tsuite."

6. Ōtani, *Iki aishi kaita*, 20–34.

7. Quoted in Uranishi, *Oda Sakunosuke bungei jiten*, 271.

8. On the building of the Benguet Road and the settling of Baguio, see chapter 7 in Corpuz, *Colonial Iron Horse*; and Reed, *City of Pines*.

9. Worcester describes this expedition and the settlement of Baguio in his book, *The Philippines Past and Present*, which includes photos from this era of the Benguet Road and Baguio.

10. Corpuz, *Colonial Iron Horse*, 143.

11. Report of the Philippine Commission, quoted in Reed, *City of Pines*, 89.

12. Worcester, *The Philippines: Past and Present*, 477.

13. Initial estimates were six months and $65,000; in fact, the road was not open for regular service until March 1905, four year after construction began, and by that time the cost had exceeded $2 million (Corpuz, *Colonial Iron Horse*, 135).

14. On the development of Davao before World War II, see Goodman, "'A Flood of Immigration,'" and Furiya, "The Japanese Community Abroad." For the number of immigrants registered in Manila, see Yoshikawa, "Development of the Japanese Commercial Sector in Manila," 411.

15. Oda, *Waga machi*, 247.

16. Quoted in Iriye, *Pacific Estrangement*, 9.

17. Yu-Jose, *Japan Views the Philippines*, 33–35.

18. Reed, *City of Pines*, 95–96.

19. Oda, *Waga machi*, 251.

20. Corpuz, *Colonial Iron Horse*, 138–39. Goodman notes another reason for the lower efficiency of Philippine labor: the fact that "during the Spanish regime, public works projects were traditionally assigned to forced labor"; see Goodman, "'A Flood of Immigration,'" 190n4, citing a 1936 dissertation by Generoso P. Provido.

21. On Ōta's life and career, see Furukawa, *Dabao kaitakuki*, and Inoue, *Hirippin Guntō to Ōta Kyōsaburō-kun*.

22. For an account of Japanese involvement in and attitudes toward the Philippines in this period, see Yu-Jose, *Japan Views the Philippines*.

23. Oda, *Waga machi*, 251.

24. Goodman, "'A Flood of Immigration,'" 171.

25. Yu-Jose, *Japan Views the Philippines*, 13.

26. Yu-Jose, *Japan Views the Philippines*, 117–38 (119 for iron tonnage; 117 for ancillary industries; 138 for population figures).

27. Quoted in Goodman, "'A Flood of Immigration,'" 183.

28. Price, "Sangyō shihai no ura ni, chi to ase no romansu," 3. Note that the *Asahi Shimbun* began publication in Osaka in 1879. The *Tokyo Asahi Shimbun* began publication in 1888 as a separate corporate entity. The two merged in 1908, but the names of the two newspapers were not unified as *Asahi Shimbun* until 1940.

29. Yu-Jose provides a translation of the textbook passage in *Japan Views the Philippines*, 15.

30. Price, "Urusai tochi mondai," 3.

31. Yu-Jose, *Japan Views the Philippines*, 90. Yu-Jose gives the reading of Furukawa's given name as "Yoshizō"; I follow the listing in the *Nihonjinmei daijiten*.

32. The phrase "brotherly amity" appears in Tōjō Hideki's speech to the Assembly of Greater East Asiatic Nations in November 1943. See Lebra-Chapman, *Japan's Greater East Asia Co-Prosperity Sphere*, 91.

33. Oda, *Waga machi*, 257.

34. I have adopted this phrase from Kaika, *City of Flows*.

35. McClain and Osamu, *Osaka*, 51.

36. Makimura, *Ōsaka kotoba jiten*, 168. The short final "o" reflects Kansai pronunciation.

37. Oda, *Waga machi*, 252.

38. Jinnai, *Tokyo: A Spatial Anthropology*.

39. For a brief history of Osaka's canals, with special attention to the Higashiyokobori, see Kana, "Urban Spatial Transformation."

40. Jinnai, *Tokyo: A Spatial Anthropology*, 98.

41. Ibid., 87.

42. Ibid., 98.

43. Kaika, *City of Flows*, 4. Two popular novels of Osaka discussed in subsequent chapters feature pivotal scenes based on historical events in which heavy rains caused urban waterways to overflow their borders. The Great Hanshin Flood of July 1938 figures in Tanizaki's *Sasameyuki*, discussed in chapter 4. In Yamasaki Toyoko's *Noren*, discussed in chapter 5, a flood that occurred in Osaka on September 21, 1934, nearly destroys the fictional business at the center of the novel.

44. On the emergence of this discourse, see chapter 1 of Iriye, *Pacific Estrangement*.

45. Peattie points out that "'*Nan'yō*' is at once an ambiguous and a precise term": Myers and Peattie, *The Japanese Colonial Empire*, 172n. In certain contexts, it was used to refer specifically to the former German colonies in Micronesia, over which Japan exercised a mandate granted it by the League of Nations after World War I. In other contexts, it was understood to include the Philippines and other territories.

46. Oda, *Waga machi*, 258.

47. The text gives "*watari*" in katakana as a gloss for the kanji compound "*togyo*"; Oda, *Waga machi*, 302. Ikutama (or Ikudama) is the colloquial name for Ikukunitama-jinja.

48. Oda, *Waga machi*, 259.

49. Bakhtin, *The Dialogic Imagination*, 272.

50. Oda, *Waga machi*, 273.
51. Ibid., 250.
52. Ibid., 250.
53. On Oda's use of Kansai dialect in narrative ground in ten works (*Waga machi* not among them), see Miyagawa, "Oda Sakunosuke no Kansai-ben," in *Kindai bungaku no naka no Kansai-ben*.
54. Bhabha, "Unsatisfied: Notes on Vernacular Cosmopolitanism," 195–96.
55. Werbner, "Vernacular Cosmopolitanism," 496. On the proliferation of cosmopolitanisms, see also Vertovec and Cohen, *Conceiving Cosmopolitanism*, and Harvey, "Cosmopolitanism and the Banality of Geographical Evils."
56. Radhakrishnan, "Towards an Eccentric Cosmopolitanism."
57. Cheah and Robbins, *Cosmopolitics*, 22–30.
58. Hanes, "Osaka versus Tokyo," 231–33.
59. Latour, *We Have Never Been Modern*, 124.
60. Dainotto, "'All the Regions Do Smilingly Revolt,'" 500.
61. Torrance, "Literacy and Literature in Osaka," 29. For an analysis of Osaka regionalism in the context of the mid-1960s, see Gardner, "From Parody to Simulacrum."
62. Dainotto, "'All the Regions Do Smilingly Revolt,'" 501.
63. Arrighi, *The Long Twentieth Century*, 11.
64. Harvey, *Condition of Postmodernity*, 351.
65. Ibid., 117.
66. Massey, *Space, Place, and Gender*, 143.
67. Ibid., 333.
68. Sugihara, *Ekkyō suru tami*, 52–60.
69. Kawamura, "Ōsaka to iu shokuminchi," 167–68.
70. Oda, *Waga machi*, 277.
71. Oda's text does not give a phonetic reading for the protagonist's name, but he is called "Sadojima" in the film and in the program for the 1961 theatrical adaptation.
72. Oda, *Waga machi*, 327.
73. Ibid., 338–39.
74. Oda, *Waga machi*, 317.
75. Ibid., 338–39.
76. "Puranetariumu shiryō-shitsu."
77. Hashizume, *Eiga* Dai-Ōsaka kankō *no sekai*, 60–61.
78. Tezuka, *Tezuka Osamu essei shū*, 20. In a longer reminiscence published in 1985, Tezuka discusses the impact of the museum and planetarium on his generation of science-fiction writers and artists, including Komatsu Sakyō. See Tezuka, "Natsukashi no puranetariumu," 74–75.
79. Sakai, *Translation and Subjectivity*, 157.
80. Latour, *We Have Never Been Modern*, 120.

Chapter 4

1. On this history, see Torrance, "Literary Accounts of the Decline of Senba," 68. Torrance's article also discusses several literary works that deal with Senba.

2. Miyamoto, "Japan's World Cities," 55.

3. Tanizaki closely based the characters and stories of the four sisters on his wife and her sisters. The parallels are described in Chambers, *The Secret Window*, and Noguchi, "Time in the World of *Sasameyuki*."

4. Hatanaka, *Oboegaki*, 166; cited and translated in Rubin, *Injurious to Public Morals*, 264.

5. Keene, *Dawn to the West*, 774.

6. Itō Sei, *Tanizaki Jun'ichirō no bungaku*, 189.

7. LaMarre, *Shadows on the Screen*, 12.

8. Hosoe, *Tanizaki Jun'ichirō*, 487–525; Hurley, "Toward a New Modern Vernacular," 361–63.

9. Ito, *Visions of Desire*, 190–92.

10. Chambers, *Secret Window*, 88.

11. Chambers, "*The Makioka Sisters* as a Political Novel," 134.

12. Komori and Hasumi, "Tanizaki raisan," 25–26.

13. Ibid., 8–10.

14. Golley, "Tanizaki Jun'ichirō," 367–68.

15. Long, *This Perversion Called Love*, 37–38.

16. Ibid., 17.

17. Ibid., 38.

18. Tanizaki, *The Makioka Sisters*, 9; cf. *Sasameyuki*, in *Tanizaki Jun'ichirō zenshū*, 15:11. Where I use Seidensticker's translation, I give the citation for both it and the corresponding passage in the *zenshū*.

19. Tanizaki, *The Makioka Sisters*, 13; Tanizaki, *Sasameyuki*, 15.

20. Tanizaki, *The Makioka Sisters*, 7–8; Tanizaki, *Sasameyuki*, 8–10.

21. Tanizaki, *The Makioka Sisters*, 41; Tanizaki, *Sasameyuki*, 64.

22. The Hanshin Electric Railway Company began business as the Settsu Electric Railway Corporation (Settsu Denki-tetsudō Kabushiki-gaisha) in June 1899 but changed its name a month later. Hankyū was established as the Minō-Arima Electric Railway (Minō-Arima Denki Kidō). It was renamed the Hanshin Express Electric Rail Corporation (Hanshin Kyūkō Dentetsu Kabushiki-gaisha), contracted to Hankyū, in 1918. The two corporations merged in 2006 to become Hankyū-Hanshin Holdings, Inc.

23. Sand, *House and Home in Modern Japan*, 152.

24. Tanizaki, *Sasameyuki*, 483.

25. Ibid., 707.

26. Ibid., 443.

27. "Something like the same race" is my literal translation of "onaji jinshu no yō na mono" (*Sasameyuki*, 457). Seidensticker translates this as "He was one of them" (*The Makioka Sisters*, 278).

28. Tanizaki, *Sasameyuki*, 456.

29. Tanizaki, *The Makioka Sisters*, 529; Tanizaki, *Sasameyuki*, 880.

30. Tanizaki, *Sasameyuki*, 249–50, emphasis added.

31. Ibid., 256, emphasis added. Here, she uses the familiar suffix "*-chan*" rather than "*-bon*."

32. Tanizaki, *The Makioka Sisters*, 467; Tanizaki, *Sasameyuki*, 776–77.

33. Tanizaki, *The Makioka Sisters*, 101; Tanizaki, *Sasameyuki*, 163–64.

34. Tanizaki, *The Makioka Sisters*, 444; Tanizaki, *Sasameyuki*, 738.

35. Tanizaki, *Sasameyuki*, 849.

36. The municipal ward Hyōgo-ku, part of Kobe city, is not to be confused with the prefecture Hyōgo-ken, of which Kobe is the capital. The names are written with the same characters.

37. Tanizaki, *The Makioka Sisters*, 494; Tanizaki, *Sasameyuki*, 825.

38. Tanizaki, *The Makioka Sisters*, 98; Tanizaki, *Sasameyuki*, 159.

39. Tanizaki, *The Makioka Sisters*, 100; Tanizaki, *Sasameyuki*, 161–62.

40. Tanizaki, *The Makioka Sisters*, 131; Tanizaki, *Sasameyuki*, 211.

41. Tanizaki, *The Makioka Sisters*, 218–19; Tanizaki, *Sasameyuki*, 359.

42. Johnson, "Illness, Disease, and Medicine," 141–42.

43. Tanizaki, *Sasameyuki*, 715.

44. See Bay, *Beri-beri in Modern Japan*.

45. Tanizaki, *The Makioka Sisters*, 118; Tanizaki, *Sasameyuki*, 190–91.

46. Chambers also points to the "illnesses that pervade *The Makioka Sisters*," explaining them as symbols of the decline that he identifies as the larger pattern of the novel; see Chambers, *The Secret Window*, 81.

47. Ito, *Visions of Desire*, 204.

48. Ibid., 207–8.

49. Butler, *Bodies That Matter*, 167.

50. Johnson, "Illness, Disease, and Medicine," 144.

51. Bourdaghs, *The Dawn That Never Comes*, 52–55.

52. Morris-Suzuki, *Reinventing Japan*, 204; quoted in Bourdaghs, *The Dawn That Never Comes*, 66.

53. Ibid., 58.

54. Tanizaki, *The Makioka Sisters*, 26; Tanizaki, *The Makioka Sisters*, 23.

55. Bourdaghs, *The Dawn That Never Comes*, 56–57.

56. Koi-san replies, "He says he wants me to have it. . . . Unless we do that, Kei-chan will never give up" (Tanizaki, *Sasameyuki*, 830). Seidensticker's otherwise remarkably faithful translation omits these lines; it does, however, include the subsequent scene in which Sachiko considers the possibility of abortion.

57. Regarding the association of the Hanshin-kan with reproductive failure in Tanizaki's works, we can think of the grotesque faked miscarriage in an earlier novel, *Manji*.

58. For more on this process, see Ueno Chizuko, *Nationalism and Gender*, and Frühstück, *Colonizing Sex*.

59. Edelman, *No Future*, 134.

60. Ibid., 8.

61. Tanizaki maintained his fascination with dialects to the end of his life. His final novel, *Daidokoro Taiheiki* (The kitchen chronicles, 1963), which revisits characters and incidents from *Sasameyuki* viewed this time from the perspective of the family maids, includes a passage listing the different words used for various vegetables and fish in Kansai and Kantō, as well as an excerpt from a dictionary kept by the daughter of the household of the Kagoshima dialect used by the maids.

62. Watanabe, "Yukiko to hachigatsu jūgonichi." Watanabe calls Tanizaki's novel a "chien no monogatari," arguing that it reflects the conditions under which he was required to write.

63. Cf. Edelman's reading of a scene of postponement (Tippi Hedren's character Melanie smoking a cigarette) in Alfred Hitchcock's *The Birds*; Edelman, *No Future*, 140–43.

64. Halberstam, *Queer Art of Failure*, 124–26.

65. Tanizaki, *The Makioka Sisters*, 148; Tanizaki, *The Makioka Sisters*, 138.

66. Tanizaki, *The Makioka Sisters*, 411; Tanizaki, *Sasameyuki*, 683–84. I have used Seidensticker's translation here but retained the original ellipses indicating Yukiko's silence, which Seidensticker translates as "Yukiko did not answer" and "Silence again."

67. Tanizaki, *Sasameyuki*, 687, my translation.

68. Halberstam, *Queer Art of Failure*, 126.

69. Ibid., 125.

70. Tanizaki, *The Makioka Sisters*, 362–64; cf. Tanizaki, *Sasameyuki*, 604–5.

71. Halberstam, *Queer Art of Failure*, 131.

72. Tanizaki, *Sasameyuki*, 23, my translation; cf. Tanizaki, *The Makioka Sisters*, 18.

73. Tanizaki, *Sasameyuki*, 482–83, my translation; cf. Tanizaki, *The Makioka Sisters*, 293.

74. Tanizaki, *Sasameyuki*, 160.

75. Tanizaki, *The Makioka Sisters*, 368; Tanizaki, *Sasameyuki*, 613.

76. Ito, *Visions of Desire*, 105.

77. "Hanshin kenbunroku," in Tanizaki, *Tanizaki Jun'ichirō zenshū*, 20:63.

78. "Watakushi no mita Ōsaka oyobi Ōsakajin," in Tanizaki, *Tanizaki Jun'ichirō zenshū*, 20:357.

79. Ibid., 357–58.

80. Ibid., 360.

81. Ibid., 351.

82. Karatani Kojin, "Yume no sekai," 69.

83. Chambers, *Secret Window*, 31–32.

84. Hammersley and Atkinson, *Ethnography*, 200.

85. Doane, "Film and Masquerade," and Doane, "Masquerade Reconsidered." For an elaboration of Doane's argument, see Kanno, "Implicational Spectatorship."

86. Chambers, *Secret Window*, 81.

87. Tanizaki, *The Makioka Sisters*, 471; Tanizaki, *Sasameyuki*, 785.

88. Golley, "Tanizaki Junichirō," 399.

89. de Man, "The Concept of Irony," 165.

Chapter 5

1. On literary adaptation in Japanese cinema, see McDonald, *From Book to Screen*. McDonald writes that the postwar golden age was sustained by the pure-literature movement, and her investigation deals mainly with adaptations of "pure" or at least "high" literature. Her chapter on Toyoda Shirō, for instance, focuses on

his 1960 adaptation of Nagai Kafū's *Bokutō kitan* (A strange tale from east of the river, 1937) and mentions several other of Toyoda's films but ignores *Meoto zenzai*, one of his most successful adaptations, which I discuss in this chapter.

2. Material from Oda's screenplay for *Kaette kita otoko* also appears in the story "Ki no miyako" (City of trees, 1944).

3. *Meshi* won Blue Ribbon awards for best film, actress, supporting actress (Sugimura Haruko), and screenplay (Tanaka Sumie), and Mainichi Concours awards for best film (along with Ozu's *Bakushū*), director, actress, cinematography, and sound recording.

4. Quoted in Isoda, *Kawashima Yūzō*, 115.

5. Michael Emmerich's recent translation of *The Bullfight* makes a valuable addition to the literature of Osaka available in English.

6. For a detailed account of these charges, see Ukai, *Yamasaki Toyoko mondai shōsetsu no kenkyū*.

7. The Nomonhan Incident of 1939, also known as the Battle of Khalkhyn Gol, was an encounter between Japanese forces occupying Manchuria and Soviet and Mongol forces. In the Shimoyama Incident of 1949, the president of the Japanese National Railways (JNR), Shimoyama Sadanori, disappeared on his way to work, and his body was discovered the next day by the tracks of the Tōbu Railway's Isesaki Line. Shimoyama had announced cutbacks in JNR personnel the day before he went missing. In the Mitaka Incident of the same year, a runaway train on the Chūō Line killed six and injured twenty. Ten workers were indicted on charges of sabotage, nine of them members of the Communist Party.

8. Yamasaki, *Noren*, 44. All translations are mine.

9. Ibid., 81–82.

10. With the introduction of the metric system in 1891, 15 kilograms was set at 4 *kan*; 1 *kan* is therefore equivalent to 3.75 kilograms.

11. Yamasaki, *Noren*, 85.

12. Ibid., 211–12.

13. It was awarded the Mainichi Concours for best film and was named "best film" by *Kinema junpō*, which also named Yamamoto Satsuo "best director."

14. *Yamasaki Toyoko: zenshōsetsu o yomitoku*, 109.

15. In Yamasaki, *Shibuchin*, 1–41.

16. Chow, *Primitive Passions*, 180.

17. Ibid.

18. Stam, "Introduction," 46.

19. Elliott, *Rethinking the Novel/Film Debate*, 150.

20. The declaration that the debates are over comes from Hutcheon, *A Theory of Adaptation*, xxvi.

21. Jameson, "Afterword," 215.

22. Cazdyn, *Flash of Capital*, 117.

23. For an analysis of local geography and landscape in *Waga machi* and of Kawashima's broader collaboration with Oda, see chapter 3, "*Waga machi:* Uemachi daichi nosutarujia," in Sakai Takashi, *Tsūtenkaku*.

24. For an extended analysis of *Ōsaka no yado* in the context of Gosho's oeuvre, see chapter 6 in Nolletti, *Cinema of Gosho Heinosuke*.

25. For contemporary assessments of Genji's novel and the phenomenon it named, see Fujii Kaoru, "*Santō jūyaku*-ron," and Kada, "Gendai: Santō jūyaku-ron."

26. Although it lies outside the immediate postwar period under consideration in this chapter, Masumura Yasuzo's 1964 adaptation of Tanizaki's *Manji* merits a brief mention for its odd manipulation of the story's time setting. The actors, particularly Wakao Ayako (as the younger Mitsuko), are dressed and styled in the contemporary fashion of the 1960s as they enact Tanizaki's story from the late 1920s. This leads to anachronisms, as when Sonoko schemes with Mitsuko about how the latter might end an unwanted pregnancy—at a time when, judging by their costumes, abortion was legal.

27. The title of Toyoda's film is sometimes translated in English as *Marital Relations* or, alas, *Love Is Shared Like Sweets.*

28. These are the 1954 adaptation of Ōgai's *Gan* (Wild geese); the 1955 adaptation of Arishima's *Aru onna* (A certain woman); *Mugibue* (Wheat whistle), the 1955 adaptation of Saisei's *Sei no mezameru koro* (Awakening to sexuality); and the 1959 adaptation of Shiga's *An'ya kōro* (A dark night's passing).

29. Oda, *Meoto zenzai*, in *Oda Sakunosuke zenshū*, 1:71. Both "*hayo*" for "*hayaku*" (quickly) and "*ageten kai na*" for "*agete kurenai ka ne*" (won't you fry [it] for me) are Kansai forms.

30. Yamasaki, *Bonchi*, 5. "*Dō yanen*" is the Osaka equivalent of "*Dō desu ka*" (How is it? How goes it?).

31. Tansman, *Culture of Japanese Fascism*, 9.

32. Fujii Shigeo, "*Meoto zenzai*," 61–63. Fujii (1916–79) was short-listed for the Akutagawa Prize in 1959 and was awarded the Naoki Prize in 1965 for the story "Niji" (Rainbow).

33. Oda, *Meoto zenzai*, in *Oda Sakunosuke zenshū*, 1:73.

34. *Noren*, along with *Hana noren* and *Bonchi*, also served as source material for the television drama *Yokobori-gawa*, broadcast by NHK from April 1966 to March 1967.

35. Deleuze, *Cinema 2*, 222.

36. Dyer, *Heavenly Bodies*, 15.

37. Dyer, "*A Star Is Born* and the Construction of Authenticity," 133.

38. Ibid., 137–39.

39. See Galbraith, *The Toho Studios Story*, 455–56, for a list of all the films in each series. On the *Shachō* series, see also Nishimura, "Shachō shirīzu kara 'sengo' o miru."

40. For a complete list of his films, see "Morishige eiga o furikaeru," 28–29.

41. Spicer, *Typical Men*, 19.

42. Morishige, *Sukima kara sukima e*, 73.

43. Morishige, "Watashi no engi hōteishiki," 88.

44. Quoted in Morishige, *Sukima kara sukima e*, 80–81.

45. Fujii Shigeo, "*Meoto zenzai*," 63.

46. Dolar, *A Voice and Nothing More*, 15.

47. Ibid., 79.

48. Ibid., 20.

49. Spicer, *Typical Men*, 102.

50. Featherstone, *Undoing Culture*, 104.
51. Miyao, *Sessue Hayakawa*, 8.
52. Dyer, *Heavenly Bodies*, 150.
53. Ivy, *Discourses of the Vanishing*, 22.

Conclusion

1. The study, conducted by Hōsei University and published on November 9, 2011, ranked prefectures according to an analysis of a variety of economic statistics, measuring such factors as safety and access to medical facilities.

2. On Hashimoto's proposals, see Matthews, "Osaka In and Out of the Nation."

3. For a discussion of the constitutionality of this act, see Repeta, "Mr. Hashimoto Attacks Japan's Constitution."

4. Butler, *Bodies That Matter*, 167.

5. The film won Japanese Academy Awards for director, screenplay, actress, and supporting actor.

Bibliography

1946–1996 "Kinema junpō" besuto-ten zenshi, 2009.

Amano, Ikuho. *Decadent Literature in Twentieth-Century Japan: Spectacles of Idle Labor.* New York: Palgrave Macmillan, 2013.

Anderson, Benedict. *Imagined Communities: Reflections on the Origin and Spread of Nationalism*. Rev. ed. London: Verso, 1991.

Aoyama Kōji. *Seishun no kake: Shōsetsu Oda Sakunosuke.* Tokyo: Kōdansha, 2010.

Aoyama, Tomoko. *Reading Food in Modern Japanese Literature.* Honolulu: University of Hawai'i Press, 2008.

Appadurai, Arjun. *Modernity at Large: Cultural Dimensions of Globalization.* Minneapolis: University of Minnesota Press, 1996.

Arrighi, Giovanni. *The Long Twentieth Century: Money, Power, and the Origins of Our Times.* London: Verso, 1994.

Asahi hōsō 50-nen ippon shi. Osaka: Asahi hōsō shashi henshūshitu henshū. 2000.

Atkins, E. Taylor. *Blue Nippon: Authenticating Jazz in Japan.* Durham: Duke University Press, 2001.

Bakhtin, Mikhail. *The Dialogic Imagination: Four Essays by Mikhail Bakhtin.* Edited by Michael Holquist. Translated by Caryl Emerson and Michael Holquist. Austin: University of Texas Press, 1981.

———. *Problems of Dostoevsky's Poetics.* Edited and translated by Caryl Emerson. Minneapolis: University of Minnesota Press, 1984.

Bataille, Georges. *The Accursed Share: An Essay on General Economy.* Vol. 1, *Consumption.* Translated by Robert Hurley. New York: Zone Books, 1998.

———. "The Notion of Expenditure." In *Visions of Excess: Selected Writings, 1927–1939*, edited by Allan Stoekl. Translated by Allan Stoekl, with Carl R. Lovitt and Donald M. Leslie Jr., 116–29. Minneapolis: University of Minnesota Press, 1985.

Bay, Alexander R. *Beri-Beri in Modern Japan: The Making of a National Disease.* Rochester, NY: University of Rochester Press, 2012.

Benjamin, Walter. "On Language as Such and on the Language of Man." In *Reflections*, edited by Peter Demetz. Translated by Edmund Jephcott, 314–32. New York: Harcourt Brace Jovanovich, 1978.

———. "The Task of the Translator." In *Illuminations*. Translated by Harry Zohn. New York: Schocken Books, 1969.

Berry, Chris. "If China Can Say No, Can China Make Movies? Or, Do Movies Make China? Rethinking National Cinema and National Agency," *Boundary 2* 25, no. 3 (1998): 129–50.

Bhabha, Homi. "Unsatisfied: Notes on Vernacular Cosmopolitanism." In *Text and Nation*, edited by Laura Garcia-Morena and Peter C. Pfeifer, 191–207. Columbia, SC: Camden House, 1996.

Borgen, Robert. *Sugiwara no Michizane and the Early Heian Court*. Honolulu: University of Hawai'i Press, 1994 (1986).

Bourdaghs, Michael K. *The Dawn That Never Comes: Shimazaki Tōson and Japanese Nationalism*. New York: Columbia University Press, 2003.

Brownstein, Michael. "The Osaka Kannon Pilgrimage and Chikamatsu's 'Love Suicides at Sonezaki.'" *Harvard Journal of Asiatic Studies* 66, no. 1 (June 2006): 7–41.

Butler, Judith. *Bodies That Matter: On the Discursive Limits of Sex*. London: Routledge, 1993.

Cazdyn, Eric. *The Flash of Capital: Film and Geopolitics in Japan*. Durham: Duke University Press, 2002.

Chambers, Anthony Hood. "*The Makioka Sisters* as a Political Novel." In *A Tanizaki Feast*, edited by Adriana Boscaro and Chambers. Ann Arbor: University of Michigan Center for Asian Studies, 1998.

———. *The Secret Window: Ideal Worlds in Tanizaki's Fiction*. Cambridge, MA: Harvard East Asian Monographs, 1994.

Cheah, Pheng, and Bruce Robbins, eds. *Cosmopolitics: Thinking and Feeling beyond the Nation*. Minneapolis: University of Minnesota Press, 1998.

Chikamatsu Monzaemon. *Chikamatsu zenshū*. 17 vols. Tokyo: Iwanami Shoten, 1985–94.

———. *Major Plays of Chikamatsu*. Translated by Donald Keene. New York: Columbia University Press, 1961.

Chow, Rey. *Primitive Passions: Visuality, Sexuality, Ethnography and Contemporary Chinese Cinema*. New York: Columbia University Press, 1995.

Cohn, Joel R. *Studies in the Comic Spirit in Modern Japanese Fiction*. Cambridge, MA: Harvard University Asia Center, 1998.

Corpuz, Arturo G. *The Colonial Iron Horse: Railroads and Regional Development in the Philippines, 1875–1935*. Quezon City: University of Philippines Press, 1999.

Dainotto, Roberto Maria. "'All the Regions Do Smilingly Revolt': The Literature of Place and Region." *Critical Inquiry* 22, no. 3 (Spring 1996).

———. *Place in Literature: Regions, Cultures, Communities*. Ithaca, NY: Cornell University Press, 2000.

de Certeau, Michel. *The Practice of Everyday Life*. Translated by Steven Rendall. Berkeley: University of California Press, 1984.

Deleuze, Gilles. *Cinema 2: The Time Image.* Translated by Hugh Tomlinson and Robert Galeta. Minneapolis: University of Minnesota Press, 1989 (1985).

Deleuze, Gilles, and Felix Guattari. *Kafka: Toward a Minor Literature.* Translated by Dana Polan. Minneapolis: University of Minnesota Press, 1986 (1975).

de Man, Paul. "The Concept of Irony." In *Aesthetic Ideology,* edited by Andrzej Warminski. Minneapolis: University of Minnesota, 1996.

———. "Conclusions: Walter Benjamin's 'The Task of the Translator.'" In *The Resistance to Theory,* 73–105. Minneapolis: University of Minnesota Press, 1986.

Derrida, Jacques. "Des Tours de Babel." Translated by Joseph F. Graham. In *Difference in Translation,* edited by Joseph F. Graham, 165–207. Ithaca, NY: Cornell University Press, 1985.

———. *The Ear of the Other: Otobiography, Transference, Translation,* edited by Christie McDonald. Translated by Peggy Kamuf. Lincoln: University of Nebraska Press, 1985.

———. *Monolingualism of the Other; or, The Prosthesis of Origin.* Translated by Patrick Mensah. Stanford: Stanford University Press, 1998.

———. "What Is a 'Relevant' Translation?" Translated by Lawrence Venuti. In *The Translation Studies Reader,* 2nd ed., edited by Lawrence Venuti, 423–46. New York: Routledge, 2004 (1999).

Doane, Mary Ann. "Film and Masquerade: Theorizing the Female Spectator." *Screen* 23, nos. 3–4 (September–October 1982): 74–87.

———. "Masquerade Reconsidered: Further Thoughts on Female Spectatorship." In *Femmes Fatales: Feminism, Film Theory, Psychoanalysis,* 33–43. London: Routledge, 1991.

Dolar, Mladen. *A Voice and Nothing More.* Cambridge, MA: MIT Press, 2006.

Dorsey, James, and Douglas Slaymaker, ed. *Literary Mischief: Sakaguchi Ango, Culture, and the War.* Lanham, MD: Lexington Books, 2010.

Dyer, Richard. *Heavenly Bodies: Film Stars and Society.* London: Routledge, 2004 (1986).

———. "*A Star Is Born* and the Construction of Authenticity." In *Stardom: Industry of Desire,* edited by Christine Gledhill, 132–40. London: Routledge, 1998.

Edelman, Lee. *No Future: Queer Theory and the Death Drive.* Durham: Duke University Press, 2004.

Elliott, Kamilla. *Rethinking the Novel/Film Debate.* Cambridge: Cambridge University Press, 2003.

Fargo, Matthew Thomas. *Makino Shinichi, Sakaguchi Ango, and Oda Sakunosuke: Modern Japanese Literature as a Joke.* Diss., University of California, Berkeley, Fall 2011.

Featherstone, Mike. *Undoing Culture: Globalization, Postmodernism and Identity.* London: Sage, 1995.

Fowler, Edward. *The Rhetoric of Confession: Shishōsetsu in Early Twentieth-Century Japanese Literature.* Berkeley: University of California Press, 1988.

Frühstück, Sabine. *Colonizing Sex: Sexology and Social Control in Modern Japan.* Berkeley: University of California Press, 2003.

Fujii Kaoru. "*Santō jūyaku*-ron: Taishū shōsetsu no mondai." *Shisō no kagaku* 1, no. 6 (June 1954): 85–87.

Fujii Shigeo. "*Meoto zenzai.*" *Eiga hyōron* 12, no. 10 (October 1955): 61–63.

Furiya Reiko. "The Japanese Community Abroad: The Case of Prewar Davao in the Philippines." In *The Japanese in Colonial Southeast Asia*, edited by T. Shiraishi, 155–172. Ithaca, NY: Cornell University, Southeast Asia Program, 1993.

Furukawa Yoshizō. *Dabao kaitakuki*. Tokyo: Dai Nihon Hōrei Insatsu, 1956.

Galbraith, Stuart, IV. *The Toho Studios Story: A History and Complete Filmography*. Lanham, MD: Scarecrow Press, 2008.

Gangloff, Eric J. "Tanizaki's Use of Traditional Literature: A Comparison of *Manji* and *Shinjū Ten no Amijima*." *Journal of the Association of Teachers of Japanese* 11, nos. 2–3 (May–September 1976): 217–34.

Gardner, W. O. "From Parody to Simulacrum: Japanese SF, Regionalism, and the Inauthentic in the Early Works of Komatsu Sakyō and Tsutsui Yasutaka." *Paradoxa* 22 (2010).

Garon, Sheldon. "Fashioning a Culture of Diligence and Thrift: Savings and Frugality Campaigns in Japan, 1900–1931." In *Japan's Competing Modernities: Issues in Culture and Democracy, 1900–1930*, edited by Sharon Minichiello, 312–34. Honolulu: University of Hawai'i Press, 1998.

———. *Molding Japanese Minds: The State in Everyday Life*. Princeton, NJ: Princeton University Press, 1997.

Genji Keita. *Santō jūyaku*. Tokyo: Mainichi Shinbunsha, 1951.

Golley, Gregory L. "Tanizaki Junichirō: The Art of Subversion and the Subversion of Art." *Journal of Japanese Studies* 21, no. 2 (Summer 1995): 365–404.

Gonda Yasunosuke. "Ginbura to Dōbura: Santo jōshū." In *Gonda Yasunosuke chosakushū* 4, 68–71 (*Chūgai Shōgyō Shinpō* 8/11/23).

———. "Minshū goraku." In *Gonda Yasunosuke chosakushū* 4, 72–82. Tokyo: Bunwa Shobō, 1974–75 (*Chūgai shōgyō shinpō* 1/23).

Goodman, Grant. "'A Flood of Immigration': Patterns and Problems of Japanese Migration to the Philippines during the First Four Decades of the Twentieth Century," *Philippine Historical Review* 1, no. 1 (1965).

Gordon, Andrew. "Consumption, Leisure and the Middle Class in Transwar Japan." *Social Science Japan Journal* 10, no. 1 (2007): 1–21.

Gottlieb, Nannette. *Language and the Modern State: The Reform of Written Japanese*. London: Routledge, 1991.

———. *See also* Twine, Nanette.

Halberstam, Judith. *The Queer Art of Failure*. Durham, NC: Duke University Press, 2011.

Hammersley, Martyn, and Paul Atkinson. *Ethnography: Principles and Practice*. 3rd ed. London: Routledge, 2007.

Hanes, Jeffrey E. *The City as Subject: Seki Hajime and the Reinvention of Modern Osaka*. Berkeley: University of California Press, 2002.

———. "Media Culture in Taishō Osaka." In *Japan's Competing Modernities: Issues in Culture and Democracy, 1900–1930*, 267–87. Honolulu: University of Hawai'i Press, 1998.

———. "Osaka versus Tokyo: The Cultural Politics of Local Identity in Modern Japan." In *Image and Identity: Rethinking Japanese Cultural History*, 229–48. Kobe: Research Institute for Economics and Business Administration, Kobe University, 2004.

Hara Takeshi. *"Minto" Ōsaka tai "teito" Tōkyō*. Tokyo: Kōdansha, 1998.

Haraguchi Ujio. *Hoshi to heitai: Heiyō tenmon monogatari*. Tokyo: Kaiseisha, 1943.

Harootunian, Harry D. *History's Disquiet: Modernity, Cultural Practice, and the Question of Everyday Life*. New York: Columbia University Press, 2000.

———. *Overcome by Modernity: History, Culture, and Community in Interwar Japan*. Princeton, NJ: Princeton University Press, 2002.

Harvey, David. *The Condition of Postmodernity: An Enquiry into the Origins of Cultural Change*. Oxford: Wiley-Blackwell, 1991.

———. "Cosmopolitanism and the Banality of Geographical Evils." *Public Culture* 12, no. 2 (Spring 2000): 529–64.

Hashizume Setsuya. *Eiga* Dai-Ōsaka kankō *no sekai: Shōwa 12-nen no modan toshi*. Osaka: The Museum of Osaka University, 2009.

———. *Modan Shinsaibashi korekushon*. Tokyo: Kokusho, 2005.

Hatanaka Shigeo. *Oboegaki: Shōwa shuppan dan'atsu shōshi*. Tokyo: Tosho Shinbun, 1965.

Hauser, William B. "Osaka Castle and Tokugawa Authority in Western Japan." In *The Bakufu in Japanese History*, 153–72. Stanford: Stanford University Press, 1985.

Heine, Steven. "Tragedy and Salvation in the Floating World: Chikamatsu's Double Suicide Drama as Millenarian Discourse." *Journal of Asian Studies* 53, no. 2 (May 1994): 367–93.

Hosoe Hikaru. *Tanizaki Jun'ichirō: Shinsō no retorikku*. Osaka: Izumi Shoin, 2004.

Hurley, Brian. "Toward a New Modern Vernacular: Tanizaki Jun'ichirō, Yamada Yoshio, and Showa Restoration Thought." *Journal of Japanese Studies* 39, no. 2 (2013): 359–96.

Hutcheon, Linda. *A Theory of Adaptation*. London: Routledge, 2013 (2006).

Inoue, Miyako. *Vicarious Language: Gender and Linguistic Modernity in Japan*. Berkeley: University of California Press, 2006.

Inoue Naotarō. *Hirippin Guntō to Ōta Kyōsaburō-kun*. Nishinomiya: Kawase Toshitsugu, 1927.

Inoue Yasushi. *The Bullfight* (Tōgyū). Translated by Michael Emmerich. London: Pushkin Press, 2013 (1949).

Iriye, Akira. *Pacific Estrangement: Japanese and American Expansion, 1897–1911*. Cambridge, MA: Harvard University Press, 1972.

Ishimaru Gohei. *Senba no bonchi: Gappon*. Tokyo: Konishi Shoten, 1919.

Isoda Tsutomu, ed. *Kawashima Yūzō: Ranchō no bigaku*. Tokyo: Waizu Shuppan, 2001 (1996).

Ito, Ken. *Visions of Desire: Tanizaki's Fictional Worlds*. Stanford: Stanford University Press, 1991.

Itō Sei. *Tanizaki Jun'ichirō no bungaku*. Tokyo: Chūō Kōronsha, 1970.

Ives, Sumner. "A Theory of Literary Dialect." *Tulane Studies in English* 2 (1950): 137–82.

Ivy, Marilyn. *Discourses of the Vanishing: Modernity, Phantasm, Japan*. Chicago: University of Chicago Press, 1995.

Iwano Hōmei. "Bonchi." In *Iwano Hōmei zenshū* 1. Kyoto: Rinsen Shoten, 1994: 105–129.

Jacobs, Carol. *In the Language of Walter Benjamin*. Baltimore: Johns Hopkins University Press, 1999.

Jameson, Frederic. "Afterword: Adaptation as a Philosophical Problem." In *True to the Spirit: Film Adaptation and the Questions of Fidelity*, edited by Colin McCabe, Kathleen Murray, and Rick Warner, 215–234. Oxford University Press, 2011.

Jinnai Hidenobu. *Tokyo: A Spatial Anthropology*. Translated by Kimiko Nishimura. Berkeley: University of California Press, 1995.

Johnson, William. "Illness, Disease, and Medicine in Three Novels by Tanizaki." In *A Tanizaki Feast*, edited by Adriana Boscaro and Anthony Hood Chambers, 139–50. Ann Arbor, MI: Center for Japanese Studies, University of Michigan, 1998.

Jones, Gavin. *Strange Talk: The Politics of Dialect Literature in Gilded Age America*. Berkeley: University of California Press, 1999.

Kada Tetsuji. "Gendai: Santō jūyaku-ron." *Keizai tenbō* 24, no. 9 (September 1952): 46–49.

Kaika, Maria. *City of Flows: Modernity, Nature, and the City*. London: Routledge, 2005.

Kamizukasa Shōken. "The Skin of the Pike Conger Eel ("Hamo no kawa," 1914). Translated by Andrew Murakami-Smith. https://ceas.sites.uchicago.edu/sites/ceas.uchicago.edu/files/uploads/Sibley/Hamo%20no%20Kawa.pdf 2013.

Kana Koichi. "Urban Spatial Transformation Observed through Focusing Osaka's Riversides." In *Memoirs of the Faculty of Engineering, Osaka City University* 46 (2008): 29–34.

Kanno, Yuka. "Implicational Spectatorship: Hara Setsuko and the Queer Joke." *Mechademia* 6 (2011): 287–301.

Karatani Kojin. "Yume no sekai: Shimao Toshio to Shōno Junzō." In *Imi to iu yamai*. Tokyo: Kawade Shobō, 1975: 67–108.

Kawahara Yoshio, ed. *Oda Sakunosuke kenkyū*. Osaka: Minazukisha Shobō, 1971.

Kawamura Minato. "Ōsaka to iu shokuminchi." In *'Sengo' to iu seido: Sengo shakai no 'kigen' o motomete*, edited by M. Kawamura, 152–173. Tokyo: Impact, 2002.

Keene, Donald. *Dawn to the West: Japanese Literature of the Modern Era: Fiction*. New York: Holt, 1984.

Kobayashi Yutaka. *Ōsaka to kindai bunka*. Kyoto: Hōritsu Bunkasha, 1989.

Koide Narashige. *Koide Narashige zuihitsu-shū*. Tokyo: Iwanami Shoten, 1987 (1930).

Komori Yōichi. *Nihongo no kindai*. Tokyo: Iwanami shoten, 2000.

Komori Yōichi and Hasumi Shigehiko. "Tanizaki raisan," *Kokubungaku* 38, no. 14 (December 1993): 6–29.

Kon Tōkō. *Akumyō*. In *Kon Tōkō daihyōsaku senshū* 3. Tokyo: Yomiuri shinbunsha, 1973.

Kōno Taeko. *Tanizaki bungaku to kōtei no yokubō*. Tokyo: Chūō Kōronsha, 1980 (1976).

LaMarre, Thomas. *Shadows on the Screen: Tanizaki Jun'ichirō on Cinema and "Oriental" Aesthetics.* Ann Arbor: University of Michigan Center for Japanese Studies, 2005.

Latour, Bruno. *We Have Never Been Modern.* Translated by C. Porter. Cambridge: Harvard University Press, 1993.

Lebra-Chapman, Joyce. *Japan's Greater East Asia Co-Prosperity Sphere in World War II: Selected Readings and Documents.* Oxford: Oxford University Press, 1975.

Lee Yeounsuk (I Yonsuku). *"Kokugo" to iu shisō: Kindai Nihon no gengo ninshiki.* Tokyo: Iwanami shoten, 1996, 2005.

Lloyd, David. *Nationalism and Minor Literature: James Clarence Mangan and the Emergence of Irish Cultural Nationalism.* Berkeley: University of California Press, 1987.

Long, Hoyt. *On Uneven Ground: Miyazawa Kenji and the Making of Place in Modern Japan.* Stanford: Stanford University Press, 2011.

Long, Margherita. *This Perversion Called Love: Reading Tanizaki, Feminist Theory, and Freud.* Stanford: Stanford University Press, 2009.

Maeda Ai. "Oda Sakunosuke, *Meoto zenzai:* Ōsaka." In *Genkei no machi: Bungaku no toshi o aruku,* 211–24. Tokyo: Shogakkan, 1986.

Makimura Shiyō, ed. *Ōsaka kotoba jiten.* Tokyo: Dai Nippon Insatsu, 2007 (1979).

Massey, Doreen. *Space, Place, and Gender.* Minneapolis: University of Minnesota Press, 1994.

Matthews, Joel. "Osaka In and Out of the Nation: Neoliberal Spatial Gestures for the Globally Competitive City-Region." In *City-Imaging: Regeneration, Renewal and Decay,* edited by Tara Brabazon. New York: Springer, 2014.

McClain, James L., and Wakita Osamu. *Osaka: The Merchants' Capital of Early Modern Japan.* Ithaca, NY: Cornell University Press, 1999.

McDonald, Keiko. *From Book to Screen: Modern Japanese Literature in Film.* London: East Gate, 2000.

Mitani Kuniaki. "Kindai shōsetsu no gensetsu: Joshō." In *Kindai bungaku no seiritsu,* edited by Komori Yōichi. Tokyo: Yūseidō, 1986.

Miyagawa Yasushi. *Kindai bungaku no naka no Kansai-ben: Kataru Kansai, Katarareru Kansai.* Tokyo: Nihon Kindai Bungakkai, 2008.

———. "Oda Sakunosuke no 'Waga machi' ni tsuite." *Nihon kindai bungaku* 73 (October 2005): 186–203.

Miyako Chōchō. *Onna hitori.* Tokyo: Zen-nihon bukku kurabu, 1970.

Miyamoto Kenichi. "Japan's World Cities: Osaka and Tokyo Compared." In *Japanese Cities in the World Economy,* edited by Kuniko Fujita and Richard Child Hall. Philadelphia: Temple University Press, 1993.

Miyao, Daisuke. *Sessue Hayakawa: Silent Cinema and Transnational Stardom.* Durham, NC: Duke University Press, 2007.

Miyoshi, Masao. *Off Center: Power and Culture Relations between Japan and the United States.* Cambridge, MA: Harvard University Press, 1991.

Morishige Hisaya. *Sukima kara sukima e.* Tokyo: Nihon tosho sentā, 1998.

———. "Watashi no engi hōteishiki." *Kinema junpō,* February 1, 1957, 86–88.

"Morishige eiga o furikaeru," *Kinema junpō* 1548 (January 2010): 28–29.

Mosse, George. *Nationalism and Sexuality: Respectability and Abnormal Sexuality in Modern Europe.* New York: Howard Fertig, 1985.
Mostow, Joshua, ed. *The Columbia Companion to Modern East Asian Literature.* New York: Columbia University Press, 2003.
Mozume Takami. "Genbun'itchi." In *Meiji ikō kokugo mondai ronshū,* edited by Yoshida Sumio and Inokuchi Yūichi, 181–193. Tokyo: Kazama shobō, 1964 (1886).
Murakami-Smith, Andrew Ladd. "Dialects and Place in Modern Japanese Literature." PhD diss., Princeton University, November 1997.
Myers, Ramon H., and Mark R. Peattie. *The Japanese Colonial Empire, 1895–1945.* Princeton, NJ: Princeton University Press, 1984.

Nabei Katsuyuki. "Ōsaka damashii: Tanizaki Jun'ichirō no 'Watashi no mita Ōsaka oyobi Ōsakajin' o hyōsu." In *Gendai zuihitsu zenshū* 6, 36–45. Tokyo: Kinseidō, 1935–36.
Najita, Tetsuo. *Visions of Virtue in Tokugawa Japan: The Kaitokudō, Merchant Academy of Osaka.* Chicago: University of Chicago Press, 1987.
Nakaishi Takashi. *Oda Sakunosuke: Ame, hotaru, kinmokusei.* Osaka: Henshū Kōbō Noa, 1998.
Nakamura Takafusa. *Economic Growth in Prewar Japan* (*Senzenki nihon keizai seichō no bunsei*). Translated by Robert A. Feldman. New Haven: Yale University Press, 1971.
Nakano Kōsaku. *Ōsaka to hachirentai: Ōsaka-shidan shōshi.* Osaka: Tōyō, 1985.
Niranjana, Tejaswini. *Siting Translation: History, Post-Structuralism, and the Colonial Context.* Berkeley: University of California Press, 1992.
Nishimura Futoshi. "Shachō shirīzu kara 'sengo' o miru: Shihon, jin'myaku, mi no narai." In *Sengo nihon eiga-ron: Sen kyūhyaku gojūnendai o yomu,* edited by Mitsuyo Wada-Marciano, 51–77. Tokyo: Seikyūsha, 2012.
Noguchi Takehiko. *Tanizaki Jun'ichirō-ron.* Tokyo: Chūō Kōronsha, 1973.
———. "Time in the World of *Sasameyuki.*" *Journal of Japanese Studies* 3, no. 1 (Winter 1977): 1–36.
Nolletti, Arthur. *The Cinema of Gosho Heinosuke.* Bloomington: Indiana University Press, 2005.
Noys, Benjamin. "Georges Bataille's Base Materialism." *Cultural Values* 2, no. 4 (1998): 499–517.

Oda Sakunosuke. *Meoto zenzai: Kanzenban,* edited by Hidaka Shōji. Tokyo: Yushodō. 2007.
———. *Oda Sakunosuke zenshū.* 8 vols. Tokyo: Kōdansha, 1970.
———. *Stories of Osaka Life.* Translated by Burton Watson. New York: Columbia University Press, 1990.
Okuno Takeo. *Burai to itan.* Tokyo: Kokubunsha, 1973.
Orikuchi Shinobu. "*Sasameyuki* no onna." In *Orikuchi Shinobu zenshū* 32. Chūō Kōronsha, 1997 (1949).
Ōtani, Kōichi. *Iki aishi kaita: Oda Sakunosuke-den.* Tokyo: Kōdansha, 1973.
Ōya Sōichi. "Osaka bunka no Nippon seifuku." In *Ōya Sōichi zenshū,* 2. Tokyo: Sōyōsha, 1981 (June 1930).

Peattie, Mark. *Nan'yō: The Rise and Fall of the Japanese in Micronesia, 1885–1945*. Honolulu: University of Hawai'i Press, 1988.

Price, Willard. "Sangyō shihai no ura ni, chi to ase no romansu: Sekai ichi o hokoru taima; kagakuteki ni ueru eikyūsei." *Ōsaka Asahi Shimbun*, November 19, 1935.

———. "Urusai tochi mondai: Norikoete susumu hōjin, mujin no tenkei o kaitaku." *Osaka Asahi Shimbun*, November 19, 1935.

"Puranetariumu shiryō-shitsu." Ōsaka shiritsu kagakukan. December 28, 2000. http://www.sci-museum.kita.osaka.jp/~kazu/zeiss/gallery.html.

Radhakrishnan, R. "Towards an Eccentric Cosmopolitanism." *Positions* 3, no. 3 (1995).

Reed, Robert. *City of Pines: The Origins of Baguio as a Colonial Hill Station and Regional Capital*. Berkeley: Center for South and Southeast Asia Studies, University of California, 1976.

Repeta, Lawrence. "Mr. Hashimoto Attacks Japan's Constitution." *Asia-Pacific Journal* 10, no. 13 (March 2012).

Rubin, Jay. *Injurious to Public Morals: Writers and the Meiji State*. Seattle: University of Washington Press, 1984.

Sakai, Naoki. *Translation and Subjectivity: On "Japan" and Cultural Nationalism*. Minneapolis: University of Minnesota Press, 1997.

Sakai Takashi. *Tsūtenkaku: Shin Nihon shihonshugi hattatsushi*. Tokyo: Seidosha, 2011.

Sakaki, Atsuko. *Recontextualizing Texts: Narrative Performance in Modern Japanese Fiction*. Cambridge, MA: Harvard University Asia Center, 1999.

Sanada Shinji. *Hyōjungo wa ika ni seiritsu shita ka*. Tokyo: Sōtakusha, 1991.

Sand, Jordan. *House and Home in Modern Japan: Architecture, Domestic Space, and Bourgeois Culture, 1880–1930*. Cambridge, MA: Harvard University Asia Center, 2003.

Sasagawa Keiko. *Meiji Taishō Ōsaka eiga bunka no tanjō*. Osaka: Kansai Daigaku Ōsaka Toshi Isan Kenkyū Sentā, 2012.

Sasai Yoshitaka. *Ōsaka shoku-bunka taizen*. Osaka: Nishi-nihon, 2010.

Seeley, Christopher. *A History of Writing in Japan*. Honolulu: University of Hawai'i Press, 2000.

Shah, Nayan. *Contagious Divides: Epidemics and Race in San Francisco's Chinatown*. Berkeley: University of California Press, 2001.

Sheldon, Charles David. *The Rise of the Merchant Class in Tokugawa Japan, 1600–1868*. Locust Valley, NY: J.J. Augustine, 1958.

Shibata Shōji. "'Monogatari'-enai katarite: *Manji* to Osaka kotoba." In *'Sakusha' o meguru bōken: Tekusuto-ron o koete*. Tokyo: Shinyōsha, 2004.

Shibata Takeshi. *Sociolinguistics in Japanese Contexts*. Berlin: Mouton de Gruyter, 1999.

Shindō Masahiro. *Shokutsū shōsetsu no kigōgaku*. Tokyo: Sōbunsha, 2007.

Shively, Donald H. *The Love Suicide at Amijima: A Study of a Japanese Domestic Tragedy by Chikamatsu Monzaemon*. Cambridge, MA: Harvard University Press, 1953.

Silverberg, Miriam. "Constructing the Japanese Ethnography of Modernity." *Journal of Asian Studies* 51, no. 1 (February 1992): 30–54.

———. *Erotic Grotesque Nonsense*. Berkeley: University of California Press, 2006.

Smith, Henry D. II. "Tokyo as an Idea: An Exploration of Japanese Urban Thought Until 1945." *Journal of Japanese Studies* 4, no. 1 (Winter 1978): 45–80.

Spicer, Andrew. *Typical Men: The Representation of Masculinity in Popular British Cinema*. London: I.B. Tauris, 2001.

Stam, Robert. "Introduction: The Theory and Practice of Adaptation." In *Literature and Film: A Guide to Theory and Practice of Adaptation*, edited by Robert Stam and Alessandra Raengo, 1–52. Oxford: Blackwell, 2004.

———. *Literature through Film: Realism, Magic, and the Art of Adaptation*. Oxford: Blackwell, 2005.

Steiner, Kurt. *Local Government in Japan*. Stanford: Stanford University Press, 1965.

Sugihara Tōru. *Ekkyō suru tami: Kindai Osaka no chōsenjinshi kenkyū*. Tokyo: Shinkansha, 1998.

Taguchi Shigeru. *Oda Sakunosuke no sekai*. (n.p., 1999).

Takagi Harue. *Tanizaki-ke no omoide*. Tokyo: Kōsōsha, 1977.

Tanizaki Jun'ichirō. *The Makioka Sisters* (Sasameyuki). Translated by Edward Seidensticker. New York: Vintage, 1985 (Alfred A. Knopf, 1957).

———. *Manji*. In *Tanizaki Jun'ichirō zenshū*, vol. 11, 393–569. Tokyo: Chūō Kōronsha, 1966–70.

———. *Quicksand* (*Manji*). Translated by Howard Hibbett. New York: Alfred A. Knopf, 1994.

———. *Sasameyuki*. In *Tanizaki Jun'ichirō zenshū*, vol. 15, 1–881. Tokyo: Chūō Kōronsha, 1966–70.

———. *Tanizaki Jun'ichirō zenshū*. 28 vols. Tokyo: Chūō Kōronsha, 1966–70.

Tansman, Alan. *The Culture of Japanese Fascism*. Durham, NC: Duke University Press, 2009.

Tatsumi Kojirō. "Baku-genbun'itchi-ron." In *Meiji ikō Kokugo mondai ronshū*, edited by Yoshida Sumio and Inokuchi Yūichi, 224–33. Tokyo: Kazama Shōbo, 1964 (1887).

Taylor, Charles. *Modern Social Imaginaries*. Durham, NC: Duke University Press, 2004.

Tezuka Osamu. "Natsukashi no puranetariumu." In *Nihon no kagakukan wa Ōsaka kara*, 74–75. Osaka: Ōsaka Kagaku Shinkō Kyōkai, 2008.

———. *Tezuka Osamu essei shū*, 1. Tokyo: Kōdansha, 1996.

Tipton, Elise K. "The Café: Contested Space of Modernity in Interwar Japan." In *Being Modern in Japan: Culture and Society from the 1910s to the 1930s*, edited by Elise K. Tipton and John Clark, 119–36. Honolulu: University Hawai'i Press, 2000.

Torrance, Richard. "Literacy and Literature in Osaka, 1890–1940." *Journal of Japanese Studies* 31, no. 1 (Winter 2005): 27–60.

———. "Literary Accounts of the Decline of Senba." *Monumenta Nipponica* 67, no. 1 (2012): 29–73.

———. "Review of *Language and the Modern State: The Reform of Written Japanese*, by Nanette Twine." *Journal of Japanese Studies* 19, no. 1 (Winter 1993): 234–39.

Twine, Nanette. "The Genbun'itchi Movement: Its Origin, Development, and Conclusion." *Monumenta Nipponica* 33, no. 3 (Autumn, 1988): 333–56.

——. *Language and the Modern State: The Reform of Written Japanese*. London: Routledge, 1991.

Tyler, William J. *The Legend of Gold and Other Stories*. Honolulu: University of Hawai'i Press, 1998.

Ueno Akira et al. "Sōsaku opera 'Meoto zenzai' o megutte." *Ongaku geijutsu* 15, no. 7 (July 1957): 94–98.

Ueno Chizuko. *Nationalism and Gender*. Translated by Beverley Yamamoto. Melbourne: Trans Pacific Press, 2004 (1998).

Ukai Kiyoshi. *Yamasaki Toyoko mondai shōsetsu no kenkyū*. Tokyo: Shakai Hyōronsha, 2002.

Uno Kōji. "Nagai koinaka." In *Uno Kōji zenshū* 1, 282–309 (*Yūben*, October 1919).

——. "Samazama no Ōsaka katagi: Arui wa Ōsaka-damashii no futatsu no kata." In *Uno Kōji zenshū* 12. Tokyo: Chūō kōronsha, 1969.

Uranishi Kazuhiko, ed. *Oda Sakunosuke bungei jiten*. Osaka: Izumi Shōin, 1992.

——. *Ōsaka kindai bungaku sakuhin jiten*. Osaka: Izumi Shoin, 2006.

Vertovec, Steven, and Robin Cohen, eds. *Conceiving Cosmopolitanism: Theory, Context, and Practice*. Oxford: Oxford University Press, 2002.

Walsh, Michael. "National Cinema, National Imaginary." *Film History* 8 (1996): 5–17.

Watanabe Naomi. "Yukiko to hachigatsu jūgonichi—*Sasameyuki* o yomu." In *Tanizaki Jun'ichirō: Gitai no yūwaku*. Tokyo: Shinchōsha, 1992.

Watanabe Tadashi. *Kinsei "kuidaore" kō*. Osaka: Tōhō, 2003.

Werbner, Pnina. "Vernacular Cosmopolitanism." *Theory, Culture and Society* 23, nos. 2–3 (2006): 496–98.

Williams, Raymond. "Region and Class in the Novel." In *Writing in Society*, 229–38. London: Averso, 1983.

Worcester, Dean C. *The Philippines: Past and Present*. New York: MacMillan, 1914.

Yamanouchi Yasushi, J. Victor Koschmann, and Ryūichi Narita, eds. *Total War and "Modernization."* Ithaca, NY: East Asia Program, Cornell University, 1998.

Yamasaki Toyoko. *Bonchi*. Tokyo: Shinchōsha, 1959.

——. *Hana noren*. Tokyo: Shinchōsha, 1958.

——. *Noren*. Tokyo: Shinchōsha, 1957.

——. *Shibuchin*. Tokyo: Shinchōsha, 1965 (Chūō Kōronsha, 1959).

Yamasaki Toyoko: zenshōsetsu o yomitoku. Tokyo: Yosensha Mook, 2009.

Yasuda Toshiaki. *"Kokugo" to "hōgen" no aida: Gengo kōchiku no seijigaku*. Kyoto: Jimbun Shoin, 1999.

Yoda, Tomiko. "First-Person Narration and Citizen-Subject: The Modernity of Ōgai's 'The Dancing Girl.'" *Journal of Asian Studies* 65, no. 2 (May 2006): 277–306.

Yoshikawa Yoko. "Development of the Japanese Commercial Sector in Manila, 1898–1920: The Case of Jose M. Tagawa." *Tonan Ajia Kenkyu* 18, no. 3 (December 1980): 387–421.

Yu-Jose, Lydia. *Japan Views the Philippines, 1900–1944*. Manila: Ateneo de Manila University Press, 1992.

Films and Television Series

Akumyō. Dir. Tanaka Tokuzō. Daiei, 1961. DVD.

Bonchi. Dir. Ichikawa Kon. Daiei, 1960. DVD.

Chi to hone. Dir. Sai Yōichi. Shōchiku, 2004. DVD.

Dia Pyonyan. Dir. Yang Yong-hi. Cheon, 2006. DVD.

Gaki teikoku. Dir. Izutsu Kazuyuki. Art Theatre Guild, 1981. DVD.

Hana noren. Dir. Toyoda Shirō. Takarazuka, 1959. DVD.

Kaette kita otoko. Dir. Kawashima Yūzō. Shōchiku, 1944. Video.

Kashima ari. Dir. Kawashima Yūzō. Tōhō, 1959. DVD.

Kazoku no kuni. Dir. Yang Yong-hi. Star Sands, 2012. Film.

Kishiwada shōnen gurentai. Dir. Izutsu Kazuyuki. Shochiku, 1996. DVD.

Kishiwada shōnen gurentai: Chikemuri junjō-hen. Dir. Miike Takashi. Yoshimoto kōgyō, 1997. DVD.

Manji. Dir. Masumura Yasuzō. Daiei, 1964. DVD.

Meoto zenzai. Dir. Toyoda Shirō. Tōhō, 1955. DVD.

Meshi. Dir. Naruse Mikio. Tōhō, 1951. DVD.

Naniwa yūkyōden. Dir. Miike Takashi. 1995. DVD.

Neko to Shōzo to futari no onna. Dir. Toyoda Shirō. Tōkyō eiga, 1956. DVD.

Noren. Dir. Kawashima Yūzō. Tōhō, 1958. DVD.

Ōsaka no yado. Dir. Gosho Heinosuke. Shin-Tōhō, 1954. DVD.

Ōsaka saikyō densetsu: Kenka no hanamichi. Dir. Miike Takashi. 1996. DVD.

Sasameyuki. Dir. Abe Yutaka. Shintōhō, 1950. DVD.

Sasameyuki. Dir. Ichikawa Kon. Tōhō, 1983. DVD.

Shiroi kyotō. Fuji Terebi, 2003. DVD.

Shiroi kyotō. Dir. Yamamoto Satsuo. Daiei, 1966. DVD.

Waga machi. Dir. Kawashima Yūzō. Nikkatsu, 1956. DVD.

Index

Harvard East Asian Monographs
(most recent titles)

351. Michel Mohr, *Buddhism, Unitarianism, and the Meiji Competition for Universality*
352. J. Keith Vincent, *Two-Timing Modernity: Homosocial Narrative in Modern Japanese Fiction*
354. Chong-Bum An and Barry Bosworth, *Income Inequality in Korea: An Analysis of Trends, Causes, and Answers*
355. Jamie L. Newhard, *Knowing the Amorous Man: A History of Scholarship on* Tales of Ise
356. Sho Konishi, *Anarchist Modernity: Cooperatism and Japanese-Russian Intellectual Relations in Modern Japan*
357. Christopher P. Hanscom, *The Real Modern: Literary Modernism and the Crisis of Representation in Colonial Korea*
358. Michael Wert, *Meiji Restoration Losers: Memory and Tokugawa Supporters in Modern Japan*
359. Garret P. S. Olberding, ed., *Facing the Monarch: Modes of Advice in the Early Chinese Court*
360. Xiaojue Wang, *Modernity with a Cold War Face: Reimagining the Nation in Chinese Literature Across the 1949 Divide*
361. David Spafford, *A Sense of Place: The Political Landscape in Late Medieval Japan*
362. Jongryn Mo and Barry Weingast, *Korean Political and Economic Development: Crisis, Security, and Economic Rebalancing*
363. Melek Ortabasi, *The Undiscovered Country: Text, Translation, and Modernity in the Work of Yanagita Kunio*
364. Hiraku Shimoda, *Lost and Found: Recovering Regional Identity in Imperial Japan*
365. Trent E. Maxey, *The "Greatest Problem": Religion and State Formation in Meiji Japan*
366. Gina Cogan, *The Princess Nun: Bunchi, Buddhist Reform, and Gender in Early Edo Japan*
367. Eric C. Han, *Rise of a Japanese Chinatown: Yokohama, 1894–1972*
368. Natasha Heller, *Illusory Abiding: The Cultural Construction of the Chan Monk Zhongfeng Mingben*
369. Paize Keulemans, *Sound Rising from the Paper: Nineteenth-Century Martial Arts Fiction and the Chinese Acoustic Imagination*
370. Simon James Bytheway, *Investing Japan: Foreign Capital, Monetary Standards, and Economic Development, 1859–2011*
371. Sukhee Lee, *Negotiated Power: The State, Elites, and Local Governance in Twelfth-Fourteenth China*
372. Foong Ping, *The Efficacious Landscape: On the Authorities of Painting at the Northern Song Court*
373. Catherine L. Phipps, *Empires on the Waterfront: Japan's Ports and Power, 1858–1899*
374. Sunyoung Park, *The Proletarian Wave: Literature and Leftist Culture in Colonial Korea, 1910–1945*

Harvard East Asian Monographs

375. Barry Eichengreen, Wonhyuk Lim, Yung Chul Park, and Dwight H. Perkins, *The Korean Economy: From a Miraculous Past to a Sustainable Future*
376. Heather Blair, *Real and Imagined: The Peak of Gold in Heian Japan*
377. Emer O'Dwyer, *Significant Soil: Settler Colonialism and Japan's Urban Empire in Manchuria*
378. Martina Deuchler, *Under the Ancestors' Eyes: Kinship, Status, and Locality in Premodern Korea*
379. Joseph R. Dennis, *Writing, Publishing, and Reading Local Gazetteers in Imperial China, 1100–1700*
380. Catherine Vance Yeh, *The Chinese Political Novel: Migration of a World Genre*
381. Noell Wilson, *Defensive Positions: The Politics of Maritime Security in Tokugawa Japan*
382. Miri Nakamura, *Monstrous Bodies: The Rise of the Uncanny in Modern Japan*
383. Nara Dillon, *Radical Inequalities: China's Revolutionary Welfare State in Comparative Perspective*
384. Ma Zhao, *Runaway Wives, Urban Crimes, and Survival Tactics in Wartime Beijing, 1937–1949*
385. Mingwei Song, *Young China: National Rejuvenation and the* Bildungsroman, *1900–1959*
386. Christopher Bondy, *Voice, Silence, and Self: Negotiations of Buraku Identity in Contemporary Japan*
387. Seth Jacobowitz, *Writing Technology in Meiji Japan: A Media History of Modern Japanese Literature and Visual Culture*
388. Hilde De Weerdt, *Information, Territory, and Networks: The Crisis and Maintenance of Empire in Song China*
389. Elizabeth Kindall, *Geo-Narratives of a Filial Son: The Paintings and Travel Diaries of Huang Xiangjian (1609–1673)*
390. Matthew Fraleigh, *Plucking Chrysanthemums: Narushima Ryūhoku and Sinitic Literary Traditions in Modern Japan*
391. Hu Ying, *Burying Autumn: Poetry, Friendship, and Loss*
392. Mark E. Byington, *The Ancient State of Puyŏ in Northeast Asia: Archaeology and Historical Memory*
393. Timothy J. Van Compernolle, *Struggling Upward: Worldly Success and the Japanese Novel*
394. Heekyoung Cho, *Translation's Forgotten History: Russian Literature, Japanese Mediation, and the Formation of Modern Korean Literature*
395. Terry Kawashima, *Itineraries of Power: Texts and Traversals in Heian and Medieval Japan*
396. Anna Andreeva, *Assembling Shinto: Buddhist Approaches to Kami Worship in Medieval Japan*
397. Felix Boecking, *No Great Wall: Trade, Tariffs, and Nationalism in Republican China, 1927–1945*
398. Chien-Hsin Tsai, *A Passage to China: Literature, Loyalism, and Colonial Taiwan*
399. W. Puck Brecher, *Honored and Dishonored Guests: Westerners in Wartime Japan*
400. Miya Elise Mizuta Lippit, *Aesthetic Life: Beauty and Art in Modern Japan*
401. Brian R. Steininger, *Chinese Literary Form in Heian Japan: Poetics and Practice*
402. Lisa Yoshikawa, *Making History Matter: Kuroita Katsumi and the Construction of Imperial Japan*
403. Michael P. Cronin, *Osaka Modern: The City in the Japanese Imaginary*
404. Soyoung Suh, *Naming the Local: Medicine, Language, and Identity in Korea since the 15th Century*
405. Yoon Sun Yang, *From Domestic Women to Sensitive Young Men: Translating the Individual in Early Colonial Korea*